PROGRESSIVISM
AT RISK

Recent Titles in
Contributions in American History

PROGRESSIVISM AT RISK

Electing a President in 1912

Francis L. Broderick

Contributions in American History, Number 134
JON L. WAKELYN, SERIES EDITOR

GREENWOOD PRESS
New York • Westport, Connecticut • London

Library of Congress Cataloging-in-Publication Data

Broderick, Francis L.
    Progressivism at risk : electing a President in 1912 / Francis L.
Broderick.
        p.   cm.—(Contributions in American history, ISSN 0084–9219 ; no. 134)
    Bibliography: p.
    Includes index.
    ISBN 0–313–26400–7 (lib. bdg : alk. paper)
        1. Presidents—United States—Election—1912.   2. Progressivism
    (United States politics)   3. United States—Politics and
    government—1909–1913.   I. Title.   II. Series.
    E765.B76   1989
    324.973'0912—dc19   88–38547

British Library Cataloguing in Publication Data is available.

Copyright © 1989 by Francis L. Broderick

Library of Congress Catalog Card Number: 88–38547
ISBN: 0–313–26400–7
ISSN: 0084–9219

First published in 1989

Greenwood Press, Inc.
88 Post Road West, Westport, Connecticut   06881

Printed in the United States of America

The paper used in this book complies with the
Permanent Paper Standard issued by the National
Information Standards Organization (Z39.48–1984).

10 9 8 7 6 5 4 3 2 1

Copyright Acknowledgment

Arthur S. Link, ed., *The Papers of Woodrow Wilson*. Published by Princeton University Press.
Scattered excerpts reprinted with permission of Princeton University Press.

To my brothers
Joseph Albert Broderick, retired Professor of Law,
North Carolina Central University Law School,
and
Senior Judge Vincent L. Broderick,
Federal District Court for the Southern District of New York,
who
preceded me into historical studies
and
led me into the study and practice of law

Contents

Preface

Dozens, perhaps hundreds, of people have made this narrative political history of the presidential election of 1912 possible—historians, journalists, participants. The footnotes and bibliography record a part of that debt. In addition, I have some specific acknowledgments to make. My son, Joseph B. Broderick, did most of the research and some of the writing for the sections on Eugene V. Debs. John Morton Blum, classmate and friend, read the manuscript with the acumen developed in a lifetime of distinguished historical scholarship and teaching. Richard N. Niebling, colleague and critic, helped me shape my prose. Early on, Richard M. Freeland made shrewd observations that led me to see 1912 in a larger context. All these folks bear no responsibility, of course, for I did not heed all their counsels; in fact, on many points, they disagreed with each other. Finally, I welcome this chance to thank the staff of the Phillips Exeter Academy for providing a scholarly base for most of my historical work, and especially for this book.

PROGRESSIVISM
AT RISK

Introduction

1912: Progressive Crossroads

By August 1912, four political parties had presented candidates for the post of President of the United States: the Socialist Party, as usual, named Eugene V. Debs of Indiana; the Republican Party, for the second time, offered William Howard Taft, the incumbent President; the Democratic Party, after a tense internal struggle, came up with Woodrow Wilson of New Jersey; and the Progressive Party—the Bull Moose Party—nominated Theodore Roosevelt by acclamation.

At stake in the ten-week campaign that followed was a national decision on the future of progressivism, a wave of reform that spread from cities and states to the nation as a whole in the first decade of the twentieth century. A complex, many-faceted movement, progressivism searched out ways to deal with the new industrial America that a nationwide economy, bound together by railroad and telegraph, had created under a Constitution written for a remote agrarian age.

The new era had affected people in different ways. Farmers became hostages to the railroads and grain elevators over which they had no control. Workers saw familial relationships in small workshops melt away in large foundries; women and children found jobs as cheap labor that would hold down costs. Small businessmen lost the capacity to compete with gigantic corporations that merged many small companies. Large bankers, especially in the large cities and most especially in New York City, provided the capital for the mergers, soon becoming influential partners, sometimes controlling partners, in the new conglomerates, and small bankers found themselves confined by what their affluent competitors did. Consumers—everybody—hung on at the tail end of the process, powerless, frequently victimized by high prices and poor quality. Needing relief from unwonted conditions of life, victims were inclined to turn to government.

The federal system created by the Constitution gave government a curious relation to the new world being created by economic growth. The Constitution divided power between states and nation, limiting national power to those areas that transcended states—war and diplomacy, currency and post office, interstate and international commerce. Even within the areas of its authority, the national government divided its mandate among the executive, legislative, and judicial branches. The arrangement was not accidental: the American Revolution had been fought to stave off the power of a central government in London that exercised more authority than the colonists cared to bear. "That government is best that governs least"[1] was a sentiment not limited to Henry David Thoreau and Thomas Jefferson. The North's victory in the Civil War and the amendments that followed, especially the Fourteenth Amendment, hinted at a potential enlargement of national power. But while the word "power" continued to mean for Americans governmental power,[2] a strong American prejudice persisted against any extension of it. By the beginning of the twentieth century, the socialists' advocacy of government as an instrument for seizing the principal means of production and distribution reinforced the negative prejudice.

The prejudice produced a product: the myth of laissez-faire. Stated in starkest form by Herbert Spencer, vastly more influential in the United States than in his native England, the doctrine held that the government's role was limited to repelling invasion, protecting persons and property against "internal enemies," and enforcing contracts.[3] The idea was propagated that this doctrine lay at the heart of American practice. In fact, of course, the national government was not so passive, especially in the Republican years that stretched, almost uninterruptedly, from the Civil War to 1913. A high, ever higher, protective tariff sheltered American industry. Monetary policy—gold and silver, greenbacks, and banknotes issued by national banks—responded to dominant political pressures and affected the real income of every inhabitant. Generous grants of land, first to railroads, later to mining and timber interests—three times as much as was distributed as homesteads—created enormous wealth for a handful of beneficiaries: handouts for the powerful. But tariffs, monetary policy, and land grants all occurred without conspicuous governmental intrusion—a few customs inspectors at the ports, a few bureaucrats in Washington, a handful of underpaid land agents. As a result, laissez-faire came to mean nothing more than the absence of governmental regulation. Thus, the powerful American fear of power impeded political supervision of private economic power, power that could affect the lives of citizens just as surely as the mandates from King George III's officials.

The states, less addicted to nonintervention than the central government, provided the earliest challenge to the new order. When railroads and grain elevators used their commanding presence to tax the livelihood of farmers excessively, agrarian states passed the so-called Granger laws that regulated the conduct and fees of railroads and elevators.

Then the federal government entered the picture. In 1886, the Supreme Court invoked the federal commerce power to preempt for the national government control over the railroads that crossed state lines. Thereafter, Congress in 1887 passed the Interstate Commerce Act, which set up a commission to supervise railroad practices. Three years later Congress acted again. In a gesture toward stemming the growing concentration of economic power, the Sherman Antitrust Act forbade "every contract, combination in the form of trust or otherwise, or conspiracy, in restraint of trade or commerce among the several states...." The two acts provided a base for near-universal satisfaction: To those who wanted the national government to set itself as the guardian against the excesses of capitalism, the laws made a show of unprecedented intervention. To those threatened with regulation, it turned out that indolent enforcement and judicial obstruction reduced the laws to toothless tigers.

The failure of both acts suggested a comity of interest between big business and political leaders, mainly in the Republican Party: business bankrolled political campaigns and politicians reciprocated with favors. Corruption in politics was no new thing. Nor was protest against it, in both parties, unheard of. Every urban state had its periodic reform movement, throwing the rascals out, restoring honesty in government for a moment. But since reformers were better at protest than at tenacious administration, their day always passed and the professionals always returned.

The first decade of the twentieth century marked a resurgence, even an acceleration, of protest that came to carry the name "progressive." A recent scholar defines the process as the "corporate reconstruction of American capitalism," the widespread replacement of owner-managers in a competitive economy by a corporate structure characterized by widely diversified ownership, divorce of ownership and management, and specialized management skills in price-administered markets.[4] On every level—nation, state, city—voters sought to get a handle on the forces that were hurting their lives, first, by making government more immediately reflective of the popular will through devices of direct democracy, and second, by using government to regulate economic institutions. Popular journals supported the reformist urge: Ida Tarbell laid bare the inner workings of the Standard Oil Company in a series that began in *McClure's Magazine* in 1903. Lincoln Steffens, in *The Shame of the Cities* (1904), exposed politicians' sale of special privileges to businessmen in city after city all over the land. Though these investigative journalists eventually acquired the pejorative name "muckrakers," they created widespread popular support, especially among educated readers, for progressive reform at every level.[5] In Toledo and Cleveland, Ohio, reforming mayors remade their cities' images. In Oregon, the legislature limited women's working hours. Governor Robert M. La Follette epitomized the change possible on

the state level: direct primaries, regulation of lobbyists, higher taxes on corporations, regulation of state banks and of railroads operating entirely within
Wisconsin. He popularized the "Wisconsin idea," the use of experts, frequently from the state university, to set the factual base for reform.

Theodore Roosevelt made progressivism a powerful force in the national
arena. Elected vice-president in President William McKinley's second term,
he was abruptly propelled into the presidency by the assassination of McKinley
in 1901. Over the next seven years he reinvigorated the Sherman Act by
antitrust prosecutions, strengthened the Interstate Commerce Act, gave national standing to the conservation of natural resources, signed the Pure Food
and Drug Act and the Meat Inspection Act. His flamboyant presence—what he
was as much as what he did—put progressivism at the top of the national
agenda. His successor, William Howard Taft, more temperate in style, slowed
the movement; some said, reversed it. Yet Taft initiated more antitrust suits
in four years than Roosevelt had in seven and a half. By 1912, the Sherman
Act and the Interstate Commerce Act were no longer in limbo.

The presidential election campaign that year dealt with the central issue
of progressivism: How should the United States "work out a strategy for
orderly social change" in the new order created by large-scale industrial and
financial capitalism?[6] Experience was lacking, for the rapid economic changes
since the Civil War had indeed created something new under the sun: a
nationwide, even international, market; a revolution in productive capacity
that outran the nation's ability to distribute and to consume; a new breed of
managers whose "visible hand," displacing the invisible hand made classic
by Adam Smith, crafted new strategies for survival and profit and whose
success bred status anxieties among the leadership that they had elbowed
aside.[7] The complexity of the new era guaranteed that the lines of battle were
never clearly drawn. Businessmen, seeking "some decently comfortable measure of stability" for their interests, real or imagined, financial or other,[8]
might end up favoring or opposing any given reform. Farmers, needing
governmental intervention, might feel the countervailing tug of their traditional independence. Workers could not be certain how their wages and
conditions of work would be best served. Urban political machines, themselves the target of progressive reform for stifling the electoral process, sometimes led the movement for social legislation so important to their
constituents.[9]

The rhetoric of 1912 addressed the issues that progressive sentiment raised.
All four candidates were, in some real sense, progressive, Taft and Debs as
well as Wilson and Roosevelt. All four could not but recognize that fundamental changes were occurring. The question that each had to propound to
the American electorate was: Where do we go from here to master a system
seemingly out of control? The campaign was a moment of education, not just
for the American people, but for the candidates, especially Roosevelt and
Wilson. Beyond the election, the path of progressivism was paved not just by

the winners, but also by the terms of the debate that the political process had forced upon all the candidates. Furthermore, the lines of argument developed in 1912 had staying power for two full generations; not until the 1970s was there a discernible reversal of the thrust.

The political process in 1912, to be sure, contained elements other than the debate over future policy. Many citizens did not vote at all. Many others voted by habit as much as by conviction: western states were likely to vote Republican, Regular Republican or Progressive Republican, the South certain to vote Democratic, regardless of the views presented to them. (The Socialists could expect, did expect, no state to support them.) Other states—New York, for example, its forty-five electoral votes the biggest prize—might go either way, but their vacillation hinged more on habit, on successful political organization, on personalities, even on local issues, than on the fine points of difference over progressivism.

Nonetheless, the campaign of 1912 offered the moment of decision on the future of progressivism. It defined the era's answer to the questions raised by the new industrial order that had grown up within the American constitutional system.

PART I

Republican Fragments

1

The Roosevelt Legacy

Theodore Roosevelt was the pivot of progressivism and, as the central figure in the drama that reached its climax in November 1912, the political prodigy of his era. A youthful president from 1901 to 1909, he made the office that had languished for thirty years after Abraham Lincoln into the focal point of American political affairs, foreign and domestic, its incumbent the conspicuous first citizen, knowledgeable about the nation's problems, preeminent in proposing solutions. A Rooseveltian presidency meant bold steps and exciting drama. No matter that the excitement of the drama exceeded the boldness of the steps, for Roosevelt's aura of activity blurred the line between accomplishment and fantasy so effectively that even he could not tell one from the other.

By 1912, he had done more things than his friends could remember, done them with enthusiasm and success: he wrote books, fought Spaniards, snooped on policemen, won the Nobel Peace Prize, closed illegal bars, overcame asthma, legislated state reforms, boxed as an amateur, hunted lions, won the governorship of New York and the presidency of the United States, romped with his children, beat political bosses at their own game, lectured European princes on their heritage and Indians on sign language, took the Canal Zone and built the Panama Canal, and ranched cattle. He held his own with cowboys and with hoodlums. He was totally at home with the upperclass swells in the most elegant salon in Washington, one of whom could write, however, without being contradicted, "You must always remember that the President is about six."[1] Indeed, around the house, even the White House, his wife Edith treated him like one of the children. A dozen interests claimed his attention, and his extraordinary verve let him find time for them all. Intensely patriotic, even chauvinistic, he developed a sense of duty that in a more overtly hierarchical society would have carried the label *noblesse oblige*. As Roosevelt faced 1912, his whole life made doing the right thing more important than success.

Born in 1858, the first son of Theodore Roosevelt, Sr., and Martha Bullock Roosevelt, young "Teedie" came as close to aristocratic standing as the American system permits. His mother was a lineal descendant of the first president of Georgia during the American revolution. On his father's side, the child went back seven generations to the original Dutch settlers in Manhattan— the Rosenvelts were there before the English took over New York. His father, a prosperous importer and prominent Republican, exchanged calling cards with the most fashionable New York families, all of them disdainful of the new rich whose wealth needed to age for a generation or two.

The family's position gave the young Roosevelt a healthy share of what Robert Coles calls a "sense of entitlement,"[2] that is, the expectation that status created a right to life's goodies: servants, private tutors, carriages, summer vacation resorts, trips to Europe, North Africa, the Middle East. Theodore would go on to college and to a profession just as surely as an Italian immigrant would go into a mill and work his sixty hours a week.

Raised in this climate of confidence, Teddy went off to Harvard in the fall of 1876. Mastering the asthma that wracked his childhood, he became a bright athletic sociable person. Though passed over at first, he won entry to the most sought after social club, Porcellian, and he adorned the social life of Cambridge, Boston, and the surrounding towns. He rode a horse well, and in his senior year he attached his horse Lightfoot to a tilbury, a small dogcart for two with which he courted Alice Lee in Chestnut Hill with as much intimacy as the era and their social class allowed. He boxed manfully, well enough to be runner-up in Harvard's lightweight championship; in the summers, he also rowed, swam, sailed, shot, climbed. He graduated just out of the top 10 percent of his class, *magna cum laude*, Phi Beta Kappa, in the spring of 1880. After a six-week hunting trip in the Midwest, Theodore married Alice Lee in the Unitarian Church in Brookline on his twenty-second birthday.

As the young couple settled into their home at 6 West 57th Street, Roosevelt undertook three chores. He started attending law classes in Columbia University's dingy quarters downtown. At the same time, he picked up two chapters of a manuscript started at Harvard, and, using the resources of the Astor Library, laboriously worked *The Naval War of 1812* to completion. His third activity set him on the truest of his careers: He was accepted for membership in the 21st District Republican Association at Morton Hall on 59th Street.

His family and his family's friends were shocked. For people in Roosevelt's social circle, politics was a dirty word. A gentleman might accept a public appointment, but he did not enter the "rough and tumble"—Roosevelt's phrase[3]—with the grubs who mucked around in the trenches of politics. Politics perverted government, creating a vile system, corrupt, venal, too soiled for a gentleman to enter. Young Roosevelt's contrary view was blunt:

If being part of the governing class brought him to ward-level politics, so be it.

Within a year, an angry sub-boss at the ward level revolted against the top banana, using the affluent, aggressive Ivy Leaguer as a willing pawn to outflank their superior. Easily nominated for a run into the state legislature and as easily elected—Roosevelt campaigned on Fifth Avenue, his new associates took care of the rest of the district—Roosevelt went off to Albany. As he entered the Republican caucus, an observer not so unfriendly as most described what he saw:[4]

Suddenly our eyes...became glued on a young man who was coming through the door. His hair was parted in the center, and he had sideburns. He wore a single eyeglass, with a gold chain over his ear. He had on a cutaway coat with one button at the top, and the ends of its tails almost reached the tops of his shoes. He carried a gold-headed cane in one hand, a silk hat in the other, and he walked in the bentover fashion that was the style with the young men of the day. His trousers were as tight as a tailor could make them, and had a bell-shaped bottom to cover his shoes.

The debonair new member recorded in his diary his reciprocal impressions of his colleagues (except for a handful close to his own age): Republicans corrupt, oily, unprincipled; twenty-five Irish Democrats "a stupid, sodden, vicious lot, most of them being equally deficient in brains and virtue."[5]

Roosevelt's social class gave him uncomplicated righteousness. Untruthfulness, petty dishonesty, sexual misconduct—no gentleman could behave in such a perverse way, for natural leaders needed to set an example for the rest of the nation.

Therefore, once in the assembly as the Republican machine's candidate, Roosevelt felt no obligation to the machine's style. He made himself a striking figure in a mediocre group—a gamecock with vivid prose, stylish dress, and an eye for the headlines. He coaxed the assembly—unsuccessfully—into a thorough probe of corruption in New York City, the headlines establishing Roosevelt as a comer. In his second year, he achieved the position of minority leader, but when the Republicans took over the following year, the machine denied his promotion to the speakership.

In the midst of the legislative excitement, Roosevelt's wife Alice died giving birth to a daughter, also named Alice. Roosevelt's mother had died just hours before. The double agony drew wide public sympathy; the assembly adjourned to express its shock. Roosevelt sold off his recently acquired house and rushed plans for completion of a new home on 153 acres at Oyster Bay on Long Island.

Returning to Albany for a final torrent of work, Roosevelt also got himself elected as a delegate-at-large to the 1884 Republican national convention. Disdaining the frontrunners, Roosevelt and Henry Cabot Lodge of Massachusetts, a two-term representative in the Massachusetts General Court, a fellow

Porcellian even more aloof than his younger friend, helped stage a largely symbolic rally for a reform candidate. The fight went nowhere, but it netted Roosevelt plenty of notice. When James G. Blaine of Maine, an able congressman and cabinet officer who had never quite lived down a deal about railroad bonds in the past, won the nomination, Roosevelt hesitated, then fully supported Blaine, even campaigning for him in New York and in Lodge's Massachusetts—much to the horror of his reformist supporters and friends. Roosevelt spurned their scorn: healthy Republican partisan spirit was "prerequisite to the performance of effective work in American political life."[6] In 1884, Republican spirit was partisan, but not healthy. Blaine lost to Governor Grover Cleveland of New York.

For the next four years, Roosevelt, his legislative days behind him after three terms, divided his time among his cattle ranch, his literary and historical productions, and a chimerical run for mayor of New York.

With more bravado than good sense, Roosevelt invested about half his inheritance from his father—roughly $75,000—in a ranch in the Dakota Territory and in the cattle to stock it; the catastrophic blizzard of 1886–1887 all but wiped out his investment. In his self-image as a devil-may-care person, courageous and decisive, financial plunging was closely allied to the stamina that he displayed on hiking trips in Maine and on the trail in the Dakota country. A city man, he matched the sheer physical output of people who had spent their whole lives in the saddle or on the trail or in the woods.

Between episodes in Little Missouri country, Roosevelt resumed his writing, his gusty *Hunting Trips of a Ranchman* appearing in 1885 and the more prosaic *Thomas Hart Benton*, finished the same year, appearing two years later. Roosevelt's forgettable biography of Gouverneur Morris came out the following year (1888); then over the next eight years, his monumental *Winning of the West* (4 vols., 1889–1896), a paean to America, its white Anglo-Saxon Protestant culture, and its destiny. Along the way minor books and articles and reviews poured from his pen, much of it remunerative hack work reflecting his wondrously acquisitive mind, always ready for new information and insight.

In the fall of 1886, Roosevelt yielded to importunate requests that he run for mayor of New York against the Democratic Abram S. Hewitt and the single tax advocate, Henry George. All the old juices started to flow again. Even as he carried transatlantic steamer tickets in his pocket, he worked to revive his political fortune by seeking to become the youthful (twenty-eight) mayor of New York. Despite spirited campaigning, he finished a poor third.

His loss confirmed, he sailed to England with his sister Bamie. Upon his return, he married Edith Carow, who had been a favorite girl friend years before he had met Alice Lee. It was a happy match, and eventually the couple had four sons and a daughter. Edith created a comfortable haven for her husband at Oyster Bay, accepting his boundless enthusiasms without occupying herself in their eccentricity.

In 1888, the presidential race brought him back onto the political stage as a bit player. Roosevelt campaigned in Illinois, Michigan, and Minnesota for the Republican Benjamin Harrison against President Cleveland. When Harrison won, Lodge, now a congressman from Massachusetts, pressed Harrison into an obscure patronage award for his friend: Civil Service commissioner at $3,500 a year. Roosevelt took it immediately, for it was in Washington, D.C., it dealt with an interesting issue, and, in the hands of an aggressive commissioner, it could certainly produce attention.

In Washington for six years (1889–1895), Roosevelt moved easily in the highest circles of political and intellectual life. His technical knowledge and his ebullient conversation gained him prompt acceptance at the Cosmos Club. He entered the most sophisticated salon in the capital, the LaFayette Square residence of John Hay and Henry Adams, two distinguished intellectuals who attracted prestigious Washington leaders. The youngster in the group, Roosevelt soon found himself welcomed as a full member in good standing, much more than a mere civil service commissioner.

The Civil Service Commission, created in 1883 in the wake of President James Garfield's assassination, protected parts of government service from the intrusions of patronage-mongering. Putting duty and public notice above party, Roosevelt stayed through Harrison's four years and, when President Cleveland returned to office in 1893, for two additional years under the Democrats. Six years was enough; by then Roosevelt felt that he was "starting to go through Harvard again after graduating."[7] When Mayor William L. Strong of New York offered him a job as one of four police commissioners, Roosevelt accepted with alacrity.

The presidency of the Board of Police Commissioners gave Roosevelt an ideal job. It dealt with the security of the people of New York. It involved a large army of 38,000 policemen for whose activities he was responsible, and soon he was shaking up the notoriously corrupt high command and snooping around at night with his reporter friends Jacob Riis and Lincoln Steffens to detect sleeping or delinquent cops. It allowed him to exploit issues of public law and morality, like the Sunday closing law for saloons, which was winked at for a fee or enforced against those who held out against a payoff. Newspapers across the nation watched the performance—and the performer. What next for this irrepressible young man?

Riis and Steffens decided to probe that dark corner—and almost had their heads handed to them as the reward for their pains. With no more than curiosity and admiration for their friend in mind, Riis asked Roosevelt privately if he was working to be president. Initially enraged by such blunt exposure, then calmer, Roosevelt gave a revealing response. He acknowledged that he wanted to be president—"Every young man does"—but he feared that even adverting to that eventual goal might make him cautious and calculating in his present job, destroying the very traits that were "making him a possibility." Roosevelt forbade Riis and Steffens ever to mention "that" to him again.[8]

By the third year, the presidency of the police commission was yielding diminishing returns. It was a local job and, despite all the national publicity around Sunday closings, pretty small potatoes. What was worse, a gridlock on policy decisions developed, the commission's meetings foundering in inactivity that Roosevelt as board president lacked the authority to prevent. Furthermore, former Senator Thomas C. Platt, the "easy boss" of New York state Republicans, told Roosevelt in an interview "entirely pleasant and coldblooded"[8] that the police board would soon be abolished as part of an urban restructuring.

What followed was characteristic Roosevelt, bold and effective. Without mentioning Platt by name, he laid bare the plan in an address to the Methodist ministerial association of New York (the members of which remembered well his stand on Sunday saloon closings). The ministers responded with sermons all over the city. The *New York Times* did a full detailing of the "Republican Plot to Oust Roosevelt."[10] The date was late January 1896, a presidential election year. Wanting to be a force at the upcoming Republican national convention, Platt could not afford the appearance of a disunited party in New York. The reorganization of greater New York was quietly shelved. Roosevelt had his reprieve. Having defeated Platt in a public fight, he shrewdly did not overplay his hand. "I shall not break with the party," Roosevelt told Lodge, "the Presidential contest is too important."[11]

Its importance for Roosevelt was enormous. Initially opposed to Governor William McKinley of Ohio for the Republican nomination—a "great misfortune" if he were to be nominated, Roosevelt told Lodge[12]—he rallied to McKinley's side after the nomination and campaigned against William Jennings Bryan, the thirty-six-year-old Democratic nominee, in the Midwest. Bryan, Roosevelt told appreciative audiences, was a demagogue as radical as Robespierre and as terrible for the nation as Thomas Jefferson. When McKinley trounced Bryan, Roosevelt received his reward. In early April, he went off to Washington as assistant secretary of the navy at a salary of $4,500.

The switch was the turning point in Roosevelt's career. Up to then, he had concerned himself with local or peripheral issues—corruption in city government, job security for government workers, discipline and graft in an urban police force. Now his move to the navy department thrust him into great decisions at a moment when relations among the great powers were constantly shifting: Spain collapsing; Europe regrouping for the war in 1914; Russia, Japan, and other powers tilting for expansion in China. American expansionists felt keenly the urgency of the moment: imperialism now or never. Those who hesitated would never have another chance; for the open lands would be gone, and America would be left to thrash about foolishly, like Germany in southwest Africa, for crumbs so lacking in nourishment that no one had bothered to pick them up.

Roosevelt was both creature and creator of the newly expansionist impulses that moved many of his age, class, and temperament. Moving to Washington, he found congenial spirits at hand. His friend Lodge was now senator from

Massachusetts, increasingly a spokesman for congressional expansionists. Captain Alfred Thayer Mahan of the Naval War College, whose classic *The Influence of Sea Power upon History* (1890) was required reading among war planners throughout the world, had drawn on Roosevelt's own writings; then in turn he helped to define Roosevelt's thinking about the crucial sinews of power. Captain Leonard Wood, an ardent expansionist, had access both to President McKinley as his assistant physician and to the army's commanding general, who was his wife's uncle. In eclipse during the Cleveland administration, this coterie reemerged under McKinley. Roosevelt, as usual, was junior in this company. But his office put him at a critical command post that gave full play to his ambition for America—and for self.

Seven weeks into his appointment, Roosevelt, speaking at the formal opening of the Naval War College in Rhode Island, called for an enormous immediate increase in major naval vessels, as many as twenty battleships. Citing the growth of the fleets of other powers, he warned that the United States was vulnerable to attack and incapable of sustained response. He wanted officers and men trained to carry out national decisions at a moment's notice. He did not shrink from the possibility of war: "[N]o National life is worth having if the Nation is not willing, when the need shall arise, to stake everything on the supreme arbitrament of war, and to pour out its blood, its treasure, and tears like water, rather than submit to the loss of honor and renown. . . . Peace, like freedom, is not a gift that tarries long in the hands of cowards, or of those too feeble or short-sighted to deserve it."[13]

The speech commanded instant national attention. Reported generally and published in full in some newspapers, hailed as liberating by the jingoist press and spokesmen and as warmongering by the peace lovers, it set the terms for national discussion. The President, privately and reluctantly, agreed with his subordinate. Secretary John D. Long did not share the general enthusiasm for the speech, but he left town soon thereafter for his summer holiday. In his absence, the Assistant Secretary became the Acting Secretary.

Over the next months the Acting Secretary made two crucial interventions: He maneuvered the appointment of Commodore George Dewey as commander of the Pacific fleet, and he helped get President McKinley to sign the contingency plan ordering Dewey, in case of war with Spain, to take control of Manila harbor. When the sinking of the USS *Maine* in the harbor of Havana, Cuba, led to war, Roosevelt looked back with satisfaction at his activities: "I have the Navy in good shape."[14]

The war once declared, Roosevelt moved from desk to field. He and Leonard Wood—Wood now a full colonel, Roosevelt a modest lieutenant-colonel but clearly the driving force—received permission from the War Department to raise and command a regiment of volunteers. Ten men volunteered for every one accepted. A rugged crew of 560 men, a few elite easterners and the rest skilled horsemen and marksmen from the "frontier," gathered under Colonel Roosevelt's leadership, crossed the Gulf of Mexico as part of a large expeditionary force, landed at Siboney, Cuba, a fishing village south of Santiago, and plunged through a jungle skillfully defended by Spanish sharpshooters. Approaching Santiago from the east, Roosevelt led his dismounted cavalry, the "Rough Riders," in a charge up Kettle Hill, then moved in support of regular troops in a charge up San Juan Heights directly overlooking Santiago. With newspaper reporters in tow, his band breached the Spanish defenses, took a commanding position, and then settled in to allow the Spanish time to surrender with honor.

For Roosevelt, the war was a great personal triumph. He got himself a Spaniard (the phrasing is his), and he gave his men leadership that made them proud of themselves and proud of him as their leader. The principal hero of the war, he was so confident that he could return to New York draped in a mantle of humility: "All I'll talk about is the regiment. It's the finest regiment that ever was, and I'm proud to command it."[15]

For the moment famous throughout America, Roosevelt, spurning the overtures of reformers, accepted Platt's support for the Republican nomination for the governorship. Platt distrusted Roosevelt—he remembered recent history, and he suspected the Colonel, even then, of hoping to parlay the governorship into the presidency. But he had a scandal-ridden state Republican administration on his hands, and no alternative candidate had anything like the public exposure of the Colonel. Roosevelt made Platt's decision easier. He promised to avoid war with Mr. Platt "or anyone else,"[16] and he came, military hat in hand, to call on Platt at his "Amen Corner" in the Fifth Avenue Hotel. From their meeting Roosevelt emerged to announce his willingness to be nominated by the Republicans.[17]

Trouble emerged almost immediately. Roosevelt was not a legal resident of the state: affidavits he had signed for tax purposes made him a resident of the District of Columbia. The party turned to Elihu Root, a distinguished New York attorney as well as a prominent Republican, to create a brief— legal quibbles on the word "resident," together with patriotic blather and what even Root called "a lot of ballyhoo."[18] By a three-to-one margin, the Republican convention let itself be convinced.

For the campaign that followed, Roosevelt, with Rough Riders in tow, put himself on display all over the state—vigorous, defiant, sure of himself—as the alternative to Democratic chicanery. The voters bought his appeal. The narrowness of his margin, less than 18,000 votes, made the victory a clear personal triumph: no one else could have saved the Republicans in 1898.

He felt the satiety of success. He had turned forty during the campaign. He was about to start drawing the salary of a governor, $10,000. He had a contract for installments of his war stories, later to be a book, *The Rough Riders*. He was to give the Lowell lectures at Harvard for $1,600. He told his English friend Cecil Spring-Rice: "I . . . shall not care if I never hold another office."[19]

As Theodore Roosevelt moved Edith and the children—Alice, and the four boys and one girl that Edith bore—to the Executive Mansion in Albany early in January 1899, neither the Boy Governor nor Boss Platt could be certain who would rule. Platt's control of the legislature, especially of the Senate through which gubernatorial appointments had to pass, gave him bargaining power that no governor dared ignore. Furthermore, the process of renomination in 1900 would be no less under Platt's control. But the governor, especially if he happened to be Roosevelt, was not without assets too. His position as first citizen carried prestige and deference. He headed the state's bureaucracy. He could point the legislature's attention, if not direct its action. He could sign or veto legislative bills, and he could call the legislature into special session. To these routine weapons, Roosevelt added the power of the press. In New York, Riis and Steffens were only the most famous of those who fell under his spell. In Washington, he had captivated the younger William Allen White of the Emporia, Kansas, *Gazette*, over lunch and palaver with "the first trumpet call of the new time that was to be."[20] Now in Albany, Roosevelt drew in the reporters twice a day, bonding them to himself by creating news and, even more, by making newsmen his friends and confidants.[21] His skills made him a worthy competitor to Platt.

Roosevelt and Platt arrived at a generally workable compromise on appointments, but on legislation Roosevelt's success made Platt vengeful. Roosevelt posted a modest early progressive record. He got civil service back on the books. He successfully led the fights for improved working conditions in sweatshops, for factory inspection, and for limiting working hours for women and children. He strengthened the state's commitment to the eight-hour day for its own employees. These were not issues likely to provoke the wrath of political machines in either party. Though machines resisted sacrificing their control of process—through direct primaries, for example—they were frequently the vehicles that carried limited social reforms through the legislatures in industrial states. But when Roosevelt outmaneuvered Platt by getting a general tax on power and traction franchises through the legislature and by using an insurance scandal to open up banks and insurance companies for extensive public scrutiny, Platt and his backers in the business community were alerted to the urgency of getting rid of Roosevelt, either by denying him renomination in 1900, or, more creatively, by kicking him upstairs into the vice-presidency in 1901, Vice-President Garret A. Hobart having conveniently died.

As 1900 moved toward the summer convention months, pressure toward Roosevelt's nomination as vice-president came from varied sources. Lodge argued for it. The Wisconsin, and later the Kansas and Pennsylvania, delegations saw Roosevelt as a progressive hero. Politicians opposed to Mark Hanna, senator from Ohio and Republican national chairman, saw nominating Roosevelt as a way of humbling Hanna. Roosevelt, and Edith even more, opposed the move; the fear of inactivity in the vice-presidential office gave both of them pause. Roosevelt had his eye on the presidency in 1904; but only one sitting vice-president, Martin Van Buren, had ever succeeded to the job. On the other hand, New York was an insecure base while the hostility of Platt persisted. And Washington was, to be sure, the hub of national policy.

Arriving in Philadelphia in June 1900 for the Republican convention, Roosevelt found the conviction quite general that he would add strength to the ticket. Even as he stammered his reluctance, his every action bid the convention to insist. The convention insisted, unanimously except for Roosevelt's vote. Platt was amused.

In the ensuing campaign, the governor toured twenty-four states while McKinley stayed home. Together they won 292 electoral votes, leaving Bryan 155.

The following March, as Platt and his entourage journeyed to the inauguration, the boss told his crew: "We're all off to Washington to see Teddy take the veil."[22] Months before, Hanna had proven to be the better prophet: "Don't any of you realize that there's only one life between this madman and the Presidency?"[23]

When President McKinley's assassination thrust Theodore Roosevelt into the presidency on September 14, 1901, the office and the man were aptly met. No man except Theodore's cousin Franklin a generation later developed so certain a concept of what a vigorous executive could bring to the office. Not even George Washington and Abraham Lincoln, Roosevelt's exemplars, had comparable perception. Coming at the end of a trail of weak presidents, McKinley excepted, Roosevelt created a new vision of what the office might be. He burst through the door that McKinley had opened a crack. Such an explosion of activity, and show of activity, in the presidential office was a novel sight for Americans. Roosevelt's youth and experience served him well. The new president was forty-two when he took office, the youngest president ever. He had led men through sniper fire. He had ranged the plains for days and days. He knew Europe at first hand. He had dealt with political machines and had survived comfortably. He knew literary success. He knew his own mind. He also knew that the display of vigor, a commodity in scant supply, would carry substantial weight with the nation. He knew what made newspapermen tick. He understood how to make himself the focus of activity from which other people could draw vicarious success. He could greet a titled ambassador and a former Rough Rider with ebullience that let each feel that he and the President shared common values, at least for a moment. Nor would either of his guests have been deceived, for Roosevelt did understand the ethic of the upper classes in Europe and America, and he did recognize the energy, the productivity, the blunt honesty (and covert dishonesty) in his western friends. Though he had only a passing relation to the academic world, he knew the language of the intellectuals. His recent experience had brought him close to the value structure of military and naval officers. He had never been close to workers or to farmers, but his acres at Sagamore Hill at least taught him the vocabulary of growth and harvest, even if he never had to face the debilitating costs of grain elevators and railroads.

So the man was ready for the post.

The times were also ready for the man. The new national economy had still not been addressed in sophisticated terms. The parties still debated the tariff, as they had for generations. They diddled with the currency, moving to gold or silver in response to whatever pressures were felt in one year or another. The Interstate Commerce Act (1887) and the Sherman Antitrust Act (1890) were both ineffective: The Supreme Court had put the Sherman Act to sleep in 1895, and the Interstate Commerce Commission lacked the teeth with which to gnaw on the railroads' abuses.

In foreign affairs, the changing relationships among European powers and the competition for Asia were international issues well beyond the consciousness of most Americans, but they were part of a new reality that was emerging in the world, and the place where they could be dealt with was the White House.

At this moment a leader arrived who thought in geopolitical terms, who worried about the escapades of industrialists and about the radical solutions they evoked from their opponents, who dealt with Hanna as he had dealt with Platt, who had energy for the great and small, and who never was slowed by self-doubts. The era of Theodore Roosevelt had arrived.

To establish his primacy, Roosevelt had to transcend the accident of his accession. The problem had two dimensions: to reach the people with drama that would make them want him for their president and to master the forty-five state organizations that would give him the chance to face the people as candidate in 1904. The first involved policy. The second involved maneuver.

The principal instrument of maneuver was the jobs available to the president in every state, indeed, in every congressional district, jobs from postmaster to federal judge. Systematically, state by state, Roosevelt exercised his options: replace Hanna loyalists with Roosevelt loyalists; sidestep local political leaders who did not toe the mark or, alternately, woo away their troops; shake the Republican South by bringing in Booker T. Washington, whom the whites had raised to the status of black spokesman for the whole race following his conciliatory speech at the Atlanta Exposition in 1895, in order to rally black delegates in the South to the new cause of Theodore Roosevelt. In his own state, he moved the political pawns around sufficiently to isolate Platt. In Ohio, Hanna tried to straddle when the state party convention considered a resolution endorsing Roosevelt for the nomination in 1904. Roosevelt, familiar enough with a fox at bay, telegraphed Hanna with exquisite clarity that "of course those who favor my administration and my nomination will favor endorsing both and those who do not will oppose."[24] Hanna, an old pro, got the message, threw in the towel, and died shortly thereafter. By the time of the convention, Roosevelt's forces were sufficiently in command to make the event a coronation.

Ultimately it was the voters, not the party, who would choose the president. For a nation that had twice given William Jennings Bryan close to 6.5 million votes, in both cases within a million votes of the Republicans' count, the new president needed issues that were, or that could be made to seem to be, of importance to the voters. The President successfully seized upon two such issues.

In his first message to Congress, less than three months after his inauguration, Roosevelt addressed the problem of industrial mergers, recommending legislation to control abuses inflicted on competitors and consumers without destroying large corporations. He even invited Congress to pass an enabling constitutional amendment if it doubted its power to regulate industry.[25] When Congress failed to act, he had his attorney general invoke the Sherman Act against the Northern Securities Company, a railroad holding company that dominated the northern routes across the western United States. This particular target had special appeal, both because it was unpopular in its region and because it fell clearly within federal authority under the commerce clause of the Constitution. Furthermore, this target allowed Roosevelt to steal a march on the Democrats: no issue since silver had given Bryan and the Democrats a throatier rallying cry than the abuses of big business.

While the suit proceeded, Roosevelt undertook a barnstorming tour through New England and the Midwest, arguing that bringing the corporations to heel would lead to a "square deal" for all the people.

Roosevelt carved out a complex centrist position. Though the Sherman Act made illegal any combination that restrained trade, he allowed himself to distinguish between "good trusts," those that served the public interest by creating efficiencies in operation, thus yielding lower prices and higher quality, and "bad trusts," those that used their control of the market to exploit consumers. The distinction involved a good deal of executive discretion based, in theory at least, on the impact of any given trust on the general economic welfare. Vertical integration—controlling the process of production from acquisition of raw materials to ultimate sale to consumers—might create efficiencies and lower costs by eliminating middlemen. Horizontal mergers— buying up competitors and removing them from the market—might open the way to price gouging. Whatever the economic justification for this distinction, it departed from the stated intent of the law, and it gave Roosevelt a curiously ambiguous reputation. Those struck by federal suits regarded him as a vindictively oppressive trust-buster, and Roosevelt reveled in the image of himself standing up to the malefactors of great wealth. But those fearful of the impact of industrial concentration on American economic life regarded him as limply half-hearted. Furthermore, his political opponents suspected political motivation in his selection of trusts chosen for attack and trusts allowed to slide past the law.

In attacking the Northern Securities Company, Roosevelt was latching onto a winning issue, for both Bryan Democrats and muckrakers were making trust-busting a staple of national debate. The Supreme Court decided for the government in 1904; the decision came in ample time for the fall election.

In the same year that Roosevelt initiated the Northern Securities prosecution, he appointed a commission to mediate a strike by anthracite coal miners against their employers. The strike ended, Roosevelt rescuing the nation from the horrors of a chilly winter. His intervention gave weight to his campaign against stubborn abusive owners whose concerns for profits exceeded their interest in the public welfare.[26]

Clearly, by the time of the 1904 election, the President had his striking domestic issue. Congress had helped. In 1903, it created the Department of Commerce and Labor, which included a Bureau of Corporations to compile reports on the conduct of corporations, and it passed the Elkins Act, which specifically forbade rebates from railroads to their most favored customers.

Roosevelt made his will felt beyond the national borders as well. In 1903 he highhandedly helped the province of Panama revolt against the legitimate government of Colombia so that Panama could grant the United States effective sovereignty over a ten-mile zone that would accommodate the canal between the Atlantic and the Pacific.

As the Republican convention approached, Roosevelt protected his right flank. He turned control of the convention over to Speaker Joseph G. Cannon, Elihu Root, now secretary of war, and Senator Lodge, two of them among his closest political friends, all three of them spokesmen for the bleakest conservatism. ("It would have been difficult to find three more reverent archbishops of high conservatism in the entire Republican apostolic succession," George E. Mowry, the great historian of progressivism, records.[27]) They made the machinery run smoothly, and Roosevelt emerged as the nominee without a struggle.

At election time, the gentle Judge Alton B. Parker, a respectable advocate of the gold standard, and the Democrats, who opposed trusts too, were no match for the muscular showoff in the White House. The Republicans, who had established themselves as the clear majority party in 1896, now watched their margin in the electoral college go up to 336 to 140, 44 better than McKinley's showing in 1900, and their margin in the popular vote soared past 2.5 million.

Once president in his own right, Roosevelt maneuvered within the conservative-progressive division in his own party to push his program of moderate reform. After initial failure in 1905, he won passage of the Hepburn Act (1906), which extended the jurisdiction of the Interstate Commerce Commission to carriers other than railroads, allowed the commission to set fair rates, and eliminated some specific abuses such as the granting of free passes. Nowhere did Roosevelt's deft sense of the possible appear so strikingly. He had offered a somewhat more comprehensive bill, and he enjoyed considerable support in Congress; considerable, but not enough to gain passage. To make his minority into a majority, he dangled the threat of raising the issue of the protective tariff. That threat brought the probusiness advocates to heel. But only on a moderate bill. A moderate bill, however, was insufficient for the progressives from the midwestern states; Senator Robert M. La Follette of Wisconsin excoriated Roosevelt for accepting half a loaf. The President invoked another metaphor: "I believe in men who take the next step; not those who theorize about the two-hundredth step."[28]

Other progressive legislation passed in the same year included the Pure Food and Drug Act and the Meat Inspection Act—also half loaves. In the last year of his presidency, Roosevelt convoked the White House Conservation Conference, which focused attention on the rapid depletion of natural resources and led to the National Conservation Commission, headed by Gifford Pinchot, who was later to become Chief Forester of the United States. He also signed the Aldrich-Vreeland Act, which set up the National Monetary Commission to recommend changes in the banking and currency systems.

In the later years of the term, and especially in the face of hard times in 1907, Roosevelt, dramatically in his private correspondence but even in his public statements as well, denounced the greed of big business, scoffed at the federal courts for their unresponsiveness to contemporary needs, and spoke out for increased federal regulation by expert bodies chosen by the executive branch—a stand that he enjoyed calling "progressive conservatism or conservative radicalism."[29]

Even more in foreign policy than in domestic legislation, Roosevelt made his will felt. His conduct in the Caribbean typified his notions for that area. Safely reelected, he issued the Roosevelt corollary to the Monroe Doctrine, which warned European nations not to try to collect even their just debts from recalcitrant Latin American countries, but then set the United States as the policeman to enforce legitimate claims. "Speak softly and carry a big stick; you will go far"—he had used the West African proverb in 1900,[30] and his policy took on the name "Big Stick."

He also thrust himself into Asian and European politics. Japan's surprising victory over the Russian fleet at the Battle of Tsushima Strait caused fear about the balance of power in the Far East, so Roosevelt responded willingly to the Japanese overture to him as mediator. His efforts won him the 1906 Nobel Peace Prize. Two years later he approved the ambiguous Root-Takashira agreement in which both Japan and the United States agreed to maintain the status quo in the Pacific, to respect each other's possessions in the Pacific, to uphold the Open Door in China, and to support by peaceful means the independence of China. It was the kind of *Realpolitik* that came easily to Roosevelt and to Elihu Root, the Secretary of State in Roosevelt's second term. In Europe, Roosevelt, at Germany's request, intervened with France to set up a conference on the future of Morocco at Algeciras in 1906, even allowing American delegates to participate.

As the Roosevelt incumbency was coming to a close in 1909, Roosevelt had made the presidency the focal point of American action, and he had made the process popular by appearing as the spokesman for all the people.[31] Few doubted that he could have the office for another year. But there was an impassable barrier. In the flush of the electoral sweep in 1904, he had said:

"On the Fourth of March next I shall have served three and one-half years, and this three and one-half years constitutes my first term. The wise custom which limits the President to two terms regards the substance and not the form. Under no circumstances will I be a candidate for or accept another nomination."[32]

Canvassing for a successor, he settled on his secretary of war, William Howard Taft.

2

The Taft Years

Theodore Roosevelt's designation of William Howard Taft as his successor rewarded a close friend with rich experience on the federal bench, in the Philippines, and in Washington and with demonstrated loyalty to the Roosevelt tradition. Though Taft had faced the electorate only once, and that long ago, his long career of public service, all of it creditable and most of it vastly successful, made him a credible choice.

Born in Cincinnati, Ohio, four years before the outbreak of the Civil War, Taft grew up in Mount Vernon on the outskirts of the city. His parents, émigrés from Vermont and Massachusetts, spent their lives in circles largely made up of former New Englanders. Will's father, Alphonso Taft, a graduate of Yale and Yale Law School, was secretary of war and attorney general in President Ulysses S. Grant's cabinet and, later, American minister in Vienna. He never achieved wealth, but the family lived a comfortable, secure life. When the time was ripe, there was no doubt that young Will, too, would attend Yale. Will was graduated second in the class of 1878, well esteemed by his classmates, an unimposing class orator, and a member of Skull and Bones, a secret society that his father had helped to found.

In the fall of 1878, Will entered Cincinnati Law School and reported on county and federal courts for the Cincinnati *Commercial*. Disdaining a law degree, he left school and crammed law into his head for five weeks, and in 1880 he was admitted to the bar. The following year he accepted appointment as assistant prosecutor of Hamilton County.

His father's son, Will was effectively geared into the political machinery of his state. His contacts and his geniality made preferment easy, and, as he wrote years later, "Like every well-trained Ohio man I always had my plate the right side up when offices were falling."[1] After a year as a prosecutor, he became collector of internal revenue for the first district, which had its head-quarters in Cincinnati. But the collectorship had the rancid taste of political jobbery for Grand Army of the Republic veterans, and Taft pulled out. Like so many people in his social class, he favored putting most government jobs outside politics into civil service. He was certain that the Republican Party was the most likely vehicle to undertake such a reform.

The Tafts were implacable Republicans. Almost no one they went with would have been part of the Democracy. Will, speaking of politics in Cincinnati and in Ohio generally, was sure that "no matter how bad the Republican legislative ticket, the Democratic members will work much more mischief."[2]

His Republican affections served him well, bringing him an interim appointment as a superior court judge in Cincinnati. In 1888, Taft won election for a full term.

On the bench where his father had once sat, now married to Helen ("Nellie") Herron, a bright, strong-minded, serious, independent daughter of a family that moved in equally well connected circles, Will adopted a pattern of strong patrician family life and committed public service. Other Tafts lived in the neighborhood, and the Herrons were even more numerous; the families traipsed in and out of each other's houses with affectionate regularity. There were servants available to help—maids and governesses indoors, housemen outside. Will's salary as a judge was a modest $6,000, but his brother Charles, already enjoying success, supplemented Will's pay, as he did for much of Will's career. In the summers, the family went off to Murray Bay in the province of Quebec; their house there eventually accommodated thirteen grandchildren. The Tafts had a secure sense of position: they came from solid British Protestant stock; they knew that hard work was obligatory and rewarding; they enjoyed the certainty of their position and their future.[3]

Will dreamed that his future would include a seat on the United States Supreme Court; even at age thirty-three, he maneuvered for an appointment. But President Benjamin Harrison demurred—at thirty-three, Taft lacked experience—at the same time offering him, unsolicited, the post of solicitor general of the United States.

Taft faced the prospect with an odd mixture of confidence and misgivings. But Nellie had no doubts; indeed, she felt impatient with her husband's reluctance to take the next step upward. In Washington, Will would be only a step away from cabinet rank. Cincinnati was too small a pool for Will's talents or for Nellie's ambition for him. So it was that in 1890 they moved to Washington, and Taft began a parade of important federal jobs.

In eighteen months an appointment to the Sixth Circuit Court of Appeals brought the Tafts back to Cincinnati. It was a homecoming in more than one sense, for Taft dearly loved the intricacies of law and the formal decorum that clothed federal courts, especially appellate courts. The law was the distillation of man's quest for order. It was the certain guarantor of liberty. The courts were its temple, and judges its willing acolytes, none more willing or proud to serve than Taft.

For the next eight years, Taft established himself as a thorough scholar of the law, aware of English and even French precedents as well as the standard American corpus. He generally favored labor's right to organize and to strike, but he drew the line at rioting and property destruction. He refused to permit secondary boycotts, for legal precedents, which weighed on him like the law itself, were against them. His stands won him a mixed reception: on the one hand, he warned his half-brother Charles against running for Congress since their relationship would "solidify the labor vote against him";[4] on the other hand, he was written off by a railroad attorney as "one of those Western labor judges."[5]

One important Taft decision affected national policy. In *United States v. Addystone Pipe* (1898), Taft's circuit court used the Sherman Antitrust Act to order dissolved a price-fixing arrangement among six manufacturing corporations that sold cast-iron pipe in the Mississippi Valley. Three years before, the Supreme Court, in *United States v. E. C. Knight* (1895), had ruled that manufacturing was an intrastate activity beyond the reach of congressional authority under the commerce clause even when the activity created a nearly total national monopoly. Ingeniously distinguishing the facts in *Addystone Pipe*, Taft ruled that the companies' plans of action, which started in manufacturing, "necessarily involve in their execution the delivery of merchandise across state lines"; therefore, they already qualified as interstate commerce "within the regulating power of congress even before the transit of goods in performance of the contract was begun."[6] Taft boldly constructed a finding at variance with the Supreme Court's, arguing that innovation by the federal government was not unconstitutional when Congress merely exercised powers that had previously lain dormant. His court ruled that the use of the Sherman Act against anticompetitive manufacturers was "within the limits allowed by the constitution of the United States."[7] The Supreme Court substantially sustained Taft's judgment by an incredible unanimous vote, recalling the Sherman Act from the oblivion to which the *Knight* case had threatened to consign it.[8]

The decision reinforced Taft's hope for promotion to the Supreme Court. But vacancies came and went, and still no call.

When President William McKinley suddenly summoned Taft to Washington in January 1900, there was no vacancy on the Court. Instead the President asked him to head a commission to the Philippine Islands, which had just been annexed as part of Spain's penalty for losing the Spanish-American War. Taft hesitated, doubted, asked around. His wife, never partial to judicial stolidity, urged him to go. So did his brothers. Elihu Root, Secretary of War, put the job to him as a stern duty. McKinley promised judicial promotion when the occasion arose. Taft accepted, little thinking that a six- to eight-month assignment would take almost four years.

Appointed civil governor of the Philippines in 1901, Taft held the responsibility for suppressing the guerrilla forces seeking Philippine independence, creating the consultative agencies that would eventually lead to representative government, dealing with an epidemic of cholera, restoring the damaged Philippine economy, and dealing with the Catholic Church (in the Philippines and in Rome) over the disposition of church lands. Representing a distant imperialist master, he needed to reconcile order and progress. The demands of the job took a toll on his health, first dengue fever, than an abscess in the perineum. Taft recovered remarkably well, well enough to evoke an exchange of cables with his austere superior, the secretary of war. Reassuring his boss after a trip to a mountain resort, the three-hundred-pound Taft cabled Secretary Root: "Stood trip well. Rode horseback twenty-five miles to five thousand feet elevation." Root shot back: "Referring to your telegram . . . how is the horse.?"[9]

As Taft sailed off to the Philippines, politics in the United States went its own curious way as Governor Roosevelt found himself buried in the vice-presidency. At that moment, Taft appeared to be the more promising agent of destiny, and, after Taft was named the first civil governor of the Philippines, no one paid more glowing tribute than Theodore Roosevelt: "A year ago a man of wide acquaintance both with American public life and American public men remarked that the first Governor of the Philippines ought to combine the qualities which could make a first-class President of the United States with the qualities which would make a first-class Chief Justice of the United States, and that the only man he knew who possessed all those qualities was Judge William H. Taft, of Ohio. The statement was entirely correct."[10] Between the time when that tribute was written and the moment when it appeared in the *Outlook* magazine, Theodore Roosevelt had become the twenty-sixth president of the United States.

Now the two stood in a direct line, Roosevelt in the presidential chair at home, Taft his viceroy in Manila, Taft's ambitions, and those of his wife, intertwined with the unpredictable dynamo one year his junior. When Taft was in Washington in 1902 to defend administration policy in the Philippines, Roosevelt, not unexpectedly, laid out a new career pattern for Taft. He wanted Taft to complete his work in the Philippines in time for Roosevelt to offer him the next vacancy on the Supreme Court.

Taft's next appointment, when it came, would be not to the Supreme Court, but to the post of Secretary of War. His preference for the judicial post remained fixed despite the opposition of his family: his wife Nellie, his mother, his aunt Delia Torrey, his brothers Henry and Charles. Twice Roosevelt offered him the coveted seat. Each time Taft had stubbornly demurred because of the delicate situation in the Philippines. In early 1903, Roosevelt would no longer be put off by his subordinate: the President summoned Taft home to become secretary of war one year hence, when Root planned to leave the office to return to his law practice. Roosevelt said that he needed Taft: "Remember too, the aid and comfort you would be to me not merely as Secretary of War, not merely as director of the affairs in the Philippines, but as my counselor and adviser in all the great questions that come up." If only there were three of you, Roosevelt added in a handwritten note: one on the Supreme Court, one in the Philippines, and one as Secretary of War.[11]

Taft returned to the United States in time for Roosevelt's campaign in 1904. He dutifully went on the stump for the President, finding without difficulty that virtue and depravity coincided neatly with Republican and Democrat. But the tension in the campaign confirmed Taft's distaste for the process: "I would not run for president if you guaranteed the office. It is awful to be made afraid of one's shadow."[12]

For the ensuing presidential term, Taft became Roosevelt's closest adviser. As secretary of war, he supervised the continuation of his own policies in the Philippines and took charge of the beginnings of the Panama Canal. He oversaw federal relief after the San Francisco earthquake in 1906. He served as Roosevelt's surrogate on the stump in the congressional election of 1906, from Ohio to Wyoming, as far south as Texas and Louisiana, as far north as Maine. During the same year he tried in Havana to make American control palatable to the Cubans. In 1907 he traveled to Japan to smooth waters riled by Japan's desire to expand and by California's persistent habit of venting its hatred of Japanese immigrants. His close contact with the President deepened their friendship and made their joint political maneuvers a delight. Roosevelt and Taft and Root, who returned to the cabinet as secretary of state in 1905, made themselves into a private trio out of Alexandre Dumas's *Three Musketeers*, Roosevelt as D'Artagnan, Root as Athos, and Taft as Porthos.

Almost immediately after the inauguration in 1905, Roosevelt began thinking about his successor. Only two men were real possibilities, Root and Taft, and, curiously enough, neither was enthusiastic.

Elihu Root had one of the finest legal minds in America. His corporate law practice in New York City made a curious backdrop for the trust-busting image that Roosevelt professed to project, but in fact Root shared many of Roosevelt's upperclass attitudes. He felt the same distaste for extremes of both corporate abuse and proletarian aggression. He regarded public service as a public trust for competent leaders, and he regretted the need to deal with unsavory types that controlled votes in the many fiefdoms of American politics. With an impenetrable mien and a sharp wit, occasionally sharp to the point of venom, he suffered fools with disdain mingled with wry tolerance. Roosevelt told Taft in 1906 that while Root would not be so strong a candidate as either of them, he would be "at least as good a President as either you or I"[13]—a level of praise, in the midst of Roosevelt's second term and prior to Taft's accession, that in Roosevelt's mind fell just this side of extravagance. In 1904, Root toyed with the idea of plotting his way to the White House in 1909. By then, he would be sixty-six years old. Root said simply that he was "not willing to pay the price."[14]

Taft, diffident about his abilities for the presidency, knew by 1907 that he would be the President's choice and, when the machinery purred with pre-election hum, the choice of the Republican convention as well. And so he was. Senator Henry Cabot Lodge, permanent chairman of the convention, guided the tally: 702 votes for Taft, 274 for everybody else.

The victory had its darker side. Taft and Roosevelt proposed a plank lamenting the "hasty and ill-considered" issuance of labor injunctions.[15] When a mushy plank was substituted, outraging organized labor, Roosevelt and Taft agreed to it to keep the peace. Even worse, Taft let control of the vice-presidency out of his hands. He wanted, ideally, "some western senator who has shown himself conservative and at the same time represents the progressive movement."[16] But the convention, having been muscled by Roosevelt more than it cared for, turned defiantly to James S. "Sunny Jim" Sherman of New York, a standpat nonentity, the only man in the convention that Taft would have explicitly eliminated from consideration.

The Republicans in Congress who viewed themselves as progressives could not fail to note the omens.

But Roosevelt, official and unofficial bandmaster for progressivism, had no doubts about Taft: "I do not believe there can be found in the whole country a man so well fitted to be President. He is not only absolutely fearless, absolutely disinterested and upright, but he has the widest acquaintance with the nation's needs without and within and the broadest sympathies with all our citizens."[17]

Roosevelt was sincere. He knew that Taft was unlike him, not the combative, vigorous, outgoing, impetuous, intense leader for whom politics was food and drink and statesmanship almost a sacrament. But Taft had his own qualities. He had loyally supported Roosevelt's initiatives, especially in the previous three years. He had successfully managed large undertakings—the Philippines, the Vatican, Cuba and Japan—and snarled bureaucratic tangles like the War Department. As judge he had weighed conflicting values resolutely, not least in the antitrust field. Taft had shown spunk and integrity in resisting the President's calls home from Manila. As friend, Taft was a joy and a boon. As lieutenant, he had never been anything but utterly dependable, loyal beyond cavil.

As lieutenant—there was the rub. Taft had become the first lieutenant of D'Artagnan. Now, with D'Artagnan still alive, indeed in his prime and younger than Porthos, primacy was passing to the older man. At issue was not a little swordplay with Cardinal Richelieu's guards, but the conduct of the newly invigorated presidential office.

As Taft campaigned for the presidency, he needed presidential stature while the figure in the White House preempted the field. Even if Roosevelt could have hidden under a bushel, Taft's affection for his superior, his respect for the office, and his own nonimperial nature would have caught him up short. To make matters worse, he had no taste for canvassing for votes for himself: Begging itself made the beggar unworthy of the gift. Roosevelt had no such qualms, and he sought to rub his lust for battle into his lethargic aide. Taft, alternately grateful and resistant, essentially went his own way.

Taft made a virtue of his preference for peace over tumult. In his acceptance speech, he pitched his campaign on consolidation, not innovation: "The practical, constructive and difficult work . . . of those who follow Mr. Roosevelt is to devise ways and means by which the high level of business integrity and obedience to law which he has established may be maintained and departures from it restrained without undue interference with legitimate business."[18] On this basis the transition from one administration to the next could satisfy both Roosevelt and Taft: for Roosevelt, the assurance of continuity, the mantle of progressivism itself falling on Taft's ample frame; for Taft, a presidential role that acknowledged the past and set out new directions for the future.

With Taft's lopsided victory in November, 321 electoral votes to 162 for the Democratic William Jennings Bryan, the nation moved on to the Taft years. Once Roosevelt had helped to install his successor on March 4, 1909, he went to Africa to hunt lions.

The administration of President Taft (1909–1913) set the agenda for the two years of political debate that led to the election of 1912. The new President looked forward to his term without zest. If he were about to preside as chief justice in the cramped room in the capitol where the Supreme Court met, he told a friend, he "should feel entirely at home."[19] But for the nagging decisions about a cabinet and the approaching complexities of revising the tariff he had no enthusiasm. Fifty-two as he entered office, he had maturity and experience, but he was not really cut out for Rooseveltian drama. Though an active man who rode horseback and who played golf before gocarts reduced the game to sedentary socializing, he did not push himself to work until he had to, only at the last meeting a deadline with a kinetic spurt of energy. He carried his 250 pounds well, even when they slipped up to and past 300 pounds. His height carried authority, and his erect carriage let his tastefully tailored clothes give the impression of dignity rather than bulk. His hair, always carefully parted in the middle, was considerably darker than his generous white handlebar moustache. His large face, wrapping itself around a chuckle until it burst out as a full laugh, could be merry and warm.

The presidency would tax his best qualities, and he could not look for compensation in the power plays, in the intricate manipulations, and in the battle of wits that Roosevelt had mastered and had come to love. For days after his inauguration, he still felt that the office was not his. "When I hear someone say Mr. President, I look around expecting to see Roosevelt," Captain Archie Butt—Archibald Willingham Butt—Roosevelt's military aide who stayed on with Taft, heard the President tell a political friend; and to his wife, Taft affirmed that Roosevelt "will always be the President to me, and I can never think of him as anything else."[20] But now President Roosevelt had become Colonel Roosevelt, private citizen. William Howard Taft was the only president the nation had.

President Taft entered office with solid Republican majorities in both houses of Congress: a forty-seven seat margin in the House of Representatives and almost a two-to-one ratio in the Senate. Yet the party label hid the turbulence within: "Republican" meant Senator Nelson W. Aldrich of Rhode Island, conservative, astute, aristocratic, and Senator Robert M. La Follette of Wisconsin, progressive, uncompromising, populist. In the House, it meant Speaker Joseph C. Cannon of Illinois, a foxy reactionary whose thirty-six years of experience let him play his colleagues like a mandolin, and George W. Norris of Nebraska, a talented progressive who carried his principles through the New Deal and into World War II.

The aggressively progressive minority—perhaps thirty in the House and eight to twelve in the Senate—lacked the strength to be decisive. But they were prepared to defy party discipline, responding to progressive pressures from their constituency that they both obeyed and led. Just after the election, La Follette's message of congratulation—an ominous cross between good wishes and stark threats—set the standard that the progressives, soon to be known as Insurgents, would hold Taft to: "The country confides in your constructive leadership for the progressive legislation needed to secure equal opportunity for all in our industrial development."[21] La Follette's telegram tugged at Taft's left sleeve. But the pressures on the other side were stronger, for Taft's determination to carry out the Republican mandate required that he work closely with Republican leadership in Congress. The insurgents watched warily this anointed heir of Roosevelt. What was lacking? Will, or competence, or both? Or did Taft merely pay lip service to progressivism to conceal a basically standpat mentality?

The answer took shape around specific issues. The first was the reelection of "Uncle Joe" Cannon as speaker of the House of Representatives. The insurgents wanted to end his dictatorial rule, exercised both as speaker and through his hand-picked Ways and Means Committee. In the larger and more unruly House, control over procedure bestowed control over substance, and the standpat rule by Cannon, openly cynical and arrogant, gave the speaker as effective a veto as the Constitution gave to the president.

Taft, favoring reform of the House's rules, wanted Cannon out of the speaker's chair. But since he had "to regard the Republican Party as the instrumentality through which to try to accomplish something," he told William Allen White, editor of the Emporia, Kansas, *Gazette*, "I cannot afford, merely to accomplish one good purpose, to sacrifice all the others, when those others are, as compared to the one, much more important."[22] He knew—and if he had any hesitation, Root reinforced the point for him—that if he fought Cannon and lost, he would begin his presidency with one black eye and with a top congressional leader ready to give him a second. So Taft hesitated, as Roosevelt urged him to do: it did not make sense to put Cannon into the position of "the sullen and hostile floor leader bound to bring your administration to grief."[23] Then principle entered: respect for a coordinate branch of government should slow the president's hand on an issue as central to congressional power as the selection of the House's presiding officer. Here

Taft differed from Roosevelt: constitutional scruples were both a barrier and an excuse. He came away from a meeting with Cannon satisfied that Cannon had promised "to stand by the party platform and to follow my lead."[24]

The insurgents watched the performance with dismay. Doubts created at the convention now deepened as Taft extended the hand of cooperation to the tightest fist raised against reform.

During the first months of the term, doubts grew into certainty when Taft met repeatedly with Cannon and Aldrich, the most prominent power in the Senate. With Aldrich, Taft felt a closeness far beyond what Cannon's crude cynicism would ever allow. Aldrich was a gentleman, strong, shrewd, imperious, when necessary a real gut fighter, but withal a gentleman with values and attitudes not notably different from Taft's own.

Thus increasingly, Taft drifted away from the progressive heritage of Roosevelt and sidled up to a conservative posture that caricatured his honest convictions.

The fight over the tariff in 1909 repeated the scenario. The Republican platform in 1908 spoke of revising the tariff, and Taft himself spoke during the campaign of revision downward to the point of compensating for cheaper production costs abroad. True to his campaign commitment, he summoned Congress into special session less than two weeks after his inauguration.

When Congress gathered, Aldrich and Lodge unabashedly denied that revision of the tariff necessarily meant downward revision; it could equally and unquestionably mean revision upward. Aldrich and Cannon had enough control to make their audacity work despite the insurgents in the Senate: La Follette and his allies. The Payne-Aldrich bill juggled rates, and, in balance, it could be argued that some downward revisions occurred. But the result fell far short of Taft's intent. A joint committee of both houses, predictably stacked with high-tariff advocates, edged rates back up. Taft could scarcely argue that he had won, and the insurgents were certain that they had lost.

Taft never took control of the process to bend Congress to his will. He lacked detailed knowledge of tariff schedules, and he could not bring himself to the elaborate tutoring that the situation required. Late in the process, he forced Aldrich and his allies to vote for a 2 percent tax on corporations and for a constitutional amendment permitting a federal income tax as alternatives to proposed income and inheritance taxes. And he gained some concessions for the Philippines. But when the moment came for final presidential action, he signed the bill into law.

Taft took grim satisfaction: no one would sing his praises; both sides would blame him. The path of duty was more attractive than praise. More attractive perhaps, but politically destructive. And deservedly so, too, for, unlike Roosevelt who could hunt with conservative hounds and run with reforming hares,[25] Taft had merely stood by the stable fence with a muffled cheer for alternate sides until the hares lost their zest and the hounds ran out of breath. William Allen White recalled a saying among his fellow "progressive conspirators": "There stands Taft like the statue of Louis XV in the Tuileries Gardens, smiling and formidable, but without heart or guts."[26]

Taft convinced himself that the Payne-Aldrich tariff was the best that could have been passed under the circumstances. Then, in the course of a cross-country trip (the longest in presidential history to that time) to show the flag, best-under-the-circumstances edged remorselessly into best until finally in a hastily thrown-together speech in Winona, Minnesota, he let himself say: "I am bound to say that I think the Payne bill is the best bill that the Republican party ever passed."[27]

The next day the President woke to headlines across the country. His ill-prepared speech locked him into place. Bad enough to have to acknowledge a politically inevitable defeat; Taft elected to claim victory. The insurgents in Congress took him at his word and asked: Victory for whom? Clearly not for the progressive forces that had helped him win over Bryan. Clearly, then, a victory for those forces of reaction for whom he was now viewed as spokes-man.

Later the same year, with controversy over the tariff still bubbling angrily, Taft fell into another unsought confrontation. This time everyone involved could feel the absent Roosevelt as a brooding omnipresence.

The Ballinger-Pinchot controversy arose over the release of coal lands in Alaska for private development. Richard A. Ballinger, Taft's secretary of the interior who released the lands, was indeed closer to the Cunningham-Guggenheim-Morgan interests that were seeking the coal lands than was advisable for a public servant. Gifford Pinchot, Chief Forester under both Roosevelt and Taft and also a member of Roosevelt's "tennis cabinet," was a conservationist whose zeal for withdrawing public lands into federal reservations matched Roosevelt's and undoubtedly exceeded what congressional policy allowed.

When Pinchot went public with his protest against his superior—a conscious act of defiance intended to produce just the public brawl that did occur—Taft, who regarded Pinchot as "a radical and a crank" even before the Ballinger controversy broke out,[28] was in another no-win situation. A Republican-dominated congressional inquiry found Ballinger blameless of malfeasance, and Pinchot was, quite properly, fired for insubordination. But the simplified version of the controversy that found its way into the press branded Taft as an anticonservationist, which he was not, and put him in apparent opposition to Roosevelt, which he was only in the sense that he doubted that the President and his agents had unlimited license to withdraw public lands.

Pinchot wasted no time in going abroad to carry his complaint directly to Roosevelt as he emerged from Africa. Roosevelt made no response publicly. Privately he indicated guarded acceptance of Taft's actions. But at home Taft suffered from the unmistakable implication that he was unfaithful to the conservation policies of his patron and, by extension, to any progressive program of action. The drama of the Ballinger-Pinchot affair, vastly simpler than the debatable complexities of the tariff, cost Taft dearly among progressives and their following in the populace.

Taft's record was nowhere so bleak as his critics maintained. He had what he liked to view as a constitutional interpretation of his office: He was the chief executive. He performed acts commanded by the Constitution and the laws. His predecessor asserted authority to take any action not forbidden by the Constitution and the laws.[29]

Their attitudes toward the Sherman Antitrust Act highlighted the contrast. Though Roosevelt initiated forty-four antitrust actions in seven and a half years, he became increasingly committed to administrative remedies for the trust problem, that is, supervision of large-scale corporate operations by expert bodies that drew their authority from the executive. Legislative definitions were too rigid, and judicial remedies too ponderous for effective monitoring of trusts, while the executive could exercise discretion, as Roosevelt did in his distinction between "good trusts" and "bad trusts." Taft's judicial bent drove him in a different direction. Though necessarily his administration exercised discretion in selecting targets for prosecution, his basic thrust was to enforce the Sherman Act as written. The purported economic benefits arising from concentrations carried little weight compared to the stated intent of the law. In four years, the Taft administration undertook ninety prosecutions.[30]

Taft's conscientious application of the law to interests that lay at the core of Republican financial support cost him considerable support in the business community. He created the image of an unfriendly force in the White House, a relentless plodder whose devotion to the law overran national welfare.

The Mann-Elkins Act, passed in 1910 with Taft's support, pointed up the dilemma of his administration. It contained genuine progressive provisions: it gave the Interstate Commerce Commission power to initiate rate changes for the railroads, and it extended the commission's mandate to telegraph and telephone companies. But it also set up a commerce court to review the ICC's decisions, which progressives deplored and conservatives welcomed. Everyone, therefore, had the basis for a grievance: while insurgents were nipping at Taft from the left, men of wealth and economic power on the right were almost equally critical.[31]

The President suffered by having none of Roosevelt's flair for interpreting and publicizing his administration. His temperament matched his experience, which had been judicial and administrative. But in the White House he held office at the will of a voting public that heard its leaders speak, and that heard their silences as well. Even when Taft toured the countryside, he did not mine the occasions for their political gold. He spoke as president, which he was, but not as politician, which he also was despite the dignity of his office. His critics, whether insurgents or disgruntled businessmen, felt no such restraint.

Even in foreign policy, a clear area of presidential initiative, his efforts gained him next to nothing politically, for with no clarion in the White House, they passed by largely unnoted. His "dollar diplomacy" did not penetrate the Chinese market, but in Latin America, especially in Nicaragua, the United States used both financial pressure and marines to maintain American suzerainty in the area. At the same time, Taft negotiated and, with considerable difficulty, got Congress to approve, a reciprocal trade agreement with Canada. But the Canadians failed to ratify it after indiscreet statements—some by Taft himself, the most blatant by Representative Champ Clark of Missouri—hinted at eventual annexation of Canada to the United States. He also negotiated arbitration treaties with England and France, but the Senate attached so many reservations that Taft was reluctant to seek assent from the Europeans. None of these undertakings had much impact in 1912, but the arbitration treaties gave Roosevelt one more grievance against his successor: their flaccid thrust was unworthy of a great nation.[32]

The major attention in the political field after Taft's first two years turned to the upcoming presidential election. The midterm elections of 1910 were a disaster for Taft: the Democrats won control of the House of Representatives for the first time in a decade and a half, and in the Senate the balance of power between regular Republicans and Democrats rested with the insurgents. For all practical purposes the legislative process went on hold. For the President, for the insurgents in Congress whom he had angered on issues of patronage as well as legislation, and for the patron whom he had disappointed, the Republican nomination became a top priority.

3

Seeking the Republican Nomination

Both President William Howard Taft, who thought that the Republican Party, and the nation as well, owed him a second term, at least a second nomination, and the insurgents, who resolved to replace him, plotted their courses to the Republican convention with anxiety, for neither could escape the enigma of Theodore Roosevelt.

Roosevelt's dynamism made him the perennial central star; he wanted to be the bride at every wedding and the corpse at every funeral, someone said at the time.[1] From the moment of his emergence from the African jungles, his triumphant tour through European capitals, and his arrival in New York harbor in June 1910, the intentions, real or fancied, of the ex-President who guardedly kept his own counsel, maybe even kept it from his own conscious mind, provided the central drama in the Republican Party.

Returning to America, Roosevelt found his party in disarray, his successor fumbling. A stream of correspondence over the previous fifteen months had lamented Taft's inadequacies, and Gifford Pinchot caught Roosevelt in Italy to give him a first-hand briefing. Privately to Senator Henry Cabot Lodge, Roosevelt acknowledged his disillusionment with Taft: Policies essential to the national welfare "have been pursued by the present Administration in a spirit and with methods that have rendered the effort almost nugatory."[2] Still, on his arrival in New York for a spectacular public welcome, Roosevelt held his peace. Within a fortnight, he called at the White House, regaling Taft's family and aides with tales of his wide swath through European courts, but avoiding policy entirely.

Tugged by progressives like Pinchot and Hiram Johnson of California and hauled by conservatives like Lodge and Elihu Root, a conciliatory Roosevelt backed Henry L. Stimson, a supporter of Taft, for the governorship of New

York and Johnson, an ardent progressive, for the governorship of California. On a cross-country tour into sixteen states in August and September of 1910, he played a double game, praising elements of Taft's performance and uttering thoughts more radical than the American public expected from a major political figure.

At a veteran's gathering in Osawatomie, Kansas, he outlined his "new nationalism," the name drawn from a fellow Harvardian, Herbert D. Croly, author of *The Promise of American Life*, which itself had drawn inspiration from Roosevelt's presidency. Setting himself as the middle figure between plutocracy and mob rule, Roosevelt called for governmental supervision of the capitalization of all corporations and for an end to corporate expenditures for political purposes. He favored expanded powers for the Interstate Commerce Commission and the Bureau of Corporations rather than fruitless efforts to prohibit combinations: "Combinations in industry are the result of an imperative economic law which cannot be repealed by political legislation." Extending his idea of administrative agencies as regulators of corporate capitalism, he called for a nonpolitical expert tariff commission "wholly removed from ... improper business influence." He wanted graduated income and inheritance taxes, more effective control of the currency, more active conservation policies, and direct primaries. A new notion of the relation between property and human welfare was imperative: "Every man holds his property subject to the general right of the community to regulate its use to whatever degree the public welfare may require it." He balanced this call for reform of business with a stern warning to labor: "We need to set our faces like flint against mob-violence just as against corporate greed; against violence and injustice and lawlessness by wage-workers just as much as against lawless cunning and greed and selfish arrogance of employers."[3]

As Roosevelt, contributing editor at *Outlook* magazine, restated his views month by month, even a careless reader could see the implicit rebuke to the inactive Taft. Then as the midterm elections of 1910 indicated that Republicanism, with Will Taft as its head, was careening into catastrophe, the previously warm friendship cooled.[4] For some weeks into 1911, Roosevelt and Taft exchanged substantive letters on national policy—Canadian reciprocity, Mexican border troubles, Panama Canal. Early in June they made a great show of public comity in Baltimore at Cardinal James Gibbons's twenty-fifth anniversary as a bishop. But that moment of intimacy was the last. From Baltimore, the Associated Press reported that Roosevelt had told the White House that he supported Taft's renomination. Roosevelt curtly denied the report the next day.[5] Friends of both—Stimson, Root, Archie Butt—hoped to keep the two men in tandem. But too much worked against the relationship. Roosevelt sensed in Taft hostility rooted in ingratitude. For his part, Taft—President of the United States—refused to view himself as an insubordinate lieutenant.

Taft defended himself by controlling the selection of delegates to the Republican national convention in Chicago in June 1912. His secretary, Charles D. Hilles, an agile determined forty-four-year-old Ohioan who had formerly been assistant secretary of the treasury,[6] had been at work on the project since 1910. Now in April 1911, Taft planned a seven-week, 13,000-mile tour through sixteen states from September through early November. In 330 speeches that ranged from set occasions to brief remarks from the rear of his train, he touted his progressive credentials, midway between insurgency and standpattism, while Hilles negotiated to establish pro-Taft dominance in state organizations that would select delegates in early 1912.

The problem of recruiting delegates differed according to local circumstances. In the territories, the southern states, and the District of Columbia, no difficulty arose, for party officials were almost invariably federal office-holders subject to the will of the administration in power. In an important state like New York, Taft threw his support to William Barnes, a dependable skilled old-line conservative. Elsewhere, as in Indiana, Taft redirected patronage to tilt the balance into favorable hands. In general, Hilles opposed presidential primaries beyond the six states where they were already in place; but in California, where Governor Johnson and the state organization, progressive victors all, leaned toward Senator Robert M. La Follette, Hilles taunted the dominant group to allow newly enfranchised women a chance to voice their views through a primary. Where primaries already existed, as in Taft's own Ohio, there was no alternative to facing up to an unpredictable primary fight. In progressive strongholds like Iowa and La Follette's Wisconsin, Hilles strengthened conservative organizations in order to catch any random fallout from competitive bickering within the opposition.

Meanwhile, but later than desirable, the insurgent forces were firming up their challenge, looking for leadership to Senator La Follette.

La Follette, a Wisconsin farm boy who had gone to the University of Wisconsin and than had got himself admitted to the bar, achieved national fame as the governor who created the most comprehensive model for progressive reform at the state level: direct primaries, a railroad commission charged with setting rates, higher taxes on both railroads and other corporations, extension of civil service, regulation of lobbyists, conservation (especially of water power), regulation of state banks. La Follette's achievement set a national standard.

Moving on to the United States Senate in 1906, La Follette, barely inside the door, used his experience in Wisconsin to oppose the Hepburn bill as a weak-kneed compromise that would delay adequate regulation. The view was typical of the man. "Half a loaf, as a rule," he said in another connection, "dulls the appetite, and destroys the keenness of interest in attaining the full loaf. A halfway measure never fairly tests the principle and may utterly discredit it."[7]

When Taft followed Roosevelt in the presidency, La Follette watched Taft's vacillation on the vice-presidency and the labor plank in the convention, then the fights over the speakership, the Payne-Aldrich tariff, and the Ballinger-Pinchot controversy. How much more evidence of Taft's true conservative coloration was needed?

In December 1910, just after the elections, La Follette circulated a proposal for a National Progressive Republican League (NPRL) as a caucus for the promotion of direct election of United States senators, direct primaries for the nomination of all elected officials, corrupt practices acts, and the trio of progressive panaceas, initiative as a way for private citizens to begin the process of law-making, referendum as a device to let the people pass judgment on prospective laws, and recall as a way to remove public officials. In January 1911, elected officials and private citizens met at La Follette's Washington home to set up a formal organization. The charter members included six governors and the bulk of the insurgents in Congress.[8]

Roosevelt was invited to throw in with the NPRL, but he stayed determinedly aloof.

By April 1911, leading progressives decided to field a candidate, and, when Roosevelt could not be smoked out, the group turned to La Follette. La Follette, confident that even Roosevelt was urging him into the race,[9] accepted the league's offer of support and announced his candidacy.

In July 1911, a year before the convention, La Follette began his campaign in earnest. Enthusiastic crowds greeted him. The workload at campaign headquarters grew constantly. Yet the newspapers never quite believed. The notion persisted that he was merely laying the groundwork for Colonel Roosevelt. La Follette denied the charge. But his words sounded hollow without a similar denial from Roosevelt himself.

In mid-October, three hundred progressives from thirty states met in Chicago to discuss a platform, to unify the organization, and to meditate on the gains thus far. They also endorsed La Follette as the logical candidate for president of the United States and urged that in all states organizations be formed to promote his nomination.

The October 28 issue of *Outlook*, Roosevelt's employer, observed archly: "This endorsement is to be regarded as a recommendation rather than the committal of the movement to any one man."[10]

The hint was ominous. Many in La Follette's camp preferred Roosevelt: Gifford Pinchot and his brother Amos were charter members of the NPRL. How many in the league would stay if the finger beckoned from New York? When some newspapers began to call for Roosevelt's candidacy, each call made it more difficult for La Follette to proceed.

Thus, persistently, Theodore Roosevelt remained, for both Taft and La Follette, a dark cloud on the horizon.

For much of 1911, Roosevelt dismissed the possibility of another run for the White House. His failure to get Stimson elected governor in New York in the 1910 election indicated that he had no local political base. Nationally, he suffered the usual fate of peacemakers: he was clobbered from both sides,

Taft Republicans blaming their defeats on his foolish radicalism, insurgents, especially in the West, indignant about his occasional defense of Taft. He retreated to Sagamore Hill, comfortable in his private status, comfortable with his generous salary of $12,000 at *Outlook* magazine. He felt a diminution of his physical powers: a bit of rheumatism, inferior tennis, less walking. He could envisage no scenario that would call Cincinnatus back from the plow. With resignation, he told one of his sons that Taft would defeat La Follette for the nomination, and four more years of standpattism would follow; or worse, the Democrats would take over: "Taft, plus the Republican Party, would do better than the Democrats could do."[11]

Publicly, Roosevelt gave no satisfaction to either Taft or La Follette. Cynics had an explanation for this forbearance: Roosevelt was dissembling to serve his ambition.

In fact, his motivation was more complex, indeed perhaps beyond fathoming. His whistling about the charms of private life had a graveyard timbre. Just fifty when he left the presidency, not yet fifty-four, he had a residue of unexpended vigor that only politics—politics as grand policy, politics as intrigue—could drain off. The British Lord Morley had spoken of Roosevelt's "combining in equal proportions the attributes of St. Paul and St. Vitus."[12] Roosevelt's being needed politics as it needed air; and the need was personal, not programmatic. Sober analysis of issues and cold calculation of votes did not exhaust the elements going into the decision,[13] for if such a groundswell of popular demand were to develop that no man with a star-spangled flutter in his heart could say Nay, Roosevelt would have to let himself be drawn in.

In late October 1911, the scene changed dramatically when Taft's attorney general indicted the United States Steel Corporation for creating a monopoly, in part by absorbing the Tennessee Coal and Iron Company in 1907. The indictment—which George E. Mowry calls the most costly political error in Taft's entire career[14]—struck Roosevelt directly, for as president he had assented to the merger as a way of easing the impact of depressed business conditions. Now he was being branded a fool if he had been duped by U.S. Steel, or a knave if he cooperated in creating a monopoly.

On the very day that the suit against U.S. Steel was filed, Roosevelt was writing to Governor Johnson in California: "I have a right to ask every friend of mine to do everything possible to prevent not merely my nomination, but any movement looking toward my nomination."[15] In late November, Roosevelt could still tell one of his former cabinet officers of a "devout wish that for my own personal comfort either Taft or La Follette, or some third party, will develop such overwhelming strength that there will not possibly be any tendency to come to me."[16] Two weeks later, Roosevelt told Lodge that he had refused to tell La Follette's emissaries, as he had refused to tell Taft's agents, that he would decline the nomination if it were offered. "I told them that . . . as Abraham Lincoln used to say, no man can justly ask me to cross such a bridge until I come to it."[17]

As the weeks of December went on, Roosevelt kept scratching at the itch. Taft was such a "floppy souled creature."[18] La Follette was erratic and extreme. The Democrats, long out of office for a sustained period, lacked experience and strength. "Down at bottom [Woodrow] Wilson is pretty thin material for a President," Roosevelt said. "He lacks the fundamental sincerity, conviction and rugged strength, and yet I think he is the strongest man the Democrats have."[19] To his friend Joseph Bucklin Bishop, to whom he had said the previous year: "They have no business to expect me to take command of a ship simply because the ship is sinking," he now wrote: "I will certainly not put myself in a position which would make it necessary for me to shirk a plain duty if it came unmistakably *as* a plain duty. As yet I am not convinced that it will be so come, and, on the contrary, believe there is practically little or no chance of it."[20] Yet the people were showing signs of awakening: "There has been a monetary flurry about nominating me simply because the average man, not finding any real and satisfactory leadership, is groping about, and turns to me as the last hope."[21] Was not this exactly the set of circumstances that might make the obligation to run overcome his own disinclination?

Still the ambivalence continued. In the first week of January 1912, Stimson came away from a visit at Sagamore Hill convinced that Roosevelt "had no thought of becoming a candidate."[22] By mid-month, however, Roosevelt wrote a long letter to Frank A. Munsey, the newspaper publisher, and sent copies to a wide circle of wellwishers. Its rambling argument and convoluted syntax showed Roosevelt in the awkward process of reversing his field: "I have all along felt that even if there should be a strong popular demand for me (as to which I can pass no judgment) yet that unless this demand were literally overwhelming it could hardly make itself effective. But it seems to me that it is better that it should not make itself effective rather than that by any action of mine I should make it seem that I desire the Presidency for my own sake, or am willing to accept it unless it comes to me as the result of a real popular movement, giving expression to a demand from at least a substantial portion of the plain people that I should undertake a given task in the interest of the people as a whole. Before I speak there should be some tangible evidence that such is the case."[23] Seeing a copy of the letter, Elihu Root, who knew Roosevelt better than Roosevelt knew himself, sent his friend a long and "very sententious and didactic" letter, as Root himself affirmed. Root could accept Roosevelt's denial of candidacy and his simultaneous refusal to rule out the nomination, he said, but, "No thirsty sinner ever took a pledge which was harder for him to keep than it will be for you to maintain this position."[24]

The sardonic Root was dead right. He was also too late.

With Roosevelt's letter to Munsey scarcely in the post, the Colonel ended his indecision and trod the path of duty. To make sure that the call hit the right notes at the right time, Roosevelt arranged for it himself. On January 18, he started a round of letters to Republican governors who had previously pressed him to declare himself. Looking for "the best way out of an uncomfortable situation," he suggested that they write to him telling him that their people wanted him to run for president and asking if he would refuse the nomination if offered—the very question he had evaded all year. "If it is the sincere judgment of men having the right to know and express the wishes of the plain people that the people as a whole desire me, not for my sake, but for their sake, to undertake the job," he said, "I would feel in honor bound to do so."[25]

Not easy to prepare at transcontinental distances, the summons to Roosevelt was finally released on February 10 in Chicago. Eight Republican governors from New Hampshire to Wyoming affirmed that a large majority of Republican voters, and a large majority of Americans, wanted Theodore Roosevelt as their president. He should, therefore, soon declare whether, if the nomination for the presidency came to him "unsolicited and unsought," he would accept it.[26]

A week before, La Follette himself had smoothed the way for Roosevelt's announcement. On February 2, the Wisconsin senator, fatigued, disheartened by defections to Roosevelt, spoke to the Periodical Publishers' Association in Philadelphia, his speech a rambling, incoherent disaster.[27] Clearly he was depressed. When he withdrew from public appearances for three weeks, the cry went up instantly that he had had a nervous breakdown. A close political friend, who had witnessed the incident, noted sadly: "It ends him for the Presidency."[28] The *Times* reported an instantaneous "scattering of the rats from the sinking ship."[29] They scattered because they preferred victory to loyalty. In the end, of course, they had neither.

As the spotlight turned to Roosevelt, he was in no hurry to respond, for too quick a reply to the governors would have suggested collusion, too much like the staged performance that in fact it was. The Colonel maintained his customary routine, days at Sagamore Hill alternating with half days at the *Outlook* office. When William L. Ward, chairman of the New York Republicans, visited Oyster Bay, Roosevelt emerged from the woods, ax in hand, the very model of a suburban squire. He accepted a call to jury duty in nearby Ocala. He addressed the American Institute of Architects. Finally, some hard news: Roosevelt would reply to the governors after a trip to Ohio on his way to a meeting of Harvard's board of overseers. On the day of entraining for Columbus, Roosevelt saw his wife Edith and their daughter Ethel off for a trip to Panama, logged a half-day's work at the *Outlook*, made his way to Grand Central Station for the trip west.

It was Candidate Roosevelt who crossed the border from Pennsylvania into Ohio. He even said as much—"My hat is in the ring"—to a reporter in Cleveland, though, curiously, the words went unreported until later.[30] Then at the Ohio constitutional convention, he set forth his platform: a repetition of the main ideas from Osawatomie, plus a new idea defiantly explicit: popular review—and potential reversal—of judicial decisions on the state level when a constitutional issue was involved.[31]

The *New York Times*, like many others, was stunned at Roosevelt's performance; recall of judicial decisions located him at the "ultimate boundary line of radicalism." The paper was not impressed that he had toned down his attack on businessmen; he was, the *Times* noted, "at pains to stitch this silken lining inside the frightful, shaggy, grissly bearskin garment in which he arrays himself when he addresses the destroying radicals."[32]

After such a performance, Roosevelt's reply to the governors was merely official. "I shall accept the nomination for President if it is tendered to me," he said in a letter dated February 24, "and I will adhere to this decision until the convention has expressed its preference.... I hope that so far as possible the people may be given the chance, through direct primaries, to express their preference."[33]

The convention's preference—there was the rub, for delegates, not American voters generally, or Republicans generally, would decide the Republican nomination. The route from Columbus to the White House had to pass through the convention in Chicago in June.

The three Republican candidates had three months to win their spurs.

La Follette refused to release voluntarily any of his supporters, though he could not restrain those who deserted flagrantly. He would stay in the race until the end, despite frantic efforts to get him to withdraw formally. Amos Pinchot, Gifford's brother, was among those shedding crocodile tears: "[I]n his [La Follette's] present state of mind he will do irreparable harm to the progressive movement and to himself."[34]

President Taft had his game plan already in operation: hold fast with existing organizations, resist raids from the buccaneering Roosevelt, and then control the convention itself.

Roosevelt's strategy was also clear: show that where Americans, especially Republicans, could choose directly, they would go overwhelmingly for him over Taft. No Republican convention could then ignore that mandate without certainty of defeat by the Democrats, and surely no Republican convention would opt for defeat.

The Roosevelt crusade started with muffled drums. The day he released his reply to the governors, he went off to Boston for four days to meet with the Harvard overseers, engage in literary discussions on Dickens, Thackeray, and Scott, and trip through elegant memories of Harvard by visits to his undergraduate clubs. Invited to appear before the Massachusetts General Court, he defended the recall of judicial decisions and took a pot shot at Taft who, he said, regarded the Constitution as a shield from the passions of the people. To reporters he revealed his intention to spend most of his time at Oyster Bay and at the *Outlook* office, leaving the politicking to his staff. He would go on tour only if necessary. Returning to New York, he announced his campaign staff: Senator Joseph M. Dixon of Montana, an able and respected legislator, became campaign manager; Ward in New York served as Roosevelt's personal representative; Cecil Lyon, who was becoming the prime power in Texas, and William Flinn, soon to assail the Penrose machine in Pennsylvania, added political experience. Munsey, George W. Perkins, close to U.S. Steel and to the Morgan interests, and Alexander H. Revell, a Chicago businessman who had soured on Taft, provided cash.

Dixon wasted no time in issuing a broadside at Taft for flaccid leadership. He challenged the Taft forces to support primaries everywhere as the surest test of the people's will; Representative William B. McKinley, chairman of Taft's campaign committee, loftily rejected the idea of changing the rules when the game had already started. Dixon circulated Roosevelt's standard reply on the third-term issue: Roosevelt had really meant to disavow only a third *consecutive* term; a coffee drinker who says he does not care for another cup does not mean never, but only right now. The *Times* hooted at this "doctrine of subsequent interpretation,"[35] and learned voices kept the issue alive.[36]

Roosevelt kept his hand in all these controversies, usually through Ward, but he busied himself with reviewing two scholarly volumes on medieval history for the *Outlook*. When reporters sought hard news, they were reduced to reporting that Roosevelt had ridden horseback for two hours.

These tactics were implausible, for they left the initiative to the opposition. By early March the southern states were falling in line for Taft: Georgia, Florida, South Carolina. Concerned about threatened defections, Taft withdrew ten appointive jobs in North Carolina from Senate consideration. Nine Republican governors, one more than Roosevelt's eight, came out for Taft. Responding to pressure from congressional leaders, Taft set up campaign headquarters outside the White House and authorized aggressive campaigning, though he forbade any personal attacks on Roosevelt. Secretary of War Stimson, giving the keynote address to the Illinois state convention, lauded Taft as the true progressive and attacked Roosevelt for his Ohio speech.

Stung, Roosevelt snapped back that he was in the presidential race in 1912 for the same reason that he had supported Stimson in 1910: to serve the public. In reply to the Taft forces' unwillingness to extend direct primaries, Roosevelt himself argued that presidential politics was not a game, the people were not spectators in the bleachers; if primaries revealed the people's will, they were central to the democratic process.

Three months could pass with this kind of parry and thrust without bringing Roosevelt any closer to nomination. "If I get the newspaper notoriety and Taft the delegates," Roosevelt noted in mid-March, "I can see our finish."[37] To exploit the primaries, Roosevelt had to show himself; he was the principal, perhaps the only, asset his forces had. Therefore, Roosevelt made the obvious and necessary decision to spend three weeks on the road. The judge in Nassau County released him from jury duty because of his military service.

Lean pickings rewarded his efforts for the next three weeks. Oklahoma had already given him ten delegates, maybe more, but no one interpreted the victory as a straw in the wind. Ormsby McHarg, a disgruntled politician denied office by Taft, toured the South to shake loose Taft's hold on southern Republicans but produced only collections of Roosevelt supporters who had bolted from regular Republican state conventions. The first state-wide primary, North Dakota on March 19, gave La Follette its ten votes. A jubilant La Follette supporter had a point: "We surely scratched the varnish off the Roosevelt boom."[38] In Indiana, where Roosevelt spent $15,000 on a last-minute newspaper blitz, Taft won from twenty to thirty delegates and control of the state convention. Meanwhile, Roosevelt stumped the streets of New York for the primary election on March 26, trying to beat back William Barnes' Republican machine, which was still smarting from Roosevelt's meddlesome intervention in 1910. On election day, the polls, in New York City at least, were manipulated with the raw muscle that Republicans liked to advertise as a monopoly of Tammany Hall. Roosevelt won a scant seven of the ninety delegates—seven against the eighty-three that presumably would go to Taft. Roosevelt's people screamed about fraud and force, demanding a whole new primary. But the state superintendent of election, try as he might, found no evidence of fraud. Roosevelt, already on his way to the Midwest in the engineer's seat of the New York Central's new electric locomotive, vented his rage: "They are stealing the primary elections from us. . . . It is outrageous."[39]

In early April, Wisconsin registered its predictable—and uncontested—result: twenty-six very solid votes for La Follette.

Illinois provided a new spark. Returning to Chicago, Roosevelt avoided reference to La Follette and concentrated on Taft and the forces of reaction. He told his audience at the court house in Clinton that "the professional bread and butter politicians are all for Taft. There never was a straighter line-up than this between the politicians and the plain people, and at least here in Illinois the plain people have the chance to speak for themselves."[40] In Springfield, he sat in Abraham Lincoln's pew, and on the stump he told crowds that 1912 was 1860 all over again: people of privilege, what Lincoln called the "old, exclusive, silk-stockinged Whiggery," against people like Lincoln and Roosevelt.[41] (Later on, Robert Lincoln, the wartime president's surviving son, found the resemblance less than striking.)[42]

The crowds started responding to Roosevelt's appeal. At stop after stop, they stood in pouring rain to cheer his attacks. Speaker and audience spurred each other on: cheers at one stop made him readier for the next, and there his heightened glow spread to his new audience, which then propelled him to the next stop. Wrong for discussion of antitrust policy, these occasions were just right for appeals to the wisdom of the people over their rulers, for promises of popular rule over those easily frightened by the "bugbear of majority tyranny."[43]

Roosevelt had a fine sense with crowds. He looked at them and saw their faces. He moved about, unconfined by modern public-address systems. Even on the back of a parlor car he kept in near-constant motion, his right arm moving up and down to reinforce a point, his whole body leaning outward to his audience as if he wanted to touch each one of them with his argument. His high voice did not produce the orotund boom that let William Jennings Bryan fill a Chautauqua tent, but for most days he could make it last as long as he needed it. He needed it in Illinois.

Rarely did it serve him so well. Even the Roosevelt forces were stunned. The Colonel carried nearly every county in Illinois, his overall majority just short of two to one. Dixon, on the scene to preside over the victory, pointed the moral: "This ends the Taft boom." North Dakota, Wisconsin, Illinois: wherever the people had had a chance to speak their minds, Taft had lost, repudiated by a popular mandate that told Republicans that to name Taft in Chicago was "to commit deliberate suicide."[44] Roosevelt and his headquarters were jubilant, for at the end of two months of doldrums, they could feel a refreshing breeze blowing off the Great Lakes, propelling them to victory. Illinois had fifty-eight votes, more than three times as many as Roosevelt had already nailed down.

Previously a blustering nuisance, the Colonel had become a noisy contender. A Taft congressman made a prediction worth remembering: Illinois will not prevent Taft's renomination, but it will guarantee that the devil gets raised in Chicago.[45]

And not just in Chicago. The instant the results came in from Illinois, New York felt the impact. Prior to the Illinois primary, Barnes, the Republican state chairman with no great love for Taft but even less for Roosevelt, had been ready to let the Republican convention commit four delegates-at-large to Taft and endorse his candidacy. Then Taft's disaster in Illinois gave Barnes a limited victory: the four delegates-at-large were uncommitted, and the convention, while recommending Taft's candidacy, stopped short of committing New York to his support.

Roosevelt returned to New York in a glow. Maine threw in twelve more votes just the day after Illinois's great tribute. The sickly campaign suddenly recuperated. Back from campaigning in West Virginia, Kentucky, and Pennsylvania, Roosevelt purred with confidence: he was not tired, he would consider no compromise candidate, he looked forward to the Pennsylvania vote on April 13 for the final knockout blow. When he arrived in Jersey City to take the ferry across to Pennsylvania Station in New York, he told reporters that if he won in Pennsylvania, he could take off for the West to nail down the nomination.

As Roosevelt returned to New York City, Taft was coming up from Washington to attend the Yale class of 1878 reunion dinner and to go on to the Union League, where 750 diners surprised no one by endorsing his candidacy. It was the kind of evening that Taft loved. His classmates were his friends in a way that most college alumni have now outgrown, and the conservative Union League gave him a reception unjostled by unorthodox ideas. Root and Nicholas Murray Butler, president of Columbia University, were the other scheduled speakers. Even-tempered harmony, as predictable and proper as the brandy, cigars, and evening dress, gave the occasion that settled shared contentment so reassuring in a troubled world. Taft's remarks fit the mood. He condemned those who lacked knowledge of the Constitution, some sincere, some demagogic, and those who laid impious hands on the Ark of the Covenant and challenged its settled ways. As Taft left the dinner, an electric eagle attached to the wall flapped its wings to join in the applause.

In Bay City, Michigan, a very different scene. When the Republican convention met on April 11, Governor Chase S. Osborn, a Roosevelt partisan, had a company of militia on hand to keep disputed Taft delegates out of the convention hall. Then, in a gesture of civility, both sides let the state committee enter the hall. At that point the Taft forces got the upper hand, for the committee allowed a sergeant-at-arms and fifty assistants in by a side door and instructed them to admit only those delegates whose admission cards had been signed by the committee secretary, a Taft supporter. Some three to four hundred Roosevelt delegates entered under that rubric, but two to three times as many Taft delegates entered.

Thereafter, ordered chaos followed as the chairman of each faction presided over parallel conventions simultaneously in a disruptive hullabaloo. A Taft delegate pulled a Roosevelt delegate off the platform, then found himself being pummeled by Roosevelt partisans in return. Neither side could hear what was said from the platform, but both sides responded on a signal from their leaders and, in a way, adopted their motions, including designation of delegates-at-large. The Roosevelt men finished first and left under police escort to avoid any roughhouse. Their departure allowed the Taft men some closing political oratory in peace.

Some Taft men called the results in Michigan a victory.

Two days later the focus switched to Pennsylvania with seventy-six votes, second only to New York. Roosevelt, fearful of the crossfire of factions in the state, watched from a distance. Meanwhile, he made the rounds of the faithful in Massachusetts and New Hampshire. In Pennsylvania, a reform group known as the Keystone Party, hoped to exploit Taft's dependence on Boies Penrose, the established boss. Penrose, certain of victory because victory in primaries is what machines were for, let the party wheels spin in their customary way, even going off on a cruise on his yacht at 4 PM, the moment for most machine leaders when the going gets tough, leading the tough to get going. Fist fights broke out all over the state, but they did not disturb the placid waters of the Susquehanna, and Penrose never knew what hit him until the state-wide tally counted him out. When the ballot count ended, a sweep for Roosevelt gave the Colonel's men fifty of the seventy-six delegates and control of the state convention and, therefore, of the party.

Roosevelt himself was thunderstruck. A bare majority had been beyond his expectations; a landslide unimaginable. Yet there it was.

Dixon put out the official analysis for the Roosevelt faction: Taft had previously given the appearance of great strength—the previous day, Taft's camp had claimed 339 delegates already, less than 200 short of the nomination—because of "snap hand-picked conventions in the Southern States, where the pie-counter habitués are always with the administration and where no Republican electoral vote has been cast since the days of Reconstruction."[46] But now the Republican states were starting to speak, states that not only sent delegates to the Republican conventions but also voted for Republican candidates in the general election. And what they were saying clearly was: We want Roosevelt. Even the pie-counter habitués were wavering, Dixon said,[47] a plausible claim for southern Republicans were notoriously faithful only to winners and, if Roosevelt was going to win, they were not going to be too remote from the pie counter.

Roosevelt himself, ever quick to consult his own hopes and hear therein the voice of the people, could feel the surge of support for his nomination. He instantly announced that he would be off to Nebraska and South Dakota, Arkansas and North Carolina.

On April 19, two more preferential primaries, Oregon and Nebraska, gave the Colonel majorities in both state conventions. In Nebraska, Taft ran neck and neck with La Follette for second place. The following day West Virginia went for Roosevelt by better than three to one.

Roosevelt's creaky rig was becoming a bandwagon. The Colonel felt bully again.

After the upset in Illinois, Taft's electoral cup, previously seen as already half full, suddenly revealed itself as half empty. His cabinet gathered early one evening, and in a meeting that lasted until 2 AM the next morning, helped the President shake his great bulk onto a more pugnacious course: immediate indictment of the International Harvester trust and open warfare, rough and tumble with no quarter given or asked, in the Massachusetts primary. The Harvester indictment significantly focused public attention on Roosevelt's explicit decision not to prosecute that trust. Now Roosevelt the attacker was himself attacked, his energy diverted to explaining his own record. The Bay State primary April 30 promised even greater advantage for Taft's campaign. It was a favorable forum, the home of Senator Lodge and Senator W. Murray Crane, both conservatives in a state less infected with progressivism than the Midwest.

Moving north through New York City, Taft stopped to watch George Arliss in his classic performance in *Disraeli*, then went on to New England savoring two small victories—he carried Rhode Island (ten delegates) and New Hampshire (eight delegates)—and one significant incursion on insurgency—in Iowa he took sixteen votes, leaving only ten for Iowa's favorite son, Albert B. Cummins.

Once inside Massachusetts, the presidential special stopped a dozen times before reaching South Station in Boston. Crowds gathered to hear and see the President, a small one at Palmer, larger ones at Springfield and Worcester. Taft played the scrapper less well than Arliss played Disraeli: he backed into the fight, almost squirmed into it. He would not rip and snort. Gutter brawls were not for presidents, he thought. Roosevelt was "an old and dear friend of mine," he said, and "neither in thought nor word nor action have I been disloyal to the friendship I owe to Theodore Roosevelt." But Roosevelt had made untrue charges, he went on, and they had to be refuted. Taft conceded that he did not want to fight Roosevelt, "but then sometimes a man in a corner fights."[48] Later on, he was reported as saying, with dubious aptness considering that he was speaking of himself, "Even a rat in a corner will fight."[49]

In the Boston Arena, Taft drew up a lawyer's full rebuttal of eleven separate charges: he quoted Roosevelt's letters showing support of Canadian reciprocity; he quoted his own letters to Roosevelt on Speaker Cannon; he matched Roosevelt's charges of bossism with references to Roosevelt's debt to Boss William Flinn in Pennsylvania; he challenged Roosevelt to take his charges of election frauds to the courts rather than to the newspapers; he acknowledged that federal office holders might incline to "support those to whose appointment they attribute their preferment," but deftly noted that Roosevelt, not Taft, had appointed more than 70 percent of those officeholders. Then he went on to defend his own administration, the laws and executive decisions that had propelled progressivism in the previous three years. Finally, when he had taxed the tolerant audience beyond reasonable patience, he taunted Roosevelt on the third-term issue: once the two-term tradition had been breached, what would keep the still youthful Roosevelt from sensing that the nation needed him for "as many terms as his natural life would permit." Finally the end of the exhaustive brief was reached, and the climax was vintage Taft, without flamboyance, without cadence—imagine Bryan at a similar moment: "One who so lightly regards constitutional principles and especially the independence of the judiciary, one who is so naturally impatient of legal restraints, and of due legal procedure, and who has so misunderstood what liberty regulated by law is, could not safely be intrusted with successive presidential terms. I say this sorrowfully, but I say it with the full conviction of truth."[50]

From the Boston Arena, Taft went to Symphony Hall to meet the overflow that could not get into the principal meeting. Then his small party—himself, his military aide, Hilles, and two Secret Service men—made its way back to the train for the return trip to Washington. And William Howard Taft put his large head in his hands and wept.

Roosevelt, in Worcester, was quick to reply. He was glad to have Taft off his lofty perch, though he was clearly unprepared to put out a full rebuttal on short notice. Besides, he knew enough about political audiences not to overtax their receptivity. But one of Taft's points needed an immediate answer. When Taft pitted Flinn as Pennsylvania's counterpart to New York's Barnes, the issue of bossism blurred in the public's mind. So Roosevelt felt constrained to portray Flinn as a courageous independent who supported Roosevelt because of Roosevelt's promise as a reformer. This defense drew fewer chuckles in Worcester than it would have in Pittsburgh.

After a weekend, both candidates were back in Boston for a final fling. The day was late for issues. The game now was presence—seeing and being seen. Taft could not shrug off his sense of impropriety, but his defense was more demeaning than the impropriety: "I have been a man of straw long enough; every man who has blood in his body, and who has been misrepresented as I have been is forced to fight."[51] Still hoarse from a cold, Taft made the rounds. The *Times* guessed that 500,000 people saw him that one day.

Many of them must have voted for him, for Taft won the primary by a slight margin. Under Massachusetts' arcane procedures, each candidate carried eighteen delegates to the convention. The victory kept Taft in the race. A defeat might have signaled a rout that would have shaken the South loose. If Taft could not win decisively in Lodge's home state, where could he win?

Roosevelt, who had carefully avoided overinvesting in Massachusetts, professed to be more pleased by Massachusetts than by Illinois and Pennsylvania. Now he felt buoyant, confident, ready to leave for Maryland in preparation for yet another primary the following Tuesday; Minnesota and California the week after that; then Ohio, mother of presidents and especially of the incumbent president; finally, New Jersey. And then on to Chicago.

Readily accessible to both New York and Washington, Maryland offered another chance for a toe-to-toe slugfest, but Taft scarcely raised his voice. He entered the state only once, picking on an unpopular native son, Charles J. Bonaparte, Roosevelt's last Attorney General. Bonaparte gave as good as he got: The people had not wanted Taft in 1908, he said, they took him only because they could not have the man they really wanted. Now, with Roosevelt running, they could have their man, and Taft would soon be out.

Roosevelt, with Taft's marathon attack in Massachusetts on the record, threw off restraint. He had special fun with Taft's charges on the Harvester trust. The stock of the International Harvester Company had jumped up two points the day after Taft's indictment—conclusive proof, Roosevelt said with more verve than accuracy, that Wall Street knew that the proposed suit was a fake. When the polls in Maryland closed, Roosevelt had won sixteen more delegates.

Then in Minnesota and California, Roosevelt won without more than raising a finger. In Minnesota, where letters from the candidate carried only a pale image of what he could have accomplished in person, he swept the state, not only overshadowing Taft (which was to be expected), but eclipsing La Follette in La Follette's own neighborhood. A trip to California—three days each way—was out of the question. Governor Johnson, strongly committed to Roosevelt now, was an effective stand-in. Roosevelt's vote there exceeded the total for Taft and La Follette combined. A new broom was tied to Roosevelt's railroad car to remind voters of the impending "clean sweep."

The next test came in Ohio, where repudiation of a sitting president by his own state would signal to the whole party that it was saddled with a loser. Taft understood the stakes, and he foresaw failure. As he left to campaign in his home state, he told his brother Horace: "I think the American people are not quite alive to the dangers of Roosevelt's success and . . . there is too short a time to teach them in the preliminaries of a primary."[52] Taft's pessimism was for his brother's ears only. To the press he was confident, though, significantly, his campaign managers were not.

Taft got to Ohio first. As his train climbed the mountains, his ire rose as well. Who was this vain egoist, this demagogue and flatterer, who masked his own ambition with a call from the people that no one else could hear? Were the American people to watch him go from third to fourth to fifth terms, then finally to the presidency for life?[53]

As Taft was speaking, Roosevelt was climbing into his private car Oceanic from Pennsylvania Station at 6:34 PM, his worn overcoat and slouch hat now part of a campaign costume that pleased his sense of the image he should project. Reports of Taft's personal attacks reached him before the train left; they clearly licensed anything Roosevelt might say in rebuttal.

By the following night, they were both in Steubenville at the same time, their trains in parallel slots at the station. They ignored each other and went their separate ways. Roosevelt minded the proprieties, careful not to let a personal attack start a sympathetic backfire.

Suddenly Roosevelt faced an intrusion from the left as La Follette entered the state in his own behalf, pointing to Roosevelt's only too apparent rich friends like George Perkins and, locally, Dan Hanna, whose name recalled a famous boss in the state at an earlier time. He reviewed Roosevelt's checkered record on prosecuting trusts. Through concentrating on Roosevelt, La Follette let his scorn fall on both him and Taft; the convention could not nominate either one, both had mortified the presidency.

Taft regained the appearance of confidence as he made the rounds, three thousand miles all told, every congressional district, seventy-three of the eighty-eight counties. His smile, not frequently visible in recent weeks, returned, and a little of the old humor. He taunted Roosevelt on the boss issue: Walter Brown, whom he characterized as the only boss in full commission in Ohio, was spending $50,000 on Roosevelt's nomination. By the end of the week of campaigning, Taft's voice grew hoarse again, and his speaking style fell back into a dull recitative. Still the crowds held. The day before the voting, Taft flung out one last jab: Roosevelt in office had not unseated one boss; he had worked with them, like any sensible man. With that final statement of political truth, Taft settled in for the night, rose to vote the following morning, chatted with Democratic Governor Judson Harmon, and left for Washington.

Roosevelt kept to an equally grueling schedule, invading even Taft's home base, Hamilton City, though dodging around Cincinnati to avoid embarrassing his own son-in-law, Representative Nicholas Longworth, who remained loyal to Taft. Fighting off La Follette with a gloved left hand, he thumped the

President with his right: Taft never found that Roosevelt was dangerous to the people, the Colonel said, until Roosevelt found that Taft was useless to the people. Roosevelt made sly use of a bit of trivia he had uncovered: Taft's father had supported Ulysses S. Grant in his bid for a third term. Roosevelt's throat grew raw too, and an automobile collision shook him up without injuring him. He fended off elusive, and utterly untrue rumors that he drank excessively. On the boss issue, he did the best he could: Brown was not really a boss at all. Closing out his campaign, he tried to leave the boss issue as the monkey on Taft's back: he, Roosevelt, would not tolerate a boss-dominated convention, and he would accept no compromise candidate but himself. With that, he went back to Oyster Bay to await the voters' will.

Roosevelt won fifteen of Ohio's twenty-one districts. For publication, McKinley pooh-poohed the result: Taft had lost his home state as Roosevelt and Cummins had lost theirs; so what? Taft remained publicly serene. He even issued a brazen victory statement with the concurrence of his cabinet: he now had enough delegates to assure him of the nomination.[54] From Roosevelt's headquarters came the word that the candidate would probably not go to South Dakota; Ohio had settled the issue of the nomination.[55]

During the following week in New Jersey, Roosevelt toned down his criticism of Taft lest he appear to be berating the underdog. Frugal two weeks before, he now had money to splurge: one hundred people on salary, two hundred automobiles available. The investment paid off: another clean sweep, twenty-six out of twenty-eight New Jersey districts. La Follette, who had urged that the nation needed surgical statesmanship, not a Rough Rider or an easy-going fat man,[56] took only about 2 percent of the vote.

At the *Outlook* office, Roosevelt declared himself fit as a bull moose. But he was not ready to talk about the postnomination campaign: better not to divide the bearskin, he said, until after the bear was dead.[57]

The great Republican debate was over, the people having spoken for Roosevelt, the party organization having remained with Taft. The convention itself now had the authority to choose between them.

The Taft congressman who commented on the Illinois primary had it right: the devil would get raised in Chicago in June. Peter Finley Dunne's Mr. Dooley was more graphic: the Chicago convention would be "a combynation iv th' Chicago fire, Saint Bartholomew's massacree, the battle iv th' Boyne, th' life iv Jesse James, an' th' night iv th' big wind."[58]

As the Republican convention opened, the tactics of the Taft forces had an engaging simplicity: Hang tough. In the face of accusation and bluster, hang tough. Taft controlled at least 555 votes (Hilles claimed another 20), more than an absolute majority of the 1072 delegates. Therefore, enough votes were in Taft's satchel to let him win. If everyone kept the bag tightly shut, then no deluge of oratory could move Taft out of the nomination.

Before the opening of the convention, the national committee, elected in the docile hour that had brought Roosevelt and Taft together in 1908, drew up the temporary roll of the convention. Of the 254 contested seats, it awarded the Colonel 19 seats, the President 235. Taft men voted Taft men onto the temporary rolls while Roosevelt, in the *Outlook*, denounced the "fraud as vulgar, as brazen, as cynically open as any ever committed by the Tweed regime on New York forty-odd years ago."[59]

Whatever might be said of Taft's shenanigans as an unedifying spectacle, Roosevelt's hands were not clean either. An astonishing 164 of Roosevelt's contests were transparent shams, McHarg, Roosevelt's agent, having fashioned competing delegations out of cobwebs and fantasy.[60] When the contests came before the committee, even a Roosevelt partisan like Senator William E. Borah of Idaho would not squander any part of his prestige by giving them the time of day. The committee rejected the whole 164 unanimously. In the popular estimate, this patent dishonesty brushed off on more legitimate contests elsewhere. And legitimate claims they were: certainly the nineteen that even the Taft forces conceded, and almost certainly the twenty-four additional claims on which Borah and Governor Herbert S. Hadley of Missouri were prepared to stake their reputations—in the convention and before the nation. The others, Root told Mrs. Lodge, were "of such a character that honest men might fairly differ in their conclusions."[61]

The difficulty for Roosevelt's future was that even with the nineteen delegates the national committee gave him and the twenty-four his team was prepared to fight for, Roosevelt could not control the convention. Taft could. Hadley told Nicholas Murray Butler, or so Butler said, that Roosevelt insisted on taking seventy-four cases to the floor of the convention because a lesser number would not give him control.[62]

Roosevelt watched and listened from New York. When he realized that the Taft forces were counting him out, he rushed to Chicago to assume command. Speaking to his supporters in the auditorium the night before the convention itself began, he accused the national committee of acting "with deliberate dishonesty." He insisted that neither set of contested delegates—not his, not Taft's—be allowed to vote until the one thousand or more uncontested delegates decided between them. "We stand at Armageddon," he said, "and we battle for the Lord."[63]

Roosevelt was not the only one to bandy biblical metaphors. Thousands of throwaways appeared in the neighborhood of the convention announcing that "Teddy will walk on the water of Lake Michigan at 6 PM. . . . Unbelievers are invited to attend."[64]

The rhetoric and the banter, even when lighthearted (as much of it was), did not obscure the prime political fact at stake: If 70 or more of Taft's 555 delegates were forced to stand mute, Roosevelt's 430 delegates plus other scattered votes would control the proceedings up to and including the nomination.

Monday, June 18, the convention opened, Victor Rosewater, acting chairman of the Republican National Committee, presiding over the temporary roll of delegates approved by his committee. Hadley sought immediately to substitute seventy or more delegates for Taft men on the rolls. Rosewater ruled Hadley out of order and forced the convention to vote on a temporary chairman. The Taft forces offered the name of Elihu Root. Roosevelt had recruited Governor Francis E. McGovern of Wisconsin, a hopeful—actually, a hopeless—gesture aimed at appeasing La Follette. La Follette, scornful of McGovern for allowing himself to be used as a dupe, spurned Roosevelt's overture.[65] Root won, 558 to 502. From that moment on, Taft, through Root, dominated the convention.

Root was a magnificent choice, a superb parliamentarian, unflappable. Though he bore the double burden of being Taft's choice and serving as the agent of the national committee,[66] he was, as a longtime political associate and close personal friend of the Colonel, immune to gross attack. Root viewed the Taft-Roosevelt quarrel with regret, but always more conservative than either of his two friends, he had to view recall of judicial decisions as irresponsible tampering with the judicial system. At that point, he knew that the path of duty led him into Taft's camp. In choosing him for temporary, then permanent, chairman, Taft made his only brilliant political decision of the year.

Root's keynote address made the tone of the convention unmistakably pro–Taft "according to rules long since established," though he linked the McKinley-Roosevelt-Taft years into an unbroken chain of accomplishment.[67] Then he refused to disqualify individual delegates whose seats were contested from voting on other contested seats, arguing, quite sensibly, that any other ruling would allow a minority to become a majority simply by contesting enough seats and that, ultimately, when every seat became contested, there would be no convention left. He permitted the convention to refer the temporary roll to a committee charged with drawing up the permanent roll, knowing well that the Taft forces were in even more total command than they had been on the national committee. The Roosevelt team screamed "steamroller," and a delegate drew laughter by emitting a reasonable imitation of a steam whistle. A Mississippi delegate raised a point of order: "the steam roller is exceeding the speed limit." Root sustained the point, offering as his excuse the hope that the convention would finish before the weekend.[68] Throughout the week, Root never faltered, performing his task with stoic sadness, for, as he told a friend just after the convention ended, "I care more for one button on Theodore Roosevelt's waistcoat than for Taft's whole body."[69] But his affection did not retard his determination to see Roosevelt defeated.

The fight came down to two political platitudes: A great popular victory guaranteed nomination only when converted into the currency of presidential politics, that is, delegates at the national convention. A corollary of this truth was clear to Taft, if not to his managers: Losing in the great popularity contest destroys hope of winning the presidential election. Taft was prepared to settle for the nomination: "Whatever happens we shall have preserved the party organization as a nucleus for conservative action in 1916."[70]

Faced with Taft's imminent victory, Roosevelt, having whiffed success, knew that he had been outmaneuvered in a game that he relished as he relished power. Having staked everything on the turn of a red card, control of the convention, he watched as the card turned up blackest of black. Both sides knew that the victor in Chicago would lose in November, so massive were the scars of the struggle. Both sides assessed the combat as determinative of the party's stance for the indefinite future. On Wednesday, June 20, Roosevelt faced the moment for decision on his own public posture. Many of Roosevelt's delegates were prepared to walk out; some were not. Borah had no taste for apostasy, however determined Johnson might be to take California into revolt. Roosevelt played with indecision all afternoon and evening. Then Munsey and Perkins helped by promising financial support: "Colonel, we will see you through."[71] The next day, one of Roosevelt's agents delivered the Colonel's request that his delegates no longer participate in the Republican proceedings. Whatever progressive arguments Roosevelt used publicly to justify his persistence, Root observed later, "The real reason was he was so damn mad."[72]

Within forty-eight hours a rump convention in Orchestra Hall gave Roosevelt its support for the nomination and for the presidency. In response, Roosevelt denounced the fraud they had all witnessed as victims. He bade them back to their communities to receive a fresh mandate for a progressive candidate to whom all honest men could rally.

The truncated Republicans moved ahead with their ritual. Warren G. Harding, a newspaper editor, nominated his fellow Ohioan in listless proceedings. Nomination for La Follette followed, then for Cummins. The latter speeches were perfunctory, though spirited in their defiance. Then the vote: 561 for Taft, 41 for La Follette, 17 for Cummins, 2 for Hughes. Roosevelt received 107 votes, and 344 more delegates abstained. Thus the deed was done. The convention raced through the motions to put Vice-President Sherman back on the ticket. The platform, hammered out while the major drama took place elsewhere, passed without dissent. It was Taft's document, talking of social legislation to protect workers, especially women, children, and the injured, but promising to respect the constitutional limitations on governmental action that interfered with any individual's "control of his own justly acquired property." The platform promised prosperity for the nation, despite rising prices. It predicted success for the party.[73]

Then all went home, the Roosevelt forces defeated, and the Taft forces all but certain of defeat.

PART II

Behaving Like Democrats

4

Woodrow Wilson

Republican fratricide, Democratic opportunity. The Democrats moved to their 1912 nominating convention jubilant over Republican acrimony. "When the Republicans fall out," William Jennings Bryan, the Democrats' perennial presidential loser, observed cheerfully, "honest men come into their own."[1]

Yet Democrats had handicaps as well. Barred from the White House for forty-four of the previous fifty-two years, they had no eligible figures of national stature, no reassuring experience of power, and, what was worse, no habit of winning. President Grover Cleveland and his coterie had retired or died off. Three presidential runs never brought Bryan even close to presidential responsibility. Even more serious was that the Democratic label covered wildly divergent views: Cleveland a "gold bug" and Bryan a "free silverite," for example. Furthermore, the progressives' assault on urban political machines came up against the galling fact that those city machines provided the votes that elected candidates, including progressive candidates.

To these anomalies could always be added the continuing impact of sectionalism: the South resentful that fidelity never brought it appropriate recognition, other sections uneasy at Republican taunts that the Democracy had supported the Great Rebellion of 1861–1865. The "West," wherever that was, resented the "East," somewhat more easily recognized as the territory east of the Appalachians and north of the Mason-Dixon line, the home of capital, the home of immigrants and of the machines that controlled them.

Still, handicaps are burdens, not impossible barriers, if Democrats could avoid defeating themselves. Ideally, the state-by-state nominating process would produce widespread assent, making the convention a relatively bloodless affair. In reality, the preconvention struggle was long and tortuous; the convention itself went through spasms of deadlock until Woodrow Wilson finally emerged as the Democratic protagonist.

Nominated and then elected governor of New Jersey in 1910 at the age of fifty-four, Wilson withdrew from an academic career that, however successful, never fulfilled his primary ambition: to be a political force like William E. Gladstone, the British prime minister in Queen Victoria's era, whose oratory and political principles reflected his view of God's moral order. The imperatives of the moral order were not Sunday dress for Wilson's parental family, but part of its routine daily life, reinforced for young Thomas—the first name was dropped in adulthood—by his closeness to his father, Joseph Wilson, a Presbyterian minister who held prominent posts in Virginia, Georgia, and South and North Carolina. The eldest of four in this close-knit family, Wilson was the cosseted favorite child. His father monitored the son's conversation, corrected his writing, introduced him to Tennyson and Dickens and to the high thinking of the *Edinburgh Review* and to the classically liberal views of the *Nation*. His mother was immensely supportive, even protective; Tommy later recalled, affectionately, the force of her apron strings. They were tight indeed, not an encouragement of maturity. Mrs. Wilson fussed continually over Tommy's health (and her own); lamented his every separation from his family; cushioned his failures, large and small, with excuses; turned her need for him into his dependence on her.

Eventually the maturing youth left home. After a depressed year at Davidson College, he ventured further north to the College of New Jersey, the most southern of the northern colleges and still a bastion of Presbyterianism. Graduating from Princeton in 1879, he attended the University of Virginia Law School for a year, then completed his law studies privately in time to be admitted to the bar in 1882. Turned off by the law's "scheming and haggling practice" and its "most vulgar methods" to make money,[2] he went off to Johns Hopkins University in 1883 for graduate training in law, government, and jurisprudence. He put aside thoughts of a political career; he determined to seek a role as "an *outside* force in politics" through "literary and non-partisan agencies."[3] Within two years he finished a major work, *Congressional Government*, published by Houghton, Mifflin in 1885 and accepted as his doctoral dissertation the following year. In this notable book, Wilson criticized the scheme of congressional supremacy that had emerged from the triumph of national sovereignty following the Civil War. More particularly, he deplored the emergence of "government by the Standing Committees of Congress,"[4] the president an impotent figurehead, the Supreme Court merely ratifying the flow of power to Congress.

Congressional Government brought Wilson wide reputation as a scholar; even reviewers who rejected his argument recognized him as a worthy antagonist. Wilson relished his impact as an "*outside* force in politics," but he could not suppress his "very real regret that I have been shut out from my heart's *first*—primary—ambition and purpose . . . a *statesman's* career."[5]

After this initial success, books and articles flowed from his study: *The State* (1889), a textbook in comparative government; *Division and Reunion* (1893), a Southerner's remarkably evenhanded discussion of the Civil War and Reconstruction; *George Washington* (1896), a popular—and inconsequential—biography; books of occasional essays; and in 1902, his five-volume *History of the American People*, primarily a money-maker to adorn fashionable parlors.

Wilson needed to supplement his professional income, for he had acquired a wife and three daughters. Just after publication of *Congressional Government*, he had married Ellen Axson. His new bride, a Georgia painter who let her own artistic talent wither to create a secure base for her husband, gave Wilson the ideal model of womanhood that he needed to perpetuate his mother's uncritical adulation and to relieve the internalized anxiety that her possessiveness had created in him. Though not without its troubled moments and one occasion of profound hurt, their marriage flourished with a depth of affection that survives in the letters of both.

Wilson and his bride moved to Pennsylvania, where he accepted an appointment at Bryn Mawr College, then further north to Wesleyan University in Connecticut. There he stayed until his call (as it was known in the days before faculty unions) to Princeton in 1890. Professor of jurisprudence and political economy for a dozen years, Wilson moved smoothly into the presidency of Princeton in 1902, there to remain for a brilliant and stormy eight years until his election as governor of New Jersey in 1910.

Wilson learned much about executive leadership in his years as Princeton's president. He achieved two great successes: reform of the upperclass plan of study and introduction of small tutorials known as preceptorials. He suffered two great defeats: he failed to displace the upperclass eating clubs with a more egalitarian house system, and he lost an internal battle over the location of Princeton's graduate college. Both losses had potential political glamor: the house, or quadrangle, system could be viewed as a battle for the sturdy democracy of undergraduate life against the effete exclusiveness of selective upperclass clubs. Even more, though with considerably less justification, the debate over site lent itself to populist rhetoric. Wilson framed the issue himself. Writing to a trustee closest to Wilson's adversary, Dean Andrew Fleming West, Wilson insisted on resisting control by people of great wealth: "I cannot accede to the acceptance of gifts upon terms that take the educational policy of the University out of the hands of the Trustees and Faculty and permit it to be determined by those who give money."[6]

By the time of Wilson's defeat on the site question, he was already well into his adventure in politics, with Colonel George Brinton McClellan Harvey his preceptor, small gatherings of industrial and political leaders in New York, Princeton, and Trenton his tutorial, and, eventually, the state of New Jersey and the whole nation as his lecture hall.

As early as 1906, Harvey, president of the publishing firm of Harper and

Brothers and editor of *Harper's Weekly*, publicly adopted Wilson as a potential presidential candidate, and in the four years thereafter he made Wilson's march to the White House an intense hobby.[7] From Harvey's point of view, the Democratic Party needed an alternative to Bryan after Theodore Roosevelt's thumping of the stolid Judge Alton B. Parker in 1904. Where could he be found? The Democrats had a governor here and there outside the South and senators and representatives who conducted guerrilla action from the disadvantaged position of the minority party in Congress. Compared with them, someone like Wilson could command attention. He was a national leader in education. He understood the structure of government. He was a fine lecturer, and he could become a splendid public speaker. Above all, he was safe.

Indeed, very safe. Under Harvey's tutelage, Wilson in 1907 drew up a "Credo" for perusal by William M. Laffan, publisher of the New York *Sun*, possibly the most conservative paper in the United States. Wilson acknowledged that modern business had on occasion contravened both good morals and sound business practices, and he accepted the need for prohibitions and punishments. Nevertheless, he rejected governmental regulation of business. He defended great combinations: "Great trusts and combinations are the necessary, because the most convenient and efficient, instrumentalities of modern business; the vast bulk of their transactions are legitimate and honest; their methods are for the most part legitimate and honest." All American history has been a "brilliant and successful" protest against the "fruitless . . . experiment of paternalism," he said. We should clear away governmental commissions and set up again the right of the individual to "that most precious of all the possessions of a few people, the right of freedom of contract," specifically, the right to sell his labor "for such price as he is willing to accept." Wilson posited an active executive as the only voice for the whole people, a voice necessarily increasing in "significance and importance." But in the era of Theodore Roosevelt, he warned against "any encroachment upon the sphere either of Congress or of the courts": Congress must work its will "without suspicion of undue or covert executive influence," and the courts must be "free from either executive suggestion or legislative dictation." The goal for all constitutional government, Wilson intoned, is the liberty of the individual.[8]

Harvey could scarcely have hoped for a more satisfying declaration. As he wrote in an editorial for the New York *World*, the leading Democratic forum, in January 1908, Wilson was the Democrat to save the party "from falling into the hands of William J. Bryan as a permanent receiver."[9]

But 1908 was too soon. Wilson was not enough of a national figure, and Bryan once again held the Democratic majority in line. Following the convention, Wilson concentrated on his fight over the graduate college, remaining aloof from Bryan's 1908 presidential bid.

As 1908 gave way to 1909 with 1910 and 1912 in the offing, the political setting for the Wilson boom improved. Witnessing the growing Republican disorder in the Taft years, Colonel Harvey groomed and promoted Wilson as a man of national stature who, all the while, offered no threat to the interests that made the nation prosperous.

Wilson, no fool, knew how high the odds were against eventual success: so long a road, so many pitfalls along the way.

Still, Harvey's enthusiasm was flattering, provocative, not unreasonable. When Wilson had turned to the academy, he had shelved his political ambitions; he had not discarded them. His years as Princeton's president rekindled his sense of self as active leader, full of projects and capable of executing them. He could move these skills to larger undertakings. In lectures at Columbia University in 1907 that appeared the following year as *Constitutional Government in the United States*, Wilson asserted that the presidential office had come to need a new kind of man. It was not "absolutely necessary that they [presidential aspirants] should have had extended experience in public affairs." The country would no longer seek "an astute politician, skilled and practiced in affairs" so much as a "representative man . . . a man such as it can trust, in character, in intention, in knowledge of its needs, in perception of the best means by which those needs may be met, in capacity to prevail by reason of his own weight and integrity."[10] Having observed Theodore Roosevelt in action, Wilson no longer thought of the president as a ceremonial figurehead: "The President is at liberty, both in law and conscience, to be as big a man as he can. . . . The Constitution bids him speak, and times of stress and change must more and more thrust upon him the attitude of originator of policies."[11] Looking at the office, the Princeton academic could see nothing inherently ridiculous in the proposition that Dr. Woodrow Wilson should be president of the United States.

From 1909 to 1912, Wilson and his agents plotted his way to achievement.

With the gubernatorial elections of 1910 in sight, Harvey surged ahead, nailing his colors to the mast in the lead editorial comment, "Looking Ahead," in *Harper's Weekly* for May 15, 1909: "We now expect to see Woodrow Wilson elected Governor of the State of New Jersey in 1910 and nominated for President in 1912 upon a platform demanding tariff revision downward."[12]

When Harvey took on the role of honest broker in the selection of New Jersey's next governor, Wilson set a tough condition: He would accept the Democratic nomination only if he could have it handed to him (in words that Harvey actually used) "on a silver platter."[13] He did not propose to expose his flank at Princeton by appearing to seek public office only to fail in the attempt.

With Wilson's condition in hand, Harvey sounded out his friend, James Smith, Jr., former United States senator and the more prominent of the two potent Democratic leaders in New Jersey. Smith did not fit the stereotypical picture of the boss: he was suave, softspoken, gentlemanly, wily rather than blunt. He and his nephew and lieutenant, James R. Nugent, the Democratic state chairman, held Essex County in thrall, just as Robert Davis ruled the Democratic roost in Hudson County. They were part of a machine that had been out of power for sixteen years following a racetrack scandal in 1893. But though the bosses were not power brokers in state government, which was ruled by their Republican counterparts, they had substantial influence over the internal workings of the Democratic Party. No candidate for governor could survive their veto.

Smith was interested, but wary: interested because an untainted candidate like Wilson could sweep an election, indeed, win "in a walk" if nominated,[14] and if he carried a Democratic legislature into office with him, the Democratic majority could return Smith to the United States Senate; wary because he was not prepared to buy a pig in a poke. Would Wilson respect existing arrangements in the party? Smith needed to know.

Wilson, through intermediaries, gave Smith the necessary assurance: "So long as the existing Democratic organization was willing to work with thorough heartiness for such policies as would reestablish the reputation of the State and the credit of the Democratic party in serving the State, I should deem myself inexcusable for antagonizing it, so long as I was left absolutely free in the matter of measures and men."[15]

Less sensitive to ambiguity than he should have been, Smith found the declaration acceptable. The deal was struck. Wilson wanted the nomination, and Smith wanted a winner in 1910. It was in the interest of each not to check out nuances of meaning too precisely. In mid-July, Wilson issued a statement for the press: he would accept the nomination for governor as a duty, honor, and privilege if "a decided majority of the thoughtful Democrats of the State" were to confer it upon him.[16]

Smith had some difficulty lining up the thoughtful Democrats. Smith's firm control extended only to Essex County. Beyond the borders he had substantial influence, but he had to deal with similar satrapies as jealousy held as his own, sometimes more tenaciously held because the little corner of power was smaller. Furthermore, the small progressive wing of the Democracy—people like Joseph P. Tumulty of Jersey City, a former assemblyman barely tolerated by Davis's organization, and James Kerney, editor of the Trenton *Evening News*—was less than enthusiastic about the latest coup of the state house ring in bringing in a candidate so clearly its creation whose record displayed little progressive commitment.[17] Finally, other candidates were not prepared to play dead for an interloper with no record.

The summer months were heavy with attacks on Wilson's candidacy. Wilson, vacationing in Lyme, Connecticut, stayed aloof from the fray, unbending only to respond after the State Federation of Labor denounced him as "the tool or agent of . . . Wall Street's interests."[18] Wilson said in rebuttal to these "willful and deliberate misrepresentations" that he had always been a "warm friend of organized labor"; he had criticized labor only as a friend.[19] Thereafter, through the September primaries, Wilson posed as an interested bystander.

Smith was more active. He held his own forces in Essex County fully in line. That was no problem. He struck a deal with Davis in Hudson County. He watched the other candidates cancel each other out by holding tenaciously to their conflicting ambitions. And finally in Trenton on the night of September 15, he achieved the majority necessary to put his candidate over. "What was my exact majority?" Wilson asked Harvey later that evening. "Enough," Harvey answered flatly.[20] The convention dutifully made the nomination unanimous. Harvey had Wilson stashed at the nearby Trenton House, his acceptance speech in hand, ready to address the convention.

Appearing before his new confederates, Wilson accepted the nomination, he said, bound by no pledges—none given, none "proposed or desired"— that would mar "serving the people of the State with singleness of purpose." Foretelling "a new and more ideal era in our politics," he embraced the Democratic platform, then listed his priorities: reorganization in administration, equalization of taxation, control of corporations. Employers' liability, corrupt electoral practices, and conservation were also important, but not dominant. He disclaimed any spirit of hostility, any attack on established interests as public enemies, preferring common counsel, dispassionate study, and action based on the common interest. But he did not shrink from citing Wisconsin's pioneering success in regulating public service corporations as a model, or from coveting for New Jersey the honor of "showing the other States how corporations can be controlled."[21]

The convention was astonished and electrified by Wilson's blunt declaration. Even the progressives were impressed. Tumulty, who had opposed Wilson's nomination, succumbed to the force of the speech: There would be a new day in New Jersey after all; "Jim Smith will find he has a 'lemon.' "[22]

Initially awkward about asking people to vote for him, Wilson soon adapted to the rigor of campaigning, travel day by day, endless introductions, constant repetition of phrases to catch the fancy of the uncommitted as well as the faithful. He resigned from Princeton, the trustees mumbling the customary inane platitudes to mask the relief that many of them felt. The Wilson family left the president's residence and settled into rooms at the Princeton Inn. From there Wilson sallied forth daily, usually by car across largely unpaved roads, frequently with State Chairman Nugent as his companion. Criticized at first for vagueness, he became increasingly precise, going well past the platform in denouncing corporations that moved toward becoming trusts, listing specific political changes that would make "that great voiceless multitude of man" into "the saving force of the nation."[23] He moved comfortably toward a progressive stance, focusing on reforms that could be accomplished at the state level, for example, regulating commuter rates by a state commission.

Wilson's Republican opponent, Vivian M. Lewis, similarly a moderate progressive in a party dominated by bosses, offered a comparable package. But he was saddled with the voters' perception of his helplessness while the

"Board of Guardians," the progressives' tag for the Republican power structure, remained in place. In truth, was Wilson any freer?

One Republican progressive, George L. Record, decided to smoke Wilson
out once and for all. Record had spent a career in the thicket of New Jersey
politics, his enthusiasm for progressivism a matured and well-informed stance
rich in knowledge of the hidden skeletons in both parties. Responding to
Wilson's careless challenge to debate any politician in the state, Record invited
Wilson to name the times and places. It was a moment of great risk. But
Wilson was not willing to play the scared hare. After three days' reflection, he
plunged into the vortex that Record had stirred up, inviting a full inquisition
by public letter and authorizing Record to publish his reply.

At that moment and from that whirlpool Woodrow Wilson emerged as a
notable spokesman for progressive principles in New Jersey and in America.

Record made the most of the opportunity. He pressed Wilson on specific
progressive reforms—primaries for all major officers and a public utilities
commission with power to fix rates. Then he narrowed in on the boss issue.
Both he and Wilson denounced the Republican "Board of Guardians"; would
Wilson also denounce the Democratic counterpart, known as the "Over-
lords"?[24]

In reply, Wilson went point by point down Record's fourteen-question list,
accepting Record's position as his own, demurring only on details. He favored
the specific reforms to regulate corporations and to spread the popular control of government. He accepted Record's description of the corrupt alliance
between corporations and machines—"Of course I admit it. Its existence is
notorious."—and of the boss system. Then he went Record one better by
framing a challenge that Record had not issued: How would Wilson relate to
the Democratic bosses on appointments and legislation? "I am very glad to
tell you," Wilson replied to the question Record had not asked:[25]

If elected, I shall not, either in the matter of appointments to office or assent to
legislation, or in shaping any part of the policy of my administration, submit to the
dictation of any person or persons, special interest or organization.... I should deem
myself forever disgraced should I in even the slightest degree cooperate in any such
system or any such transaction as you describe in your characterization of the "boss"
system. I regard myself as pledged to the regeneration of the Democratic party which
I have forecast above.

Record was thunderstruck. He knew at that moment that Wilson had won
the election of 1910.[26] He, along with other "New Idea" Republicans and
undernourished Democratic progressives, also knew that a new day for progressivism had emerged in New Jersey. James Smith, Jr., understood too. Like
the Samaritans in the book of Hosea, he had unleashed the wind, and now
he was reaping the whirlwind. With the election a scant twelve days away,
there was nothing he could do but ride out the storm and hope for calmer
days.

On election day, Wilson beat his Republican opponents by more than 49,000 votes, his 233,933 votes representing just under 54 percent of the total for five candidates. Though the state senate remained Republican by one seat, he carried a Democratic assembly into office with him.

The nation showed interest, mild interest, in the performance—the college fellow moving on his first try from the academic life of Princeton to the political turmoil of the state house in Trenton. A flash in the pan? Or step one for a man of destiny?

If the election was step one, then steps three and four—nomination for president by the Democratic Party and election as president by the voters of America—were obvious but not inexorable, for destiny had to ride on step two, the performance of the forty-third governor of the State of New Jersey.

Wilson's first test came even before his inauguration, and his adversary was his late sponsor, James Smith, Jr. Smith determined to have the newly elected legislature, now controlled by the Democratic caucus over which he had long exercised suzerainty, perform its constitutional function (and elect him United States senator) without deference to the apathetic nonbinding preferential referendum just won by James F. Martine, a perennial office-seeker who would have stood out as a nonentity in any random collection of political entities. If Smith won his seat, he would reveal where real control of power lay in New Jersey. Conversely, a successful rebuff to the boss would tell the state, and the nation beyond the borders, that Governor-elect Wilson would be master in his own house and that his house would be a home for progressivism. The issue was stark and dramatic. A wily governor might even have provoked the controversy for his own purposes. But Smith's resolve made it unnecessary for Wilson to go looking for a fight. Furthermore, Smith's record made Wilson's job a bit easier: when Smith had been in the Senate previously, he had deserted his party and voted with the Republicans on the tariff of 1894, the tariff being the historic touchstone of Democratic identity. Wilson had the issues. Did Smith have the power?

Wilson gave Smith a deadline for disavowing his candidacy. When the deadline passed, Wilson went public with a bombshell, more than three weeks before his inauguration. He recognized that he had no legal role in making the choice for the Senate, he said.

But there are other duties besides legal duties. The recent campaign had put me in an unusual position. I offered, if elected, to be the political spokesman and adviser of the people. I even asked those who did not care to make their choice of Governor upon that understanding not to vote for me. I believe that the choice was made upon that understanding; and I cannot escape the responsibility involved. I have no desire to escape it. It is my duty to say, with a full sense of the peculiar responsibility of my position, what I deem it to be the obligation of the Legislature to do in this gravely important matter.

Clearly the people had expressed their preference for Martine. "For me, that vote is conclusive," he went on. "I think it should be for every member of the Legislature. Absolute good faith in dealing with the people, an unhesitating fidelity to every principle avowed, is the highest law of political morality under a constitutional government.... It is clearly the duty of every Democratic legislator, who would keep faith with the law of the State and with the avowed principles of his party, to vote for Mr. Martine."[27]

Wilson's argument was impeccable. The Democrats, having ridden the preferential primary issue for progressive acclaim, now had to live with the consequences. As Wilson made the rounds of the state pressing his case, there was little that his opponents could reply except to sputter indignantly about his ingratitude. Ingratitude to a political boss was not, in 1910–1911, a debilitating accusation.

Across the Hudson River, the newly elected Governor John A. Dix of New York ducked a comparable fight. The *Independent*, watching both contests from its vantage point in New York City, noted the difference: Dix, like Taft, regarded himself as an executive with no responsibility as a legislative leader; Wilson, like Theodore Roosevelt, actively pushed the people's interest before the legislature. The American people, the *Independent* noted, liked their elected leaders to lead, not to find excuses for passivity. Wilson, unlike Dix, was already being touted as a presidential possibility.[28]

When the New Jersey legislature assembled in early January 1911, Martine won his senatorial seat.

Thus even as Wilson was entering his gubernatorial office, he had already made himself felt within the state and observed across the nation. The college professor was no babe in the woods in dealing with power and with powerbrokers. He knew an issue when he saw it. And he won.

Once in office, he won even more, using Record and other progressives in both parties who had carried the banner of reform for almost a decade[29] to set a legislative agenda that in four months rescued New Jersey from the backwaters of political reaction. The "mother of the trusts" turned on her children and took on a new family, the people of the state who had previously been frozen out of influence in government.

The record of the 1911 New Jersey legislature was dazzling; it consisted of four major acts: an employers' liability and workmen's compensation act, a public utilities act that gave a state commission detailed authority that rivaled the force of acts anywhere in the nation, revision of primary and general election procedures, and a corrupt practices act that imposed stringent procedural limits on people running for public office. In addition, Wilson secured regulation of the cold storage of food stuffs, indeterminate sentences for convicted criminals, reform of school systems, and authorization for the commission form of government in New Jersey cities. Wilson was elated; the total constituted "one of the most remarkable records of legislation, I venture to think, that has ever distinguished a single legislative session in this country."[30]

Many of the measures had passed the Republican Senate without a dissenting vote. Wilson wrote his unrestrained appraisal to his friend, Mary Allen Hulbert Peck, a social adornment of the American colony in Bermuda whom Wilson had met on vacation in 1907. Even recognizing that the times had been ripe for great changes, he could not conceal his delight with the result, "as complete a victory as has ever been won, I venture to say, in the history of the country." He knew who was at the center of the accomplishment: "I wrote the platform, I had the measures formulated to my mind, I kept the pressure of opinion constantly on the legislature, and the program was carried out to its last detail."[31]

Wilson was right. It was an extraordinary achievement. In less than four months, he had used the momentum of his election and his early triumph over Smith to make New Jersey a minor Wisconsin. It was the kind of record that a man could take to the nation.

5

The Democratic Primary

Less than two years separated Woodrow Wilson's inauguration as governor of New Jersey from election day in 1912. He had only seventeen months before the Democrats would gather in Baltimore to name their candidate; seventeen months on a tricky path, pitfalls abounding, snipers alert, moments of failure so palpable that the final goal all but disappeared from sight.

The imponderables were enormous. Would William Jennings Bryan, thrice the Democratic standard-bearer, be a factor? About a year after his defeat in 1908, he had announced publicly that he would never seek the nomination again.[1] Still, Bryan being Bryan, neither his friends nor his foes could be certain, for the presidential bug carries an infection that, like lust, is finally laid to rest only in the tomb. If not a candidate, would Bryan, loved and detested within the party, influence events significantly, or was he a flickering flame that would light no one's way to victory? Would the progressive mood in the country survive into the following year? If it did, then Wilson had not simply to ride that wave but to channel it. How many candidates could command national attention in the press, on the platform, among power-brokers? How extensively would favorite sons, local candidates holding their own state delegations for maximal leverage at the convention, intrude on the process? Could Wilson juggle his state responsibility and his national ambition? That Wilson fill the gubernatorial office glitteringly was necessary but not sufficient for his purpose: a lackluster performance could disqualify him, as it did Governor John A. Dix in the more populous New York, but a brilliant performance gave no guarantee of advancement. Was money available for a modest base of operations? Could Wilson milk his southern origins in competition with real southerners? Could Wilson walk the fine line, progressive enough to win the reformist wing of the party, conservative enough to qualify as safe-and-sane?

Inexperience protected Wilson from realizing the complexity of his problems. As he eyed the White House from Trenton, he had to believe that if he spoke his convictions with candor in all parts of the country, preference would follow.

Even before the New Jersey legislature had completed its work, Wilson ventured beyond the state to share his views: off to New York to address the Kansas Society and the Kentuckians in New York, down to Washington for a session at the National Press Club, over to Philadelphia to draw favor from both wings of the badly divided Pennsylvania Democracy, south to Atlanta to define the interests common to all.

Then in Indianapolis, Indiana, just as the New Jersey Senate was passing the direct primary act unanimously, he pulled together the main elements of his political stand, not too aggressive, not too partisan—and not too specific. "Now your whole process of reform, your whole process of legislation is a process of adjustment, a process of accommodation, a process of bringing things together in handsome cooperation, instead of in ugly antagonism. That is your vision of the thing that is to be done, not destroying any part of the great body politic, or the body social, but unifying those living and sensitive things into one organism, through which will flow unobstructed the life blood of a free people." While affirming that "We are not fighting property," he denied that corporate capital was private; actually corporate boards of directors "are simply licensed and privileged by the community to act as trustees and representatives of the community in the combinations of the power of wealth."[2] Later in April, his legislative victories behind him, he told the social and business leadership of Virginia that the nation was reconstructing its economic life, protecting its women and children, forcing publicity on corporate operations, breaking the bond between corporations and political agents.

As he made the rounds, Wilson's manner became confident, even jaunty; at Norfolk, he cast aside his prepared address and spoke with a directness that caught his audience by surprise. Toastmasters almost routinely topped off his accomplishments in New Jersey with a climactic introduction of "the next President of the United States."

Already a tiny campaign was operating out of New York: two publicity agents put in place by Walter Hines Page, editor of *World's Work*, and William F. McCombs, a New York lawyer who had been a student of Wilson's at Princeton. Wilson played the reluctant bride—even he spoke of his "maiden coyness"—permitting a small mailing station, unwilling to have his associates acknowledge, much less suggest, that he was running for president.[3] Over the next twelve months the operation grew larger, and McCombs became what in anyone else's entourage would have been called a campaign manager. He paid much of the initial costs himself, and when his debts became too heavy and larger sums became necessary, he turned to Wilson's friendly Princeton trustees. Cleveland H. Dodge finally tossed in $51,000 of his own and solicited $34,800 from the others. In June McCombs moved the operation out of his own office to a cubbyhole at 42 Broadway, and the following month William G. McAdoo, not a Princeton man himself but the father of one, joined the team, taking time from his job as president of the Hudson and Manhattan Railroad Company. McCombs stayed close to the office, but McAdoo eventually visited twenty-four states in the South and West.

The long-range chore for the new office was to get Wilson's message, and the messenger, into the mainstream of political America: not just the northeast, where Wilson was becoming a familiar figure, but into the South, where his antecedents gave him entry, and into the vast West beyond the Alleghenies, and especially beyond the Mississippi, remote territory for which the name Woodrow Wilson had even less meaning than the name of New Jersey itself.

The immediate chore in the spring of 1911, therefore, was to set up a western tour for Wilson, arranged largely through Princeton contacts.[4] Alumni were well spread around the nation, and alumni of other eastern colleges, especially Yale and Harvard, were ready to hear in him the voice of intellectual America. Colleges were eager to hear the former Princeton president. Newspaper editors found him good copy. When he made a speech, it was well modulated, carefully prepared, then delivered with the kind of rhetorical skill that had made Wilson a popular teacher. Insurgent Democrats—like those in the important states of Pennsylvania and Texas—recognized Wilson as an asset, for his bright literacy and progressive statements reinforced their local efforts; in addition, they could see a new day nationally if the Governor of New Jersey plunged ahead successfully as a spokesman for their shared goals. For true insurgents in either party everywhere, he was an alternative to the standpattism of William Howard Taft. Even those not ready to buy into Wilson's ideas were willing to make a slight affiliation with what might eventually be a winner.

In May, Wilson went off on the hustings—Kansas City, Missouri, Denver, Los Angeles, San Francisco, Portland, Seattle, Minneapolis, then back to Lincoln, Nebraska, Bryan's base—"quite like a campaign speaking tour," he acknowledged to his friend, Mary Allen Hulbert Peck.[5] In Denver with little more than an hour's preparation he produced an eloquent address commemorating the three hundredth anniversary of the King James Bible. Elsewhere he committed himself to the standard repertory of progressive measures: primaries, short ballot, initiative, referendum, and recall of elected officials (though not of judges). He renewed his argument for regulation of corporations: "The corporations must recognize, when they ask the public to invest in their stock and securities, that they are public and not private organizations. We must bring about a condition where the officer of a corporation shall be protected in his corporate acts so long as they are within the law, but shall become an outlaw, subject to the same prosecution, con-

viction and punishment as a private citizen, when he begins to act unlawfully."[6]
Nothing much was said to ruffle conservative feathers; few voices explicitly
defended corporate outlaws. Like a good Democrat, he attacked the tariff as
a "system of patronage," but he warned that "in the revision of that tariff it
won't do to upset business conditions throughout the country."[7]

At every stop the press was curious about Wilson's presidential ambition.
The governor generally brushed off the inquiries diffidently. But when he
told an interviewer in Denver, "Really, I have not thought about the Presidency," the New York *Sun*, no longer a friendly organ, hooted in derision.[8]
Thereafter, Wilson backed off cautiously, noting for the San Francisco *Chronicle* that he had never heard of the nomination being refused.[9]

Wilson returned from the West through the Carolinas: a commencement
address at the University of North Carolina and a visit to his boyhood home
in South Carolina. Coming North, he stopped in Washington, D.C., to chat
individually with one hundred congressmen, including the Speaker of the
House, Champ Clark, and Representative Oscar W. Underwood, chairman of
the Ways and Means Committee. Finally, at the end of the first week in June,
he was back at his desk in Trenton.

Just over a week later he returned to Harrisburg, Pennsylvania, where he
shared the podium of the State Federation of Democratic Clubs with Speaker
Clark. Their host, Congressman A. Mitchell Palmer, introduced them both as
presidential timber. Clark spoke blandly, as usual. But Wilson, picking up a
theme not widely reported when he spoke in South Carolina, attacked the
"money monopoly." Control of credit, he said, "is dangerously concentrated
in this country. The large money resources of the country are not at the
command of those who do not submit to the direction and domination of
small groups of capitalists, who wish to keep the economic development of
the country under their own eye and guidance. The great monopoly in this
country is the money monopoly."[10] His speech carried him well beyond his
previous positions, well into the bluntest progressive rhetoric.

Progressives might welcome his remarks, but the New York *World*, almost
desperately anxious to be friendly, rebuked him for appealing "to public
clamor instead of to public intelligence." What had happened to his judgment?
"Does Governor Wilson think that playing to the gallery will promote his
Presidential candidacy? Does he believe that efforts to win Mr. Bryan's approval and to capture his following will increase his political strength? Is he
Bryanizing himself?"[11]

Bryan was unquestionably on Wilson's mind; he had been from the beginning. Old hand that he was, Bryan kept in constant touch with the national
scene. Even before Wilson's inaugural, Bryan tested the waters: "I am expecting to come East early in March," he wrote Wilson on January 5, 1911,
"and would like to see you for an hour or so on political matters. The fact
that you were against us in 1896 raised a question in my mind in regard to
your views on public questions but your attitude in the Senatorial case has

tended to reassure me. . . . In the meantime I would like to have your opinion of the various planks of the Denver [1908 Democratic] platform."[12] Wilson replied to Bryan's satisfaction, allowing Bryan to look forward to their subsequent meeting. That meeting occurred in Princeton in March when Mrs. Wilson summoned her husband home in haste from Atlanta to dine with the Great Commoner. The two shared a platform in Burlington, New Jersey, the following month—indeed, the occasion had been created for just that purpose—and Wilson used the moment to recall Bryan's historic role: "Mr. Bryan has borne the heat and burden of a long day; we have come in at a very much later time to reap the reward of the things that he has done. . . . It is because he has cried America awake that some other men have been able to translate into action the doctrines that he has so diligently preached."[13] Bryan was not at home when Wilson visited Lincoln, Nebraska, but Charles W. Bryan, his brother and sidekick, welcomed Wilson warmly. Thomas B. Love, the progressive leader of the Wilson movement in Texas, touted Wilson's virtues to Bryan, and old friendship lent force to his words.[14] But throughout Bryan kept his own counsel. Wilson was clearly one of the people to watch, and Bryan was watching, just as he was watching others as well: Clark, Underwood, Governor Judson Harmon of Ohio, Mayor William Jay Gaynor of New York City, and ex-Governor Joseph W. Folk of Missouri.

As the summer of 1911 gave way to autumn, Wilson continued to roam. In Wisconsin and Texas, where progressives were clearly in control, he felt confident of his favored position. In Pennsylvania, a complex internal struggle forced the whole party into his camp, for the progressives felt obliged to adopt Wilson when the conservatives showed signs of using his candidacy as a way of retaining control. From New York, McCombs redoubled his efforts, writing to leaders in state after state, keeping in touch with the leadership in New York, sending McAdoo into the South and West, setting up a branch office in Washington that gradually took over communication with hundreds of newspapers all over the nation.

For all of 1911 Wilson kept his campaign low-key. He responded to requests for speeches around the country. He spoke out on the issues as a concerned Democrat. He kept himself informed about political activity with whatever correspondents cared to write. In his exchanges with Mrs. Peck, Wilson played alternating roles, now detailing his campaign moves, then doubting that he wanted the presidency. Wilson guarded his emotional commitment, for clearly in the American context the nomination for president was not going to come on a silver platter, as the governorship of New Jersey had. The long odds made him reluctant to admit his yearnings, even to himself. So his role in 1911 remained equivocal: enough in the fight to take advantage of every occasion to exploit possible gains, not so much committed that he could not withdraw without too much loss of face.

For the thirteen to fourteen months after Wilson's election as governor, the procedure—it was not articulated enough to be called a game plan—

worked admirably. As orator and leader, giving palpable form to the otherwise inchoate dreams of the people, he was creating the image of Woodrow Wilson as a public power. He developed a line of self-deprecating remarks to defuse effusive introductions. One of his daughters fed him a limerick that became a staple of subsequent speeches:

> For beauty I am not a star
> There are others more handsome by far.
> But my face I don't mind it
> Because I'm behind it.
> It's the people in front that I jar.

His well-rehearsed stands on major public issues allowed him to speak spontaneously with good effect, and his skilled platform manner permitted him to be somber with the serious and jovial with the uncommitted. His years in the classroom served him well: he built logic, coherence, and occasional eloquence into his public statements, and he caught the mood of an occasion with deft accuracy.

Indeed, with a style very different from Theodore Roosevelt's—vastly more reserved, more formal—he did for Democratic audiences what the peripatetic Roosevelt was doing on the Republican circuit: establishing a public presence that made him the most conspicuous, certainly the most intelligent and well trained in his party's stable.

To close out the year 1911, the *New York Times* and the New York *World* sent reporters over to New Jersey to pull together the views of the man "most widely discussed" for the Democratic nomination. His campaign managers accepted the interviews as the authoritative Wilson, and in pamphlet form they were widely disseminated the following year. The *World*'s reporter tried to catch his appearance as well as his views:[15]

Physically, the Governor of New Jersey is a tall, spare man, one might also call him lean. He has long limbs, a long neck and a very long, narrow, big-boned face, with a high forehead and long, square jaw. The ears are somewhat overnormal in size, with very small lobes and are large and well rounded at the top. They are set high up on the sides of the head, and this, with the prominent cheek bones and aggressive chin, give the jaw an appearance of great length.

The face is a pleasing one. Very refined but not exactly handsome, and yet it is hard to tell why. The eyebrows are beautifully arched and the mouth is uncommonly well shaped for a man. It is sensitive but firm. The eyes are blue gray, although generally very kindly, at times take on a hard, piercing expression. The tip of the nose is most mobile, and twitches whenever the Governor lays emphasis on a word.

In the interviews, the governor established his Democratic authenticity by naming the tariff as the essential issue, a "tariff for revenue" as the ultimate goal. Under the existing tariff, prices remained high, driving up the cost of living, and opportunities remained restricted, confining individual dreams. He did not back off from his comments on the money monopoly, but he declined to elaborate on any alternative to the banking reforms being articulated by Senator Nelson W. Aldrich of Rhode Island. He acknowledged that trusts were economic and efficient, but their efficiency gave them the power "to throttle competition and establish virtual monopoly in every market that they have coveted." Monopolistic use of trusts could be stopped by punishing every person guilty of a criminal offense. "I do not think that 'war' should be made on anything; our problem is one of equitable readjustment. I do not understand that the policy of our law was ever directed against combinations as such, or against their mere size, but only against combinations in restraint of trade. Combination has proved an extremely successful means of economy and efficiency, but restraint of trade is another matter and affects the healthful operation of our whole economic system." He wanted to break the ties between corporations and political machines: the progressives' full program of popular control through primaries, initiative, referendum, and recall. And only the Democratic Party could be entrusted with the task, for the progressive element controls the party; the Republicans had a progressive wing, to be sure, but "The Republican Party in the Nation is controlled by the reactionary forces."[16]

Bryan, who could hear the grass grow in Nebraska, undoubtedly saw the interviews.

A new factor entered into Wilson's connection to Bryan: Colonel Edward M. House, a political amateur from Texas looking for a winner on the national scene to whom he could attach himself. Ideologically remote from Bryan, House nevertheless kept lines open to him based on prior social contacts and on shared commitment to Democratic victory. House and Wilson first met at House's hotel in New York in late November 1911. They hit it off immediately. As a result, Wilson acquired a counselor; House, a plausible candidate. The day following their meeting, House—the "Colonel" was honorary, but persistent—was already working on Bryan, badmouthing all Wilson's potential opponents even as he pointed to some "identical" views that Bryan and Wilson shared.[17] Within a fortnight he added William Randolph Hearst, J. P. Morgan, and "everybody south of Canal Street" to the anti-Wilson camp.[18] Thereafter, House promised McCombs to "make it my particular province to keep in touch with him [Bryan] and endeavor to influence him along the lines desired."[19] In fact, Bryan kept lines out to dozens of political operatives; House was only one among many. If it amused House to think he was the crucial contact, the fiction cost Wilson—and Bryan—nothing. When the convention met at the end of June, House was sailing for Europe, and Bryan—and Wilson—functioned without his counsel.[20]

Bryan was balm. Bryan was poison. To Mrs. Peck, Wilson stated confidently that "[O]f course no Democrat can win whom Mr. Bryan does *not* approve."[21] And to another correspondent he acknowledged: "The hazard in the whole case is what Mr. Bryan may do or say, but I do not see how I can control that to any degree." Then he added his fatalist strategy: "I can only go my own way and speak my thoughts, and let the rest be taken care of by the powers which really preside."[22]

"[T]he powers which really preside": there was the key. Wilson's gubernatorial campaign, his fight with Smith, his legislative triumphs, his speeches across the nation—in short, his public posture—positioned him aptly at the center of progressive thought. But his new posture carried a price. His treatment of James Smith, Jr. did not endear him to political leaders elsewhere. His legislation in New Jersey and his subsequent speeches, especially the Harrisburg speech on the "money monopoly," warned off a whole spectrum of conservative opinion on which George Harvey had counted. The New York *Sun*, at the most conservative end of the spectrum, treated Wilson like a pariah, and even the New York *World*, more in sorrow than in anger, could not be happy with his toadying to Bryanism. Governor Judson Harmon of Ohio inherited the mantle that Harvey had intended for Wilson.

In a progressive moment, Harmon was scarcely dangerous. Wilson's real competition in the Democratic scramble came from the nation's capital, where Oscar W. Underwood of Alabama, chairman of the House Ways and Means Committee, was the resident Democratic expert on the central Democratic issue, the tariff. Deft and intelligent, he harassed the Taft administration even as he held his own forces in line. He had considerable regional appeal in the South.[23]

James Beauchamp Clark of Missouri, Speaker of the House of Representatives, offered the more formidable danger. He was a Democrat holding a top national office—an oddity in American political life. Champ Clark as speaker was the only Democrat who could claim, even remotely, the national position preliminary to the presidency. To be sure, Clark had been sent to Congress from the ninth congressional district of Missouri, which not even its residents could view as the hinge of national power. But once in Congress, he had been chosen by his peers, the representatives of the nation, as their chief, making him the number one Democrat in the land. In addition, Clark had a long record of fidelity to Bryan and, to the extent that he had a discernible record, it was progressive rather than conservative.[24]

The difficulty, at one level, was that Clark was a person of overwhelmingly modest talent. He filled the Speaker's chair satisfactorily; with the aid of a parliamentarian, he dealt fairly with friend and foe alike, and he was widely appreciated as a raconteur whose fund of Missouri lore filled many a pleasant moment for his colleagues. He had a campaign ditty, the "houn' Dawg Song," the theme of which was that "they gotta quit kickin' my dawg aroun' "—it presumably stigmatized opponents who had a contrary intention. He was best remembered for helping to scuttle reciprocity with Canada by publicly supporting Taft's hard-won treaty as the first step in American annexation of the neighboring dominion.[25] James Bryce, the British ambassador, author of the classic *American Commonwealth*, though Clark to be inferior in character and ability to all his principal foes: "He possessed no eminent gift beyond that of a genial western manner cultivated with extreme care, the gift of more or less humorous and sometimes shrewd speech, and the reputation of being a genuine 'son of the soil.' "[26] Wilson regarded Clark as "a sort of el[e]phantine 'smart Aleck.' "[27]

The *New York Times* dealt with Clark by maliciously reprinting, word for word, part of what he said in a speech to a Jefferson Day dinner in Louisville, Kentucky, during the height of the primary.[28] After defending the Democratic stand on tariffs and labeling Taft the last of the standpat presidents, Clark went on, recalling that Kentucky was his native state where

[I] toiled as a farm hand from a time when little more than a child, clerked in a country store, taught school before I was 15 in the old-fashioned log cabin, and then went forth to seek my fortune in the Imperial Commonwealth of Missouri, whose people received me with open arms and loving hearts and have showered honors upon me without stint....

But Missouri, great as she is, and proud of her as I am, cannot singlehanded and alone nominate a candidate for President. Where, then, should the Missourians, many thousands of whom are Kentuckians or the descendants of Kentuckians, look for help? Surely to old Kentucky, to whom Missourians are bound by ties of friendship and of blood....

In this crisis of my fate to whom should I, four generations of whose ancestors sleep among the Kentucky hills, turn for succor in achieving the supreme honor of the Republic? Most assuredly to Kentuckians, who are flesh of my flesh and bone of my bone—to Kentuckians, the proudest and most clannish people in the wide, wide world...the support of Kentucky would be to me beyond all price, more precious than rubies, sweeter than honey and the honeycomb.

Since Abraham Lincoln was gathered to his fathers, no Kentuckian has had a chance to be President, and all her great sons have missed the glittering prize. In this exigency of my career I come to Kentucky for aid with the implicit confidence with which a child could go to its mother for assistance.

Bumpkin or not, Clark threatened to scuttle the Wilson boom.

Clark opened his presidential campaign late in 1911. Early the next year he established his credibility as a candidate by elbowing aside ex-Governor Folk as Missouri's favorite son and then, operating through a network of congressmen, especially in the Midwest and West, established rudimentary state organizations to plead his case. He stayed out of the South, in effect conceding it to Underwood. In the states where he focused his campaign, Clark had a double appeal: as an organization Democrat, he preferred no threat to established political machines; as a long-standing supporter of Bryan, he had a claim to the progressive label at least as authentic, probably more authentic, than Wilson's. Clark had a further notable asset: the journalistic and financial support of William Randolph Hearst, publisher of urban newspapers from New York to San Francisco. Hearst had approached Wilson, but Wilson had rebuffed him without even a show of finesse.[29] Hearst knew now to match scorn with scorn: his magazine ridiculed Wilson's post-Princeton appeal to the Carnegie Foundation for an academic pension; it dredged up his derogatory remarks about immigrant groups from southern Europe in the *History of the American People* in order to rile Italian, Polish, and Hungarian societies in opposition to his candidacy. It portrayed Wilson as a weathervane responsive to whatever political breeze happened to be blowing at any moment.[30] Indeed, with Hearst as his herald, Clark did not need to speak.

In the face of Clark's growing prominence, Wilson continued confidently, especially after two threatening incidents passed: one, a public row with his old mentor, George Harvey; the other, a bit of deviltry involving William Jennings Bryan.

During a political conversation with Wilson and Henry Watterson, editor of the Louisville *Courier-Journal*, who was active in pushing Wilson's candidacy in the South, Harvey asked Wilson whether the continued association of *Harper's Weekly* with his candidacy was detrimental. Asked the question bluntly, Wilson acknowledged that the identification did create certain problems. Harvey indicated that he would soft-pedal his advocacy; shortly thereafter, Wilson's name disappeared from the magazine's front-page banner where it had appeared for months. Under stimulus from the ever rambunctious—and somewhat doddering—Watterson, the incident reached the public as a sharp break, and "Marse Henry" did what he could to magnify the issue of Wilson's ingratitude. In fact, the attempt backfired, for most of the public that cared at all regarded the break with a publisher known to have close connections with Wall Street as more of an asset than a liability.

Even as Wilson was fumbling with soothing notes to Harvey, the New York *Sun* was gleefully publishing the "Joline letter." Adrian Hoffman Joline was a former Princeton trustee, alienated from Wilson in the later years. Replying to a letter from Joline in April 1907, Wilson had said: "Would that we could do something, at once dignified and effective, to knock Mr. Bryan once for all into a cocked hat!"[31] Without Joline's connivance, the letter was leaked to the press just before a Jackson Day dinner in Washington where the Democratic leadership, the top brass and the lowly copper, gathered to preen and to look over presidential aspirants. Political sophisticates smirked, waiting for the fur to fly when Wilson and Bryan came face to face. But both Wilson and Bryan proved themselves masters of the occasion. Associating Bryan's work with Andrew Jackson's, Wilson intoned his tribute to "the character and the devotion and the preachings of William Jennings Bryan. . . . He had the steadfast vision all along of what it was that was the matter and he has, not any more than Andrew Jackson did, not based his career upon calculation, but has based it on principle."[32] Bryan, not to be outdone, called Wilson's remarks "splendid, splendid,"[33] almost explicitly closing the book on the Joline affair.

Not a foe, Bryan refused to enlist as an ally of Wilson. Wilson's opponents continued to try to drive a wedge between them, but Bryan recognized the ploy for what it was: an attempt to divide the progressive forces. He wrote off Governor Judson Harmon as the tool of the forces of reaction, the Judge Parker for 1912, and he put Representative Underwood in the same category. The winnowing left Wilson and Clark. On that choice Bryan kept his cards very close to his ample breast. He warned his brother Charles to keep the *Commoner* "absolutely neutral" between the two.[34] The primaries were still ahead, and Bryan had no intention of saddling himself with a loser.

Nonetheless, Wilson came away from the Jackson Day dinner in euphoric high spirits. He had the impression that thirty-two of the fifty-two members of the Democratic National Committee "declared themselves" for him. He regarded his performance as a great triumph. "I was made the lion of the occasion," he told Mrs. Peck, and the probabilities of his nomination have been strengthened "many-fold."[35] Two weeks later he confidently reported "A constantly growing and strengthening boom."[36]

He continued his travels. In Michigan, he spoke in Detroit, Ann Arbor, and Grand Rapids; in Ann Arbor, he made his bid for progressive Republicans, welcoming them as Democrats who, as he said on another occasion, merely retained implausible piety on the protective tariff.[37] In the course of his visit to Massachusetts, he made a nonpolitical call on Governor Eugene N. Foss, addressed the City Club, crossed the river to Harvard where a multitude crowded into Sanders Theater to hear him playfully reply to the taunt that he was merely a schoolmaster. He made a quick trip to Virginia, reminding the General Assembly of his origin, defining his stand against business in cautious, moderate terms: "I am not here to enter an indictment against business. No man indicts natural history. No man undertakes to say the things that have happened by operation of irresistible forces are immoral things, though some men have made deeply immoral uses of them. I am not here to suggest that the automobile be destroyed because some fools take joy rides on it. I want to catch the fools."[38] Returning through Philadelphia, he shared the platform with Senator Robert M. La Follette at the publishers' banquet at which La Follette's rambling tirade all but ended his claim on the Republican nomination. In the rest of February, Wilson found time to visit Kentucky, to help Chicago Democrats celebrate Lincoln's birthday, to appear in New Hampshire and Connecticut as well as to return repeatedly to the more convenient Pennsylvania and New York. He knew he was overtaxing himself; he promised himself a respite.[39] But pressure from McCombs led him on a long trek to Missouri and Kansas, back to Tennessee, west again to Iowa. In Missouri, he kept a discreet distance from challenging Clark: "I am not going into any state that has a favorite son or that has instructed its delegation for another."[40] In Kansas, he reminded Bryan's neighbors how deeply he shared the nation's "underlying affection" for the Great Commoner.[41] In Iowa he teased Republicans who were squeamish about bolting the Republican Party because "they wonder what the old man would think about it if they voted the democratic ticket."[42] Everywhere Wilson received cordial, even enthusiastic receptions, and he felt confident of his momentum, even in the face of attacks.

Wilson sought to deal with the attacks, not always successfully. He tried to defuse his comments on southern and eastern European immigrants by obsequious claims that the plain words in *The History of the American People* did not mean what they clearly said, and he even approached his publisher to arrange for corrections in future editions.[43] Sometimes he satisfied his critics; more often he did not. Thomas E. Watson, an old Bryan ally and a drumbeater for Underwood in 1912, attacked Wilson for being anti-Southern and pro-Negro, to say nothing of being subservient to the Catholic Church.[44] Wrong on all counts, Watson never let facts overtake his judgments, and Wilson could never catch up with the poisonous whispers that Watson stimulated. Nor could he silence the untrue reports that he had voted against Bryan in 1900 and 1908. Almost as serious, for it repelled Bryan himself,[45] was Wilson's failure to reveal the sources of his campaign fund. No other candidate was any more forthright, to be sure, but none was so solicitous about Bryan's approval. Evasively, Wilson supported a congressional bill, which had no chance of passing, that required full disclosure. Since, in fact, Wilson's money came principally from bankers, industrialists, and real estate men, he could not have gotten any mileage from the explanation that the contributors were principally old Princeton friends and friends of old Princeton friends.

As state primaries and state conventions neared in the spring of 1912, it became clearer that the nomination would hinge not on the favorable impression that a witty and confident Governor Wilson could create in public appearances, but on control of state organizations. Successful on the platform, Wilson had no comparable knack for bargaining in the cloakroom. Even busy and enthusiastic agents like McCombs and McAdoo, the latter traveling extensively to make contact with party leaders, had indifferent success: McAdoo, well after the fact, lamented that "in nearly every state I went, the delegates were instructed against the governor."[46] Wilson's success, like everybody else's, hinged not on the fervor of Wilson sentiment in a given state, but on leaders organized to bargain in his behalf. Wilson could control New Jersey's fate except for dissidence in James Smith's Essex County. Pennsylvania would be solid because both factions used Wilson's candidacy as a rallying point for their own fight. Wisconsin fell into line, in part because McCombs poured lavish resources into the state, much more because Wisconsin's progressive wing, led by Joseph E. Davies, had made its commitment to Wilson the previous year when the alternative seemed to be Governor Harmon. Texas was as secure as Colonel House promised.[47] Senators Thomas P. Gore and

William H. Murray thoroughly organized Oklahoma for Wilson, though they kept peace in the family by conceding half the state's delegates to Clark. Oregon and Delaware added their scant total, sixteen delegates. Kansas displayed the anomaly of state organization: though Wilson won fourteen of the twenty delegates elected to the Baltimore convention, the state convention instructed the whole delegation to support Clark at least at first.

McAdoo sensed the danger: "The only thing that gives me concern about your prospects," he warned Wilson in early March, "is the lack of organization everywhere."[48] Both he and Wilson[49] wished that Bryan would throw his organizational weight into the battle. (In fact, Bryan had little.) But while Bryan supported Wilson in Ohio, where the alternative was the conservative Judson Harmon, he generally held to his stand of impartiality between Clark and Wilson. Wilson tried to enlist well-disposed senators in a more active alliance. Senator Francis G. Newlands of Nevada replied eagerly, but without much result: Nevada eventually went for Clark, the impact of the Hearst paper in San Francisco, the *Examiner*, making itself felt across the border. Senator Hoke Smith of Georgia organized Democrats for Wilson; Tom Watson won the state for Underwood.

The crucial fight occurred in Illinois, the third most populous state, where Wilson made his most dramatic commitment to the stump.

In the first week of April, Wilson went off to Illinois, pleased by encouraging reports from New England and confident of major breakthroughs in the Midwest after Wisconsin's showing for him that very week. Illinois had set up a presidential primary: the voters, not the bosses, would declare the state's commitment to the Democratic candidate. He started his tour at Springfield with a ceremonial homage at the tomb of Abraham Lincoln. He reaffirmed that he had never voted anything but a Democratic ticket. In Peoria he picked up the theme of popular government: initiative, referendum, and recall of elected officials. From there he went on what he called a "flying canvass" through the state with fifteen rear-platform speeches, followed by three mass meetings in Chicago. To a crowd largely of Polish-Americans, he repeated his familiar slogan on immigration: America, the home of the free and the eager.

The conventional wisdom on the street was that with Hearst fighting for Clark, the Bryan people in Illinois were working for Wilson and that Wilson, therefore, would do well downstate while Clark carried Chicago. Speaker Clark did not appear in the state for the primary, but his campaign manager, Senator William J. Stone of Missouri, spoke for him, charging that Wilson had been disloyal to the party. The local Hearst paper picked up the charge, leaving Wilson the option, which he took, of implying that Stone, and beyond him Clark, was merely the local tool of the Hearst interests. Wilson assured one and all that the decision on the nomination would not be made by Mr. Hearst: "William R. Hearst has 'decided' I am not to be nominated. What an exhibition of audacity. What a contempt he must feel for the judgment and integrity of the American people. But it is delightful to realize the people of

Illinois on next Tuesday will decide who is to be nominated and Mr. Hearst—a nonresident—can only have his say in his newspapers."[50]

The following Tuesday the people of Illinois voted: Wilson 75,527, Clark 218,483. Only Peoria went for Wilson.

In Buffalo, New York, for a "nonpolitical" speech, Governor Wilson said only: "The result of the primary in Illinois, showing a substantial victory for Speaker Clark, comes as a great surprise to me. I fully expected to carry the State."[51]

The Illinois primary changed the Democratic political profile. Until then, Wilson had been presumed to be the frontrunner, Harmon, Underwood, and Clark dividing up the rest of the vote. Harmon never broke out of Ohio—the more he spoke, the fewer votes he commanded—and Underwood's appeal remained narrowly southern. Only Clark remained as the beneficiary, especially in the Midwest and the West, of anti-Wilson sentiment and of most organizational strength. Over the next three weeks, Clark and Wilson balanced victories and defeats: New York kept its own counsel, though it was assumed to be hostile to Wilson when the pro-Wilson delegates (including State Senator Franklin D. Roosevelt) were smothered by Charles F. Murphy, the leader of Tammany Hall. Pennsylvania dutifully balanced off Illinois. Oregon declared for Wilson, but the victory did little to console Wilson for his beating in Nebraska, Bryan's home territory. Wilson added Delaware and South Carolina to his total. Meanwhile, Underwood pursued his victories in the Old South; returning to the House chamber after his victories in Georgia and Florida, Underwood enjoyed the rousing cheers of his colleagues, and even the least observant could see Clark smiling approvingly from the speaker's chair. Clark scored further victories from Massachusetts to California, the latter by almost three to one, giving his candidacy a transnational character that his managers did not hesitate to exploit. Wilson felt his goal slipping away, saying to one correspondent: "The Powers have shunted me. I do not repine; but I do feel like a man in leash."[52]

In mid- and late May, Wilson made a comeback: twenty-four out of twenty-eight votes in New Jersey (Smith's influence still strong in Essex County), all of Texas's forty votes, even Utah as well.

At the end of May, the *New York Times* made its best guess on the distribution of delegates, instructed, pledged, favorable: Clark 389, Wilson 245, Underwood 84, Harmon 36 (Ohio and 8 scattered votes); the favorite sons—Marshall of Indiana 30, Baldwin of Connecticut 14, Burke of North Dakota 10; uncommitted and uncertain 128 (including New York's 90).[53] There were still some doubtfuls to be heard from. In the next week and a half, the totals changed slightly, Wilson picking up South Dakota, North Carolina probably, and Minnesota, for a total probably around 300, 100 to 150 less than Clark.

The New York *World* was reading the same numbers with a sense of panic. In mid-April, the *World* had warned that Clark's nomination would guarantee

Republican victory and Democratic suicide. Now with Clark the frontrunner, it threw off its doubts about Wilson and favored his nomination because it feared Theodore Roosevelt, the "most cunning and adroit demagogue that modern civilization has produced since Napoleon III" (Wilson too feared the former president's "present insane distemper of egotism").[54] It was prepared to overlook Wilson's excesses on the money trust and his "too eager chase after the nomination"; his essential positions established him as "instinctively and temperamentally a Democrat," the very "sort of man who ought to be President."[55] The *World* struck a responsive chord, its editor, Frank I. Cobb, reported a few days later: letters of commendation came pouring into the *World*'s office. Cobb wrote to Wilson, "Unquestionably the thoughtful, intelligent, disinterested element of the party in the East is largely on your side, and the volume of independent Republican support that you can command is not the least interesting element."[56]

But independent Republican support would not be helpful at the Democratic convention in Baltimore. For that game, the only chips that mattered were Democratic delegates certified and secure. Of those Wilson had not nearly enough.

6

The Convention in Baltimore

The Democratic convention, as it met in Baltimore at the end of June, shaped up into a conflict of will and skill between Woodrow Wilson and Champ Clark, a duel in an atmosphere created by the public clamor of William Jennings Bryan and by the public silence of New York's leader, Charles F. Murphy, and his reticent partners from Indiana and Illinois, Thomas Taggart and Roger C. Sullivan.

Governor Judson Harmon of Ohio had clearly been pushed aside as a threat to anyone: he had won only four delegates outside his own state, and even his hold on his favorite-son delegation was tenuous.

Representative Oscar W. Underwood of Alabama had his batch of southern loyalists; by themselves they could never bring him victory. Only if Wilson and Clark deadlocked in an irreconcilable feud might the delegates of either or both turn to the talented Alabaman as a compromise.[1]

Around the edges of the convention lurked the improbables, looking for clouds that might contain bolts of lightning: Governor Thomas R. Marshall of Indiana, Governor Eugene N. Foss of Massachusetts, even Mayor William Jay Gaynor of New York City, each in a posture of readiness.

Beyond the avowed candidates there was always the roving presence of William Jennings Bryan—Nestor, Lear, and Falstaff all rolled into one figure, boisterous, inscrutable. Thrice the party's candidate, thrice its custodian of defeat, Bryan had few tokens of power in the specialized forum of the convention, but out in the countryside tens of thousands still stirred at the mention of his name, and millions had actually voted for him. Neither king nor kingmaker, Bryan had a way of blurting out an agenda. He was a public brawler, and his putatively spontaneous outrage generated unpredictable responses.

Equally inscrutable at the moment were the votes controlled by three political bosses: Taggart, Sullivan, and the godfather of them all, Murphy, custodian of ninety votes at Baltimore.[2]

Murphy faced a maze. The choice of his patrons on Wall Street was Governor Harmon; Harmon may also have been Murphy's personal choice. But after Harmon's dismal showing in the spring, he clearly belonged on the sidelines. As a political leader, Murphy was under pressure to find a candidate who could win. Clearly the year called for a progressive, whatever "progressive" meant; progressive appearances had to be at least plausible, something more than flummery. As Murphy looked over the frontrunners, each had appeal, each had flaws.

Clark, Speaker of the House, took moderate stands, and he probably lacked the wit or the will to become more radical. His close association with William Randolph Hearst, however, created a threat to Murphy in New York, where Hearst and Murphy competed for power.

Wilson was more of an anomaly. The old Wilson, whom George Harvey had unearthed, would have suited Murphy. The new Wilson, running against political machines and threatening the composure of the business community, had less appeal. Astute and reticent, Murphy would bide his time.

Uncertain and uncommitted on a candidate, Murphy was, however, certain and committed on one central goal: to keep the Democratic Party out of the clutches of William Jennings Bryan.

Wilson and Clark, the central figures in these maneuverings, recognized the complexity of the days ahead.

Clark assumed—had to assume—the posture of frontrunner. He entered the convention with the most votes, many won in head-to-head competition with Woodrow Wilson. Bryan's anointing of both Clark and Wilson apparently eliminated a veto from the left. At the same time, Clark enjoyed wide support from party professionals; indeed, as speaker of the House, chosen by the Democratic majority, he was the ultimate product of organizational politics. And his support drew on every major section of the nation. The context of 1912 served him well, for Democratic political leaders, smelling victory, had the luxury of choosing a docile, unthreatening figure. Clark's game plan, therefore, called for his nomination on the first or second ballot: he could use his committed strength plus the support that his managers could attract in the usual way to create a majority. Then a bit of Democratic folklore would provide the final impetus: never since 1844 had a candidate supported by a majority of the delegates failed to win the assent of enough others to create the two-thirds, and then normally the unanimous, designation of his peers.

Clark carried a major handicap, to be sure: He was a bulb of such meager wattage that it was hard to imagine his lighting the way to victory. Against William Howard Taft, himself no spellbinder on the stump, Clark might prevail. But the notion of Clark arguing national policy with Theodore Roosevelt was enough to make even strong men weep. The *New York Times*, ready to live with Harmon, Underwood, or Wilson, could not conceive of the Democrats' opposing the "ursus horribilis" with a chipmunk: "Of all his [Clark's] utterances, only the things he ought never to have said are remembered."[3]

Wilson faced a more complex situation. Suitor for Bryan's embrace, Wilson received nothing more than equal status with Clark, a paltry endorsement that made him a pariah among many who preferred an unquestionably moderate Democratic Party. Nor could he claim a popular mandate, like Roosevelt's against Taft. Illinois had awarded Clark the better claim. Wilson had his hard core: Texas, Pennsylvania, South Carolina, and Oregon backed him solidly, and twenty-four of New Jersey's twenty-eight delegates passionately. In addition, his managers knew of support within delegations uncommitted or bound by the unit rule to support others—eight to twenty in New York, half a dozen in Ohio. They could look for second-choice support among many southerners, for Wilson had genuine southern credentials, and by 1912 progressivism in the South had developed a substantial following.[4] But trailing Clark by one hundred or more votes, Wilson faced a hard climb.

Yet he had real assets. To begin with, no party would be ashamed to run him. His range was impressive: he could talk to lawyers or journalists or businessmen or political activists or college students or religious groups or random crowds gathered behind his train, talk to each in language suitable for the occasion and with ideas substantive enough to warrant debate. Who could hold a candle to him? Certainly not Underwood, known, if at all, for a single, albeit important issue, the tariff; certainly not Marshall or Foss or Harmon, the other state governors; and, above all, certainly not Champ Clark himself. Furthermore, he fielded a superb political team for the convention. Keeping Joseph P. Tumulty at his side in Sea Girt, Wilson put William F. McCombs in overall charge in Baltimore. McCombs functioned from his suite in the Emerson Hotel. A substation was set up in the Stafford Hotel, where the Texas delegation was staying; it was a mile closer to the convention hall. Congressman A. Mitchell Palmer of Pennsylvania, thought to have acute parliamentary skills, operated from the speakers' platform, while Congressman Albert S. Burleson of Texas organized and recruited delegates with the help of William G. McAdoo and Senator Thomas P. Gore of Oklahoma, who was blind but farseeing. The team had varied strengths: McAdoo had already established a working relationship with Bryan, and McCombs never allowed himself to become too removed from Murphy. Wilson supporters had already put together an index of all the delegates with as much useful detail—"Very vain. Treat him like a big man, and you can handle him"[5]—as they could ferret out. Committed Wilson delegates, especially those from Texas and Pennsylvania, were assigned to five names each from other delegations: conversation, camaraderie, prodding, proselytizing. As new supporters appeared in other delegations, they were drafted into recruiting and reporting; at one time, caucuses at the Texas headquarters were attended by delegates from fifteen to twenty states and, boasted one leader later, "practically no man that ever came to us afterwards slipped back."[6]

Outside the convention hall, Wilson could count on a friendly press to balance the Hearst papers and the New York *Sun*. Most important of all, the Baltimore *Sunpapers*, under the editorship of Charles H. Grasty, plugged for Wilson as actively as discretion permitted. Grasty had thoughtfully mailed his paper to all delegates for the four weeks prior to the beginning of the convention, and it, along with the *New York Times*, rushed early each morning to Baltimore by special train, was to be the daily reading for the delegates during their stay in Baltimore. The New York *World*, perhaps the most influential Democratic journal in the nation, was friendly; its message that a "Tammany–Wall Street" candidate would "revive Rooseveltism"[7] served Wilson's cause. The national chain of Scripps–McRae newspapers helped balance the influence of the Hearst empire.

Assets and liabilities would play themselves out in the unpredictable days ahead.

As the delegates were leaving home for Baltimore, Bryan made the first of three attempts to seize the initiative for the progressives by denouncing and by inviting all potential candidates to denounce the choice of Judge Alton B. Parker as temporary chairman, a position that carried the task of making the keynote address. Bryan chose to regard the selection of Parker as a conservative plot to set the tone of the convention. His deft maneuver forced candidates to identify themselves as adherents of one wing of the party or the other.

For Harmon and Underwood, Parker presented no problem in ideology: they promptly rejected the notion of protest. Clark refused to rise to Bryan's bait. Agreeing on the need for a progressive candidate, Clark told Bryan that he would not intrude on the wisdom of the convention delegates themselves in making the choice.

From Baltimore, McCombs recommended equivocation similarly prudent. In fact, prior to Bryan's proposal, Wilson had already made such a statement to the Baltimore *Evening Sun*.[8]

But then, to the dismay of the Baltimore team, especially McCombs, Wilson replied bluntly to Bryan: "You are quite right." Right, presumably, that, in Bryan's words, Parker was "in the eyes of the public most conspicuously identified with the reactionary element of the party," right that Parker should be rejected.[9]

The bold decision, impulsive or strategic, cut the ground from under McCombs' hopes for the future. In McCombs' view, Bryan was, at best, a fading star. While it was conceivably true that no candidate could get the nod over his veto, Bryan most certainly lacked the standing to designate the candidate. At the same time, the suspicion would not down that Bryan's ambiguous support of Clark and Wilson was a holding action prior to a deluge of oratory like the "cross of gold" speech in 1896. So Wilson put himself in the position of playing Bryan's game: if the game was to inveigle the Democrats into nominating the Great Commoner himself, Wilson was a sucker; if the game was to rally progressive forces and to smoke out fair-weather progressives from the real item, Wilson was passing Bryan's test at the cost of making Bryan's enemies his enemies in a battle that Bryan would probably lose on the convention floor. The staff in Baltimore had planned to stitch together bits and pieces of blocs and delegations. Wilson played a plunger's game.

Less than two weeks before, Wilson had told Mary Allen Hulbert Peck that he gained "a clearer vision and a steadier hand" by playing the political game as if he had no stake in it. He went on to say: "Just between you and me, I have not the least idea of being nominated, because the make of the convention is such, the balance and confusion of forces, that the outcome is in the hands of the professional, case-hardened politicians who serve only their own interest and who know that I will not serve them except as I might serve the party in general."[10] If he was right, better to lose the nomination living out the progressive role than whimpering with flabby equivocations.

When the selection for temporary chairman reached the convention floor,[11] Bryan himself was Parker's competitor, one more hint that Bryan hoped to use the keynote address as his passport to the nomination. The conservatives won for Parker, 579 to 510. Clark's supporters divided about equally between the two candidates; all but twenty of Wilson's delegates voted for Bryan. Wilson had established himself as the progressive candidate—the progressive candidate in a convention with a conservative majority.

Smugly, the conservatives assumed that they had reduced Bryan to passivity. They misjudged their man—as they had many times before.

Before Bryan could make his next dramatic disruption, the pro-Wilson forces won a significant victory by securing the convention's rejection of the unit rule, a device that allowed states to require their entire vote to go to a single candidate even if voters in a primary had mandated otherwise. Mayor Newton D. Baker of Cleveland, a Wilson delegate whose vote was in danger of boosting Harmon's total, successfully led the fight for abrogation of the unit rule, and the convention accepted his argument by just about the same margin that had elected Parker.[12]

Bryan, convinced that the selection of Parker, like the choice of Elihu Root at the Republican convention, demonstrated the linkage of Wall Street with conservative political machines, went on the offensive once again. Prior to the nominating speeches for the several candidates, Bryan rose from his seat in the Nebraska delegation and secured unanimous consent to offer a motion—a departure from the convention's rules. Twenty-five thousand people, all white, overpoweringly male, watched as he moved his bulk down the narrow aisles to the speaker's area, a modest platform of pine boards and gaspipes. A Washington wife noted his thick neck, his rigid jaw; all the fine features that had made him handsome sixteen years before "have hardened and grown coarse—not the least sensual or vicious, just big."[13] On the walls, portraits of Washington, Jefferson, and Jackson—Democrats did not have recent heroes—stood out from the red, white, and blue bunting. On all sides of the delegates, spectators who had gained admission by right, by favor, or by a small bribe to the gatekeepers, strained to see the Great Commoner in action. Once on the platform, Bryan turned expansively to them all and let his voice fill the huge arched armory.

He moved that the convention declare itself "opposed to the nomination of any candidate for President who is the representative of, or under obligation to, J. Pierpont Morgan, Thomas F. Ryan, August Belmont, or any other member of the privilege-hunting and favor-seeking class."[14] In addition, Bryan further resolved that the convention demand the withdrawal of delegates constituting or representing these interests. Morgan might be safely remote in New York, but Belmont and Ryan were there on the floor, Belmont a delegate from New York and Ryan from Virginia.

The convention went into an uproar, outrage and delight contributing to the tumult. Bryan fanned himself, calmly amused that the Democratic convention could not duck his challenge without appearing to admit his implied charge.

But Murphy too was not without tactical skills. When Bryan withdrew his second resolution, even he recognizing that forcing the withdrawal of duly elected delegates went too far, Murphy let the word spread that New York would cast its ninety votes (including the one held by Belmont) for Bryan's resolution. The conservatives suspected that Bryan was setting the stage for a bolt from the convention and some kind of deal with Theodore Roosevelt. The defeat of the Bryan resolution on the convention floor would have given him exactly the excuse he needed, with results that no prudent political leader could predict. So the convention adopted Bryan's resolution by better than a four-to-one margin. Murphy had deprived Bryan of his opportunity to bolt. But Bryan had saddled the convention with a resolution that could be invoked later.

Early Friday morning, June 28, the nominating speeches having taken up all the previous night, the forces in conflict displayed their deadlock with the vote on the first ballot: Clark 444 1/2, Wilson 324, Harmon 148 (including 90 from New York), Underwood 117 1/2, Marshall of Indiana 31, Baldwin of Connecticut 22, 3 scattered (including 1 for Bryan). 547 votes constituted a majority. 728 were needed for a two-thirds vote. Clark was within striking distance of his majority, and Wilson lacked the one-third necessary to block Clark's nomination.

All the principal actors—Clark, Wilson, Underwood, and Murphy—faced difficult tactical decisions. The conventional wisdom at the convention was that if Clark did not win on first couple of ballots, his delegates lacked staying power. The issue for Clark was where additional delegates were to come from. The obvious source was New York's ninety votes, lodged safely for the moment with Harmon but subject to change whenever the spirit moved Boss Murphy. The Clark people assumed they had a deal because of the Parker vote; they regretted that they had not made the deal more explicit and binding. If New York brought Clark within striking distance of a majority, a few more votes could be arranged; then Clark, majority in hand, could use Democratic precedent to demand the nomination. The steps were clear, none clearer than the first step, New York's payoff for Clark's position on the Parker resolution.

For the Wilson tacticians on the floor, the road was less clear. Wilson was clearly the underdog, very much at the mercy of forces over which his handlers had little control. Having managed a quite solid vote against Parker, they had alienated not only New York with its ninety votes but the fifty-eight votes from Illinois under Boss Sullivan and the thirty from Indiana responsive to Boss Taggart. It was assumed that the bosses, who conferred constantly, would stay together. Wilson's leaders hoped for a break from Underwood, Wilson appearing as the secondary southern candidate; but Underwood gave no sign of folding his tent. Bryan was a possible source of help: Bryan owed Wilson a response for his help on the Parker issue. But Bryan kept his own counsel—no commitment. Anyway, Bryan controlled no votes directly: under the unit rule, even his own vote as a delegate from Nebraska had been committed to Clark. The Wilson forces were in for a long fight, their success vastly uncertain.

Underwood had no choice but to wait. Sitting in his office in the capitol just across the corridor from the speaker, he spurned reminders that if Clark became president, he, Underwood, would become speaker of the House. Similarly, he was not tempted by the notion of being anyone's vice-president.

The most complex decisions belonged to Murphy. Should he go with Clark, plausible as a progressive but no boat-rocker, to whom he was indebted on the Parker resolution? What of Clark's drawbacks: the striking indifference of his qualifications—serious but not crippling—and his friendship with Hearst—close and possibly destructive of Murphy's control of the politics of New York State?

If not Clark, could Wilson be Murphy's choice? Wilson was not personally unacceptable to Murphy, and Murphy did not have to go further than his own organization to be in touch with enthusiastic Wilson support: Senator James A. O'Gorman and McAdoo held two of the ninety votes in the New York delegation. But now a victory for Wilson would be a victory for Bryan, and the defeat of Bryan at the Democratic convention held as high a priority as the defeat of Roosevelt had held at the Republican convention.

Irresolution guided Murphy through nine tortured ballots. At Sea Girt, Governor Wilson was receiving meager bulletins by phone and telegraph. His wife and three daughters gathered around him in the rambling two-and-a-half-story frame house. He shared news with Tumulty, fended off reporters' questions, walked or golfed for recreation. The reporters commuted back and forth from a tent, where telegraph wires had been set up, across a large lawn to the porch that surrounded the first floor of the house. They got little enough for their pains: anecdotes, limericks, and showcase good-fellowship that filled a void when something had to be paid. The scan of the verse or the wit of the story served as substitutes for political substance.

Both reporters and the governor could see that in nine ballots, Wilson's total had grown by 25 votes while Clark's had remained essentially static. Wilson's 350 votes brought him nowhere near his goal, but he professed satisfaction that the progressives—he and Clark together—seemed to be in control. His situation reminded him of a traveling friend who asked a man by the side of the road how far it was to the next town. Twenty miles was the reply. He drove on, stopped again, asked again. Twenty miles was again the reply. When, after a half hour's further travel, he received the same reply the third time, the traveler commented to his companion: "Well, John, I'm mighty glad we are holding our own."[15]

After the ninth ballot, Wilson went upstairs, but before he got to bed, Tumulty called up to him that Murphy had finally taken New York's ninety votes out of Harmon's column, where they had been dozing, and had awarded them to Clark.

In Baltimore the moment for the bandwagon had come, and Clark's supporters went wild, swarming all over the convention hall for thirty-five minutes while Clark's daughter Genevieve appeared on the platform as a stand-in for the candidate-to-be.

The Wilson party, forewarned about the imminence of New York's switch, stayed cool and silent, letting the rally spend itself without drawing counterfire, hoping the bandwagon would stall going uphill. North Carolina followed New York: ten votes for Wilson, no defections. Oklahoma was next, more equivocal as its delegation was polled, but more for Wilson than for Clark. William H. Murray ("Alfalfa Bill" to his friends), in explaining his vote, snarled his commentary on Clark's new friends: "I don't care how we vote, but I do insist that Oklahoma will not join hands with Tammany Hall."[16] Cheers erupted from all over the hall, and now it was the turn of the Wilson forces to demonstrate. (At the Republican convention, Bryan had said that a convention felt about demonstrations the way a big man felt about a small wife who had the habit of hitting him: it was permitted because "it seemed to please her and it did not hurt him.")[17]

As the tenth ballot ended, Wilson held his 350 1/2 votes, and Underwood's 117 1/2 votes were intact. Together, their votes were enough to keep Clark short of his two thirds.

Still, Clark now had 556 votes, 9 more than a majority. The majority of a Democratic convention had expressed its will. Precedent decreed that the nomination follow.

The break to Clark on the tenth ballot drove Wilson's hopes to their nadir.

Without a hint to the reporters, Wilson wrote out a message to McCombs: the Wilson delegates, especially those from New Jersey, need feel no compunction about changing their votes, for they had done all for Wilson that any man could have expected of them. The same thought was occurring to McCombs, frail, sleepless, and despairing in Baltimore. Early Saturday morning, before hearing from Wilson, he called the governor with the sad announcement that the game was over. He requested, and Wilson gave, specific authorization to release the Wilson delegations.[18] Later that morning, the Governor broke the gloomy atmosphere at the breakfast table in Sea Girt with a little gallows humor. The postman had brought a catalog from a company that sold coffins. Commenting on the remarkably prompt service, Wilson passed the catalog around to his wife and daughters for their help in choosing a defeated candidate's coffin.[19]

When McCombs shared Wilson's decision with McAdoo later that mid-Saturday morning, McAdoo hit the roof. "You have betrayed the Governor," he remembers saying. "You have sold him out." Grabbing the nearest telephone, he called Sea Girt: Clark had a majority; he did not have the nomination. McAdoo convinced Wilson to countermand the earlier instructions to McCombs and to insist that the struggle continue.[20] McCombs accepted Wilson's decision and went back to work. Saturday's *Times* contained not a hint of any loss of nerve; in fact, there on page three was McCombs confident of continuing gains and eventual success.[21]

Clark's campaign manager, Senator William J. Stone of Missouri—"Gumshoe Bill" to people in the trade—determined to try a direct approach, a telegram to Wilson (and other candidates): citing the precedent of seventy years, he asked Wilson on behalf of the Missouri delegation, "in the interest of the party and in vindication of the democratic principle of majority rule to assist in making his [Clark's] nomination unanimous by the withdrawal of your candidacy."[22] What's your reply, the reporters asked Wilson eagerly. "There will be none," the governor answered laconically.[23]

Back at the convention, the delegates were weary from sessions lasting far into the night. The summer heat was draining their energies as the greedy Baltimore hotels drained their purses. Ballots droned on without respite, and there was still the platform to be adopted.

After the tenth ballot, Bryan called Wilson to say that Wilson's only hope for winning was a dramatic step: a strong statement that he would reject the nomination if it came with the help of New York's ninety votes. After consulting with Mrs. Wilson and with Tumulty, Wilson telephoned a message to McCombs' assistant: The deadlock was being maintained to allow New York to control the nomination and the candidate, he said. The only way to establish a candidate's independence is to "declare that he will not accept a nomination if it cannot be secured without the aid of that delegation. For myself, I have no hesitation in making the declaration. The freedom of the party and its candidate and the security of the government against private control constitute the supreme consideration."[24] A second time Wilson played the plunger's game: he would win or lose on the basis of a defiant public stand.

In fact, whether Bryan ever received the message is uncertain. McCombs later claimed that he had pocketed it, and in view of his hopes to strike a deal with Tammany, his claim is plausible.

In any case, Wilson's message coincided remarkably with Bryan's subsequent tactics, for during the fourteenth ballot, a new prairie wind blew in from Nebraska. For a third time Bryan threw the convention into pandemonium.

Gaining the floor, Bryan threatened to bolt the party—without quite using the word, which might have justified expelling him from the convention—if the party went with a ticket named by the bosses of Tammany Hall. For once Bryan gave up his customary histrionics. He read quietly from a statement he had written out: "I shall not be a party to the nomination of any man, no matter who he may be or from what section of the country he comes, who will not, when elected, be absolutely free to carry out that anti-Morgan-Ryan-Belmont resolution and make his Administration reflect the wishes and the hopes of those who believe in a government of the people, by the people, for the people."[25] Bryan made clear that his anathema applied to any candidate whom New York supported. With that, he withdrew his vote from Clark and gave it to Wilson, then sat down in his delegate's seat "with his palm-leaf fan, without a tremor in his finger . . . with a little of the consciousness of power playing at the corners of his mouth and with the light springing in his eyes . . . the figure of a master . . . a figure of stone."[26]

Though the Wilson forces cheered Bryan's sensational outburst and though their leaders struck a confident, even jubilant, pose, they had little enough reason to be elated. Bryan's support netted Wilson the barest handful of actual votes; even Bryan's own vote was less an endorsement of Wilson than a repudiation of Clark. Yet Wilson, as apparent beneficiary, bore the anger that Bryan generated.

Prior to Bryan's speech, McCombs had been trying to stay in touch with Murphy through J. Sergeant Cram, a Harvard-educated, old-New-York-family buddy of Murphy who was said to have taught Murphy how to eat peas with a fork.[27] But, especially after Bryan's latest outburst, these efforts went nowhere. Murphy did not hanker for a bargain, Furthermore, when and if the New Yorker were to change his mind, Bryan had made clear that he would blast anyone who gained New York's favor.

When the twenty-sixth and final ballot was recorded late Saturday evening, Wilson had gained 83 1/2 votes over his first tally, to be sure, but he still trailed the Speaker by 56 votes. Even more sobering, the Wilson team could not foretell any way of winning.

For whatever consolation it was worth to Wilson's managers, Clark's situation was even sadder. After being left dangling by New York for nine ballots, Clark expected to win the nomination after New York's break on the tenth.

Indeed, he wrote out a telegram of acknowledgment, expecting to send it to the convention after the next ballot.[28] Instead his bandwagon stalled, and in the face of Bryan's attack, rolled backwards. The *Times* noted that "the Speaker's leg was being sawed off inch by inch."[29] Kansas and half of Nebraska had gone over to Wilson, and Massachusetts had withdrawn its forty-three votes, using its Governor Foss as a safe haven.

Outraged by Bryan's charge of complicity with Wall Street, Clark demanded proof of retraction. Desperate, the Speaker left Washington secretly to make a dramatic appearance before the convention in defense of his honor and in an all-but-open attempt to stampede the convention into nominating him by acclamation late Saturday night. Minutes before his arrival, Senator Ollie James, the permanent chairman, adjourned the convention by agreement between Wilson and Clark advisers. Palmer on the convention platform properly feared a situation over which he had no control, and even some Clark advisers thought the moment, near midnight just before the sabbath, inopportune.

Thus, the convention approached the week's end and a day of rest with no resolution and no clear route to resolution. The week's balloting had produced only a tightened deadlock: Clark 463 1/2, Wilson 407 1/2, Underwood 112 1/2, Foss 43, Marshall 30, Harmon 29, Bryan 1.

The White House watched every move with attention. At Oyster Bay Colonel Roosevelt denied any plot with Colonel Bryan to defeat the conservatives in both parties.[30]

Sunday was a day of rest for the delegates, but not for their leaders. Speaker Clark returned to Washington, disavowing any connection with Wall Street and predicting, without convincing anyone, that he would recover lost ground. Representative Underwood stood pat. Bryan spoke of the need for a compromise candidate, disclaiming any preference, but offering James, O'Gorman, and Senator John W. Kern of Indiana as acceptable progressives. He softened his position on New York slightly; it was only crucial that New York not provide the margin that gave any candidate victory. New York had a reciprocal requirement: that the ticket not be tainted with Bryanism. McCombs turned to Wilson for help: Would he make a commitment not to appoint Bryan Secretary of State? Wilson would make no such commitment, especially on Mr. Bryan "who has rendered such fine service to the party in all seasons."[31] Wilson's reply seriously cramped McCombs' maneuvers, for Wilson was seriously tainted with Bryanism. But the governor's instinct was sound. Bryan would certainly have learned of Wilson's commitment. What would have happened to Wilson's candidacy if Bryan had created a fourth tumult, tossing Wilson into the same tumbrel that was hauling off Clark?

In Baltimore the leaders, all except Bryan, huddled in a hotel suite. Palmer pressed Wilson's claim, but he could not overcome Murphy's determination not to buckle to Bryan. Three hours passed. No one budged. The meeting broke up. Late that evening the bosses made one last attempt at compromise.

Summoning Palmer to a secret meeting, they demonstrated that neither Wilson nor Clark could win in the present situation. Why not settle the nomination on a Wilson man, Palmer himself? An ambitious man, then only forty, Palmer must have been tempted by the offer. But he rejected it instantly. The next day he was back on duty for Wilson. The bosses sounded out Senator Charles A. Culbertson of Texas. He turned them down cold.

The sentiment grew on Sunday that Wilson was, after all, in the driver's seat. The *Times*, until then ready to go with Harmon, Underwood, or Wilson, demanded that the delegates, in obedience to their own will and their own judgment, nominate Wilson on Monday.[32] The Baltimore *Evening Sun*, which had been insinuating what its editor called Wilson "poison"[33] into the delegates for weeks, threw off its pretense and called for the Democrats to settle on a winner: "Wilson is a four-square, honest, exceptionally able man, who will offer justice to all men and injustice to none."[34] The New York *World* spoke editorially of Wilson's nomination as "a matter of Democratic life or death." Wilson's nomination was "the crucial test of the Democratic party's fitness to live."[35] The press was full of reports that Wilson men were scurrying around other delegations, as indeed they were, perhaps even trading promises for votes. The possibility of deals was thrown up to Wilson by the reporters at Sea Girt. He was certain that his managers were using nothing but argument, he said, nothing that could not be done in the view of the whole country: "There cannot be any possibility by any trading done in my name,; not a single vote can or will be obtained by means of any promise."[36] Still, the realistic correspondent for the *World* noted the "unprecedented lack of communication"[37] between the governor's cottage and the headquarters at the Hotel Emerson.

On site in Baltimore Grasty of the Baltimore *Sun* tied Bryan up all Sunday afternoon and evening with chatter and supper, Grasty reminded Bryan that Wilson was "the one man that New York could not taint."[38] Senator Francis G. Newlands of Nevada assaulted the conservatives' distrust of Wilson's candidacy. Working on "A man who stands in a position of exceptional strength with the Illinois delegation"—and there was only one man, Roger C. Sullivan, who fit this description—Newlands argued that since the conservatives could not get the nomination for a man of their stripe, they should settle for "a Progressive who, whilst determined upon a radical cure, will apply all the palliative remedies necessary to save the life of the patient."[39] Sullivan had no stake in Clark's candidacy. The primary in Illinois had focused primarily on control of the Democratic Party, Sullivan's faction against the forces of Mayor Carter H. Harrison of Chicago and William Randolph Hearst, and in that fight Sullivan thought that the preferential primary "cut no figure...at all." While the Harrison-Hearst commitment to Clark was intense, Sullivan did not similarly espouse the Wilson cause.[40] Still, since Clark had enjoyed the full support of Hearst and Harrison in the fight in Illinois, they, and not Sullivan, would be the beneficiaries of a Clark victory in Baltimore. Furthermore, though committed to Clark by the vote in his state, Sullivan owed the Wilson camp a favor, for the Wilson delegates had helped seat some Sullivan delegates in a raw steal from the Hearst-Harrison forces. There was plenty of Wilson sentiment within the Sullivan camp—probably dozens of Illinois delegates preferred Wilson, and Sullivan's son was a Wilson fan since his days at the Lawrenceville School, just down the road from Princeton. Responding now to Senator Newlands, the man "of exceptional strength with the Illinois delegation" promised to bring his votes into line at the proper time. Meanwhile, Taggart of Indiana was offered the vice-presidency for his governor, Thomas Marshall, in return for Indiana's twenty-nine votes (one vote went to Senator Kern).

Sunday's maneuvers started to pay off when the convention reconvened on Monday. Four ballots into Monday's session, Wilson passed Clark in the balloting—Wilson received the news with what he called "a riot of silence"[41]—as Taggart delivered his votes as scheduled, and Iowa switched fourteen of its twenty-six from Clark to Wilson.

Now Wilson was the frontrunner, as Clark had been, but without a majority, which Clark had had. Now Clark and Underwood could veto Wilson, as Wilson and Underwood had vetoed Clark. Underwood's chances brightened slightly: he could expect Clark's position to deteriorate, and he had a claim on Wilson's delegates if it became clear that Wilson could not be nominated. A prominent Texas delegate had promised his fraternity brother from the University of Virginia, the vice-chairman of the Georgia delegation, that he would help throw Texas's forty votes to Underwood if Wilson fell out of the race;[42] comparable, if less binding, conversations occurred all over the floor as a way of keeping Underwood's votes firm against Clark. But Underwood could wax only if Wilson waned, and the New Jersey governor kept gaining little bundles of votes, including some from Underwood.

Clark was a spent force, his prospects dim and his delegations riddled with subversive Wilson support. Clark came to Baltimore for an assessment. Senator Stone urged him to withdraw, for Bryan, having knocked Clark off, was now going to do the same to Wilson, probably in the hope, however chimerical, of winning the prize himself. The probable result, however, would be the nomination of an obscure dark horse or of a conservative, perhaps Underwood, no favorite of Clark's after Underwood's conduct over the previous three days. As Clark declined, his delegate support went softer. Political resentments generated by the convention aside, many Clark delegates were undoubtedly ideologically closer to Wilson than to any feasible alternative. Clark did not withdraw. But it did not matter.

The *Times* reported Monday morning that the convention seemed eager to break to Wilson. Only Bryan was the barrier: scores of delegates were anxious to nominate without making the nomination seem like a victory for Bryan. New Yorkers were convinced that, Murphy's irritation aside, a Bryan-tainted nominee could never carry New York.

From New York came an unexpected oblique signal. Wilson had nine and perhaps, if Murphy's stern eye were averted, as many as twenty votes within New York's ninety. One of Wilson's supporters, John B. Stanchfield, a Tammany stalwart that McAdoo counted as part of his cell, was chosen to give New York's answer to Bryan's Saturday attack. To wild applause on the convention floor, Stanchfield denounced the Nebraskan as a "selfish, money grabbing, favor-seeking office-chasing, publicity hunting marplot."[43] The signal was manysided: The convention was ready to applaud an attack on Bryan even more vicious than Bryan's attack on Belmont-Ryan-Murphy. A pro-Wilson delegate pronounced the malediction, separating Wilsonism from Bryanism. The maneuver proceeded only because Boss Murphy permitted it to occur. Those looking for omens saw one. The Wilson managers sent a messenger to warn the governor urgently against any free-wheeling intervention: Bryan was now knocked into a cocked hat, and Wilson held the hat.[44]

Still, Monday and the forty-second ballot passed with no breakthrough: Wilson 494, Clark 430.

Tuesday, July 2. McCombs, irritable and exhausted, looking, according to an ally, like a "skinned snipe,"[45] begged Sullivan to move Illinois, threatening to withdraw if Sullivan did not. "Sit steady, boy," the old pro told him.[46] On the forty-third ballot, Sullivan gave Wilson fifty-eight votes—and a majority in the convention. Virginia and West Virginia joined in.

Now Wilson had 602 votes, a tantalizing 126 votes short of the nomination. New York's vote was still frozen because of Bryan's interdict. Together Clark and Underwood could block Wilson's progress. Either could nominate him. Neither, in the pro-Wilson mania created by the Democratic press and in the excitement and fatigue present on the convention floor, could now map out a scenario for his own victory. The only alternative to Wilson was some obscure dark horse.

After the forty-fifth ballot, Underwood's managers withdrew his name. Then Senator Stone released Clark's delegates, retaining Missouri's right to stay true to Clark for one final vote. Harmon's votes dropped into place, and Massachusetts forgot about Governor Foss. Wilson's count soared to 990, now safely including New York's 90.

At 3:30 PM after the forty-sixth ballot, Senator James announced that Woodrow Wilson was the Democratic nominee for president of the United States.

With Wilson's reluctant consent, the convention nominated Thomas Marshall of Indiana for vice-president, honoring the agreement that had brought Indiana's votes to Wilson in the crucial march to overtake Clark. Underwood, Wilson's choice for vice-president, had saved Wilson's managers considerable embarrassment by refusing to let his name be considered. The platform, largely a reflection of Bryan's views, was adopted almost as an afterthought.

Underwood and Clark sent messages of congratulation. The *Times* declared that the battle between Murphy and Bryan had ended in a draw. Bryan himself, addressing the convention yet again, this time to decline the vice-presidency, gave his valedictory, surrendering the leadership of the party to its new spokesman, whose name he never uttered.

In Sea Girt, Saturday's despondency forgotten, Wilson was ready for the new day. The leader of a far western delegation wired him: "The switch of the progressive leadership from Bryan to Wilson means that the progressive movement is passing from emotionalism to rationalism. Bryanism is dead, a new Democracy is being born." For reporters gathered around the governor's house, Wilson commented with his new authority: "I think my western friend phrases it about right, and he does it quite aptly."[47]

PART III

Wilson's Active Opposition

7

The Bull Moose at Armageddon

Theodore Roosevelt, having been "beaten to a frazzle" (to use one of his favorite expressions) by the Taft forces in Chicago, watched the Democratic convention in Baltimore with more than passing interest. A conservative nominee—Judson Harmon of Ohio or Oscar W. Underwood of Alabama— would have left Roosevelt in sole possession of progressive banners. A somewhat more progressive ticket headed by a comic choice like Speaker Champ Clark would have given the Colonel a field day on the stump. (The Socialist candidate, Eugene V. Debs, could be safely ignored; indeed, ignoring him was the safest approach.) But Woodrow Wilson at the head of a united Democratic Party offered formidable opposition: with both Bryan and the Democratic organizations behind him, he could count on the usual Democratic votes; in addition, his progressive credentials, however recently acquired, would compete directly with Roosevelt's.

The issue of electibility surfaced within Roosevelt's own camp. With the results in Baltimore still up in the air, Governor Chase S. Osborn, an original supporter, wrote a public letter to Roosevelt expressing doubt that the Colonel should stay on in the contest if the Democrats were to nominate a progressive.[1] Even worse, once the Democratic nomination was set, Osborn described the central issue in the campaign as "Wall Street vs. Wilson."[2] Other governors from the original eight soon deserted as well. (Osborn eventually returned to the fold.) Roosevelt stood firm in the face of the defections. On the day of Wilson's nomination, he personally handed out a statement at Sagamore Hill saying that he would go on. The next day the *New York Times* sneered that he had no issue other than his "vindictive passion against President Taft."[3]

The Colonel saw the situation differently. The reactionaries sought to eliminate him from politics, he told Osborn, because he was the prime symbol at the moment for progressive ideas: "Among my opponents they may prefer Taft to Clark, and Clark to Bryan or Wilson, and one of the latter more than the other; but these preferences are in their eyes not very important, and their one purpose is to use any one of the men they deem strongest in order to beat me. Their victory lies in eliminating me from politics."[4] His own desires were not the issue. "On personal grounds, I should be most heartily glad if it became my duty to get out of this fight, but . . . for me to express any willingness to do so would be interpreted by the overwhelming majority not only of my friends but of my enemies into an avowal of weakness on my part. They would think that I was flinching from the contest, that I was not game enough to stand punishment and face the possibility of disaster."[5] Two-thirds of his supporters, the Colonel said, would go back to Taft, or "would simply abandon the whole field and vote the Socialist ticket or something of that kind." He would not ignore the reality of the Democrats' platform and of the boss rule that made Wilson's nomination possible. The issue was not Wilson—individually he was an "excellent man." The issue was the restoration of Democratic bosses to power in Congress and in the states.[6] "If you work for Wilson nationally," he told a popular Protestant minister who eventually joined the Wilson Republican Progressive League, "you are working for Murphy in New York, Taggart in Indiana, Sullivan in Illinois, and, in short, for bosses everywhere."[7] Equally objectionable, in his view, was the Democratic platform, "one of the worst I have ever seen."[8] To allow progressive policy to fall into those hands on these principles, he believed, would accomplish the purposes of the reactionaries without even a fight. On the other hand, if he ran, even unsuccessfully, he is said to have told a friendly journalist, "the cause of liberal government would be advanced fifty years."[9]

Roosevelt understood how unlikely success would be. Writing privately to a friend abroad just before the Progressive convention, he acknowledged that Wilson would probably win. He would take the majority of the progressive Democrats and not only the reactionary Democrats but some reactionary Republicans who did not believe that Taft could be reelected.[10]

The complications for the ensuing fight proved to be even denser than originally foreseen. Eventually the new party would have to field its own slate of presidential electors in almost every state because President Taft rejected a cooperative arrangement that would commit Republican electors to whichever candidate, Taft or Roosevelt, polled the most votes in each state. Roosevelt was even more adamant. Such an arrangement would repel Democratic voters, he said. Furthermore, since Taft was the "receiver of a swindled nomination," Roosevelt would not cooperate with him: "I won't go into a friendly contest with a pickpocket as to which of us shall keep *my* watch which *he* stole."[11]

A more difficult problem, ultimately insoluble, arose over the question of fielding full slates of candidates—governors, mayors, city councilors—under the label of what was to become known as the Progressive Party. Roosevelt felt a special pressure to build local organizations that would run candidates "from President to School Superintendent"[12] in every state, for without creating the local networks, the Progressive Party could be viewed, would be viewed, as nothing more than the vehicle for putting Theodore Roosevelt in the White House again. The crusade had to promise a new day, and the promise had little force if a victory for Roosevelt left the old Republican structure in place.

But Republican professionals like the insurgent caucus in Congress and the governors who had urged Roosevelt into the race were reluctant to leave the party, however slight their affection for Taft. "They represent nothing more than sound and fury," the Colonel lamented, "they have not the heart for a fight, and the minute they were up against deeds instead of words, they quit forthwith."[13]

Whatever the costs in defections, Roosevelt felt certain that unless any existing state Republican organization was prepared to repudiate Taft and support him—the situation in Governor Hiram Johnson's California, for example—he had to insist on top-to-bottom slates. He had to dream that eventually his new party would become one of the two national parties, replacing the Republicans as the Republicans had replaced the Whigs. Whatever the cost among party professionals, Roosevelt's stand increased his stature among the enthusiastic amateurs for whom vision meant more than booty.[14]

The creation of the new party dated from the official "Call to the People of the United States" issued on New York on July 7 by Senator Joseph M. Dixon as chairman of the Provisional National Committee. Sixty-three signers from forty states joined in the appeal: three governors, Johnson of California, Joseph M. Carey of Wyoming, and Robert S. Vessey of South Dakota, Carey and Vessey the only two left from the original eight; two senators, Dixon and Miles Poindexter of Washington; six newspaper editors or publishers, none from a major journal; and three Democrats, only one of whom, Judge Ben B. Lindsay of Denver, had any substantial recognition nationally. Roosevelt himself did not sign, but even an unattentive ear could hear familiar cadences. Dixon was radiant with hope: the scars from the Democratic convention would not heal, and Taft would not carry a single congressional district. The new party to be born in Chicago on August 5 would open a new era. Dixon did not know whether Roosevelt would go to Chicago; he may have been the only voter in America with any doubt.[15]

In the four weeks before the convention, Roosevelt shuttled back and forth from Oyster Bay to the *Outlook* office. Heeding counsel from his advisers, he decided against travel and speeches lest he make an already complicated situation unmanageable. Instead, people came to him: old friends, reformers, politicians; experts with a cause, like Charles R. Van Hise, a University of Wisconsin authority on the control of business concentrations; favorably inclined newspaper editors and publishers.

All over the nation, from New York to California and from Georgia to

Washington, rebels in each state were calling conventions and caucuses to name delegations equal in size to their congressional delegations (no territorial delegations would be recognized), and party leaders were attempting to sort through their relation to the old party. Mindful that a party of schismatic Republicans could never attract Democratic voters, Roosevelt urged the new party to nominate at least some Democrats on every state ticket. There was even talk of a Democratic vice-presidential nominee if Roosevelt was named to head the ticket. Since the campaign was taking on the trappings of a crusade, virtue and the appearance of virtue were both essential.

From the Midwest, a snappish Senator Robert M. La Follette cast doubt on both. In *La Follette's Weekly Magazine*, the Wisconsin leader started his tilt toward Wilson, contrasting William Jennings Bryan's "moral leadership" in Baltimore with Roosevelt's rule-or-ruin tactics in Chicago. La Follette scorned the moral chasm that Roosevelt saw separating Taft and himself; in fact, La Follette charged, both men had obviously fraudulent delegates and both had ample experience in recruiting them; Roosevelt could not fully oppose Taft's frauds without partially lifting the curtain on his own.[16] La Follette would not cease to regard Roosevelt as the cowbird who had laid his eggs in the nest that La Follette had built.

Roosevelt could ignore La Follette. Most known progressives had gone over to Roosevelt, and the few that remained with La Follette could not be won over anyway.

Escape from another issue was not so easy—the role of black delegates in the upcoming convention. Roosevelt needed a formula that would retain the support of northern black progressives while acknowledging that white southern progressives required a lily-white party since southern states had just completed the virtual disfranchisement of black voters through devious constitutional devices. In a long public letter, Roosevelt pronounced his verdict: full participation for black delegates from northern states, total exclusion of black delegates from southern states. Characteristically, Roosevelt wrapped his decision in a cloak of righteousness. Since only the new party could achieve progressive goals and since the new party could emerge in the South only by breaking the Democratic stronghold and by undermining corrupt Republican patronage, he said, the ultimate interests of southern blacks would be best served by their acceptance of white dominance until a progressive triumph benefited all Americans, black and white. Momentarily regressive, the formula, in his view, was ultimately benign.[17]

Despite the angry protests of blacks, the credentials committee assembled in Chicago in early August endorsed Roosevelt's formula, and Roosevelt held resolutely to his position: the new party would not encourage white hatred for blacks—the Democratic position—or black hatred for whites—the Republican position; it looked forward to the day when a new distribution of power and resources would let every man be treated like a man.

The hopes for that new day permeated the first Progressive Party convention as it assembled in Chicago on August 4. As the Colonel and Mrs. Roosevelt motored from Oyster Bay to take a modest stateroom—no private car—to Chicago, hundreds of delegates, men and women, black and white, gathered to organize themselves in an orderly way. The delegate contests were already settled, though protests in the corridors and on the floor about the black exclusion had not halted. The mood was anticipatory, pending the arrival of the leader. Little of P. T. Barnum, the *Times* noted; the assemblage of "ex's" and women and young people looked more like Sunday school teachers than like the tough types usually hanging around political rallies.[18] Red bandannas, which were to become a symbol for the party (much to the annoyance of the Socialist Debs), made their first appearance; the *Times* noted sourly that many people did not know enough to let the bandannas hang below their chins, not down the backs of their necks.[19] William Flinn of Pittsburgh was there, calculating but sedate, the *Times* observed,[20] along with ex-Attorney General Charles J. Bonaparte and ex-Senator Albert J. Beveridge from Indiana, a recent convert to third-party opposition to Taft; and George W. Perkins, Roosevelt's financial angel. More typical of the impending mood was Jane Addams from Hull House in Chicago, a prominent social worker who would give a seconding speech for Roosevelt after the Colonel had been nominated as "a National asset."[21] Miss Addams held court in the front row, confident that the new party would give women their rightful place. When Roosevelt himself arrived in the city, a small crowd greeted him on his way to a huddle with the inner circle of leaders in the presidential suite at the Congress Hotel. Roosevelt still entertained hopes for a Democratic running-mate, but the consensus at the convention favored a Republican, Hiram Johnson probably, Beveridge's ambitions having been preempted by his nomination for governor in Indiana. The convention awaited the promise of Roosevelt's speech the next day, the mood being set by shattering choruses of the "Battle Hymn of the Republic" ("Mine eyes have seen the glory of the coming of the Lord") that followed Beveridge's keynote address. Beveridge, temporary and then permanent chairman, denounced "invisible government" serving the purposes of corrupt political machines and special interests.[22] The stage was set for the entry of Colonel Roosevelt the next day.

When the Colonel appeared to make his "Confession of Faith" in the cavernous auditorium, the audience left him stranded on the stage for almost an hour while they cheered and sang and waved their banners and bandannas. In reply, Roosevelt smiled his toothiest grin, smiled sheepishly at Mrs. Roosevelt (sitting in what had become known in the Republican convention as the "millionaires' box"), waved his campaign hat in general greeting to all and in specific recognition of familiar faces. Bemused by the intensity of the demonstration, he repeatedly sought to get on with the proceedings, but the people had their hero—both lawgiver and vehicle, the *Times* commented[23]—

before them, and they had a message to give him before his message to them. Once he commanded their attention, he did not disappoint them, nor they him.

First, a tirade against the old parties, "husks, with no real soul within either, divided on artificial lines, boss-ridden and privilege-controlled, each a jumble of incongruous elements, and neither daring to speak out wisely and fearlessly what should be said on the vital issues of the day." No differences separated the controlling bosses of both parties: they acted as competing corporation lawyers, but "They come together at once as against a common enemy when the domination of both is threatened by the supremacy of the people of the United States."

The time was ripe, he said, for a genuine progressive movement, beginning with greater popular rule: woman's suffrage, presidential primaries, popular election of senators, short ballots, corrupt practices acts limiting corporate giving to campaigns; wise resort—neither wanton nor frequent—to initiative, referendum, and recall; popular review of judicial decisions of constitutional questions. He called for legislation mandating minimal working conditions and for constitutional amendments, if necessary, to accommodate the demands of social justice like a living wage. He nodded to farmers as well: "Everything possible should be done to better the economic condition of the farmer, and also to increase the social value of the life of the farmer, the farmer's wife, and their children." He accepted the Sherman Act, but not as the sole remedy: "as now applied it works more mischief than benefit." Instead, now drawing explicitly on Van Hise, he updated his call for governmental supervision of business through an industrial commission, quoting Lincoln on the distribution of the task: "Whatever concerns the whole should be confided to the whole—to the general government; while whatever concerns only the State should be left exclusively to the State." He defended the protective tariff; he looked to a permanent nonpartisan commission of experts to set rates at levels that protected American industry from foreign competition. He mocked the Democratic tariff policy as a "quack remedy" as futile as free silver had been sixteen years before. He wanted national regulation of the currency system, "safeguarded against manipulation by Wall Street or the large interests." He favored conservation and development of Alaska. He approved of an increased navy and merchant marine.

"Surely there never was a fight better worth making than the one on which we are engaged," he said in conclusion. "It matters little what befalls any of us who for the time being stands in the forefront of the battle. I hope we shall win, and I believe that if we can wake the people to what the fight really means we shall win. But, win or lose, we shall not falter. Whatever fate may at the moment overtake any of us, the movement itself will not stop. Our cause is based on the eternal principles of righteousness; and even though we who now lead for the time fail, in the end the cause itself shall triumph."

Roosevelt felt no need to temper his speech to passing expedients, for "We stand at Armageddon, and we battle for the Lord."[24]

The New York *Sun* responded predictably: Roosevelt's "Confession of Faith" was a "manifesto of revolution," full of "wild and dangerous charges" that would lead to state socialism. Roosevelt would not be president again, the *Sun* observed thankfully. "But to think that such a man has been President, could be President elsewhere than among those congenial sons of mischief and cunning, the Yahoos!"[25]

Roosevelt had a more sober view. He treasured his radicalism as ultimate conservatism, a long-held middle road between destructive plutocratic exploitation and destructive proletarian violence. "I have always believed," he told a friend, "that wise progressivism and wise conservatism go hand in hand, and that the wise conservative must be a progressive because otherwise he works only for that species of reaction which inevitably in the end produces an explosion."[26]

Wise progressives and wise conservatives staged a small tug-of-war over part of the platform. Some Progressives, having more faith in competition and more fear of bigness than their candidate and his "right-hand man," George Perkins, wrote into the draft platform a strong endorsement of the Sherman Act and a list of undesirable practices to be prohibited. In the inner circle of Roosevelt's advisers, Perkins protested, and, in the face of considerable pressure from the other side, Roosevelt agreed to the deletion of the undesirable practices. As released to the newspapers in amended form, the platform contained no references at all to the Sherman Act,[27] but when it appeared in formal campaign documents, the controversial plank, even naming some offensive practices, reemerged in most versions.[28] The more radical Progressives like Gifford Pinchot suspected that the devious hand of George Perkins had attempted to erase the will of the majority and that, intentionally or inattentively, Roosevelt had acquiesced.

The formal nomination of Theodore Roosevelt and Hiram Johnson the next day was anticlimactic. Perkins, with strong support from Roosevelt, was named chairman of the national executive committee. Working together, the party of the Bull Moose—the catchier title caught on immediately—was to create a stampede in the nation. When Roosevelt came to accept his call, the crowd greeted him anew with the "Battle Hymn of the Republic." Then, just as nine governors were gathering at Sea Girt to hear Governor Woodrow Wilson accept the Democratic nomination for the presidency, Roosevelt stepped forward in the auditorium in Chicago, thanked the delegates for the great honor, and, "of course," accepted.[29]

8

Eugene V. Debs: Educating for Socialism

The Socialists were already in place for the fall campaign. Even as the Democrats and the Republicans continued their fractious internal battles, the Socialist Party of America readily nominated Eugene Victor Debs for president. Meeting in Indianapolis, Indiana, in May, the Socialists, compromising or papering over their differences, emerged from a lively convention with enough, just enough, unity to carry them through the campaign ahead. Always building for the future, they approached the campaign confident of their own ultimate success, not this year, but certainly this generation.

A splinter group speaking for the working class without attracting more than a fraction of it, the Socialists possessed more ideological factionalism than national appeal. While Americans generally view socialism as the outer reach of radicalism, godless in intent, violent in method, subversive of all goodness, law, and order, American socialists themselves correctly perceived greater complexity.

At one end of the spectrum were Christian socialists and "colonizers." Christian socialists viewed socialism as the secular means to establish the brotherhood of man on earth; they opposed the class struggle, deplored violent industrial disputes, and supported evolutionary change. Colonizers, following an old American tradition that dated back to nineteenth-century utopian settlements like New Harmony, Indiana, dreamed of small cooperative communities serving as models for the rest of America.

At the other extreme of the spectrum were socialists from the western states where industrial struggle meant injunctions, vigilante groups, labor spies, dynamite, and shotguns. In the mines of the West, class war was already in progress.

Between the two extremes, a right wing and a left wing (they called each other "yellow" and "red"), conservatives and radicals, gradualists and revolutionaries, differed principally on tactics: gradual gains for the working force through legislation, achievement of public office, and cooperation with existing trade unions, especially the crafts loosely organized in the American Federation of Labor (AFL); or through large-scale industrial unions committed to aggressive tactics against employers and through seizure of the machinery of the state.

Each wing believed that the other invited disaster.

The conservatives feared that the radicals' violent posture alienated workers whose notion of property had developed in an agrarian age and mobilized repressive government against even marginal gains for the working force. As gradualists in a democratic nation, conservatives felt certain that the franchise widely held would, over a long but not immeasurable period of time, yield the full panoply of socialist goals.

The radicals, skeptical about the impact of capitalist elections, sought direct confrontation in the factories and mines where the physical concentration of workers, brought together by the greed and need of capitalists, made the workers' force unanswerable. Once assembled in large industrial unions, the workers, they believed, could use organized political power to take over the state. For the left wing, existing craft unions, specifically the AFL, were not only divisive, screening off skilled workers from exploited unskilled workers, but even counterproductive. Bought off by concessions denied to unskilled workers, skilled workers protected their own hides, allowing capital to continue its greedy rule. In a time of labor violence, people on the left wing regarded gradualism as betrayal, "slowcialism" as bogus socialism.[1] Their opponents called them "impossibilitists."

Eugene Debs bridged the factions, giving full satisfaction to none. Usually aloof from day-to-day intraparty politicking, he proved acceptable, though sometimes only marginally acceptable, to all major groups and, through his lecture tours across the nation year after year, perennially popular with the membership at large, who treasured his attractive personality, oratorical effectiveness, and buoyant stamina. Having run three times previously, Debs brought to the events of 1912 a mature understanding of what was at stake: less the presidency itself than the opportunity to lay out the issues when America was attentive, more or less.

Debs's prior career had prepared him to run without hope of victory and to lose without fear of despair.

Born in Terre Haute, Indiana, in 1855 to parents who had emigrated from Alsace eight years before, he left school at age fourteen; thereafter, he took charge of his own education, retaining his father's attention to French and German classics—Goethe, Schiller, Eugène Sue, and Victor Hugo—and adding an interest in railroading. A chance vacancy as a fireman on a switch engine on the Vandalia Railroad led him to roles as an officer in the Brotherhood of Locomotive Firemen and as editor of its *Locomotive Firemen's Magazine*. The brotherhood's failure to work in tandem with other railroad craft unions encouraged Debs in 1893 to help found the American Railway Union (ARU), an industry-wide union of all white men who worked for the railroads below the level of manager, bound together to guarantee hours of work and scales of pay, to lobby for favorable legislation, and to provide insurance for its members. The ARU defied the craft exclusiveness of the AFL, and by seeking to put all railroad workers in a single organization, hoped to eliminate scabbing by one trade group against another. Within a year, the ARU had 150,000 members in 465 lodges, and Debs had scored great victories against the Union Pacific Railroad and the Great Northern Railroad.

The following year the ARU collapsed as the result of the Pullman strike. In May 1894, the workers at the Pullman Palace Car Company in Pullman, Illinois, struck over wages and working conditions at Pullman and over the feudal, almost totalitarian, regulation of life in the company town. With some trepidation, more pushed by its membership than pulled by Debs, the ARU refused to handle trains that carried Pullman cars. Defying a federal court injunction to end the boycott, Debs and six associates were sentenced to the McHenry County jail in Woodstock, Illinois, he for six months and they for three. What the press called "The Debs Rebellion" was over.

Debs went to prison uncowed. "We are, by chance," he said, "the mere instrumentalities in the evolutionary processes in operation through which industrial slavery is to be abolished and economic freedom established."[2]

For Debs, the confinement was restful, a moment of repose in a career of endless travel and organizing. The genial jailor made confinement as unrepressive as possible: each night the felons were locked up, but during the day they came and went freely, wearing their own clothes, eating with the jailor's family, exercising and playing ball in the street behind the jail. They read in the morning, debated at night. The strike had made Debs a national figure, and the flood of mail each day required the services of a secretary. Books and pamphlets came in profusion. Reporters from important papers sought Debs's views on labor and politics. Henry Demarest Lloyd sent all the prisoners a copy of his *Wealth against Commonwealth*, an early comprehensive attack on big business in America. The socialists made a bid for Debs's attention: Victor L. Berger from Milwaukee, Wisconsin, visited for hours, leaving behind a copy of Karl Marx's *Capital*.

Debs was between ideologies. His prior career had carried him through the phases of the labor movement: from insurance to negotiating conditions of work, from craft organizations to large industrial unions. As editor of the *Locomotive Firemen's Magazine*, he had dealt with a whole range of panaceas that crossed his mind and desk: Henry George's single tax on the economic rent earned from land, free and unlimited coinage of silver from the Populist program, Edward Bellamy's benign view of a utopian socialist state, the Democrats' traditional tariff reduction, civil service reform being pushed by middle class "good government" types, nationalization of railroads and telegraphs—each of them plausible at the moment of statement, all of them inadequate to deal with the rise of violence against labor in the mines, factories, and railroads of America. Now in 1895, his enthusiasms were still scattered. He assured a Texas Populist convention that he was "committed unequivocally" to free silver, though he preferred another battle cry, "Free men." He also assured the Cleveland *Plain Dealer* that he liked bloomers: "They seem cool and comfortable and there is something about the air of a girl who wears them that reminds me of the Declaration of Independence."[3]

Passing his fortieth birthday as he sat in the Woodstock jail, Debs had stability, but uncertain direction. Terre Haute remained a comfortable home base, his mother and father supportive, his brother Theodore a confidant and even mothering hen, his wife Kate loyal to her husband though remote from his commitments. Kate was effective in keeping the Debs Publishing Company barely solvent—it was never any more prosperous—when her husband was absent. Gene was the center of his family and a rising force beyond it. Popular in his home town, well known beyond, Debs was piecing together a living from his editing and organizing and speaking. He acquired skill as an orator in an age that heeded oratory, indeed welcomed it as entertainment. He knew instinctively how to work a crowd, for he felt a kinship with working people that made their concerns his concerns, their good sense a partially articulated form of the divine truth that existed within all free men. He could talk their language. He could—and did—match them drink for drink, and then some. He was generous with his funds, with his time, and with his empathy. When Debs departed from a place, he left warmth behind. The day he left Woodstock jail, four inmates wrote him a formal letter of thanks: "Your presence here has been to us what an oasis in a desert is to the tired and weary traveler, or a ray of sunshine showing thro' a rift in the clouds."[4]

Now, past forty, his American Railway Union in shambles, his publishing company scarcely making ends meet, his own ideas less clear than future retrospection suggested, Debs emerged from prison to a tumultuous welcome in Chicago. Defeated as a labor organizer, he was esteemed as man and orator. "God was feeling mighty good when he created Gene Debs," James Whitcomb Riley, the Hoosier poet said, "and He didn't have anything else to do all day."[5] Debs spent some time in Terre Haute, assessing his future. Politics remained an option. In both 1894 and 1896, he resisted pressure to run on the Populist ticket for the governorship of Indiana, but in the latter year he supported the Populist presidential ticket—Bryan and Thomas E. Watson of Georgia—identifying free silver as "common ground upon which the common people could unite against the trusts."[6]

When McKinley trounced Bryan, the election effectively eliminating the Populist Party as a force in national life, Debs saw clearly that the industrial masters of America ruled; they even made their rule palatable to the voters.

Amiable reforms did not work; workers needed a program that went to the roots of social disorder.

Debs announced for socialism in the *Railway Times* for January 1, 1897: "The issue is Socialism versus Capitalism. I am for Socialism because I am for humanity. We have been cursed with the reign of gold long enough. Money constitutes no proper basis of civilization. The time has come to regenerate society—we are on the eve of a universal change."[7]

The birthing process for an organization for socialism was protracted and tortured. The first try, the Social Democracy of America, fell into the hands of the colonizers. A minority, Debs and others, bolted in 1898 to form the Social Democratic Party, a group that had some limited success in Massachusetts: a mayor in Haverhill and two representatives to the General Court. Then at the 1900 convention, the party leaders, including Victor Berger, put Debs forward for the presidential nomination as a way of containing the intrusion of the "Kangaroos," a breakaway faction of the Socialist Labor Party (SLP) headed by Morris Hillquit of New York, which had defected in a dispute over cooperation with existing trade unions. The SLP majority, under the Marxist leadership of Daniel DeLeon, held that a revolutionary movement should draw workers away from "pure and simple" unions. At odds with DeLeon, Hillquit did not find a ready home within the Social Democratic Party either, for if Hillquit was too reformist for the doctrinaire DeLeon, he was too ambitious and manipulative for his new Social Democratic colleagues; they suspected that the Kangaroos viewed cooperation as a tactic leading to takeover of the SDP. The Kangaroos were similarly wary of their new allies, with equally good reason.

A unity slate of Debs (Social Democrats) for president and Job Harriman (Kangaroos) for vice-president led to cooperation in action that did not exist in ideology. Despite continued backbiting through the summer and fall, the two groups maintained an uneasy alliance through the election of 1900, which garnered just under 97,000 votes.

Once the campaign ended, Berger and his faction continued their campaign to exclude the Kangaroos. But pressure from the rank and file who were weary of the internal bickering forced both sides to a Unity Convention in Indianapolis in July 1901. From it emerged the Socialist Party of America (SPA).[8]

The SPA sought broad middle ground. Membership in the party was open to anyone who recognized the existence of the class struggle in America. Protestant ministers joined to create a heaven on earth. Professionals, like Berger and Hillquit, arrived at their socialism through study rather than through experience in the work force. Small businessmen fought against the growing monopolization of American business. Politicians sought office. Labor leaders joined if membership served their advancement within their own organizations. Workers sought some improvement in their living and working conditions. Farmers sought to recover the equity they were losing to middlemen. Distant from both the utopianism of the colonizers and the narrow dogmatism of DeLeon's Socialist Labor Party, the SPA accepted wide diversity of opinions and substantial autonomy for state organizations. Unable to achieve ideological unanimity, the party learned to live without it.

Debs held aloof from Indianapolis. The SDP convention the previous year had given him his fill of bickering leadership. Berger, with his superior learning and equally superior manner, intimidated Debs, for his habit of lecturing Debs like a benighted pupil intruded on Debs' sense of self. Had Berger spent six months in prison? Did Berger traipse across the nation to spread the truth? Debs felt distrustful of leaders anyway, himself included. "I do not want you to follow me, or anyone else," he frequently told his audiences, "if you are looking for a Moses to lead you out of this capitalist wilderness, you will stay right where you are. I would not lead you into the promised land if I could, because if I could lead you in, someone else would lead you out. You must use your heads as well as your hands, and get yourself out of your present condition."[9] The true strength of the party, he believed, lay with the workers whose daily lives bore the ravages of capitalism. He was equally distrustful of official party platforms, and he was indifferent to them. The party officially supported craft unions. He favored industrial unions, and he refused to be sidetracked. His national tours propagandized for both industrial unions and socialism, as if the two were simply two sides of the same coin.

That Debs's views could capture his party became apparent in the second national convention in 1904, meeting in Chicago to select its presidential ticket. Avoiding the divisive issue of craft unions, the party committed itself to the class struggle, to the work of unions in the industrial field, and to eventual seizure of the government. Immediate demands—the intermediate way stations—were muted.[10] Debs was the unanimous choice for president, and for his running mate, the convention named Ben Hanford, the creator of the mythical "Jimmie Higgins," the rank-and-file worker who did scut work for the party.

Debs was, in many ways, the ideal Socialist candidate, for he was available and effective. Unlike Berger or Hillquit, who had jobs and interests to protect in their back yards, Debs made his living by lecturing, by writing articles for labor and socialist periodicals, and by organizing. Travel was his normal vocation, and his life went on pretty much the same whether there was a campaign in progress or not. Socialist organizations locally provided him a platform. Issues remained largely unchanged. His fee for speaking did not vary markedly. He drove himself with equal vigor.

Once on the road, he was a national asset that built up local organizations, for crowds that came to hear him were a potential source of votes, even of members, on the state level. Debs moved crowds, and they moved him. He told them that they were the final depository of wisdom and goodness, and they responded with cheers that assured him that he was their voice. His language carried the message in terms that people could understand. His manner told them that he was one of them. His energy carried the message from coast to coast, making the miners of Colorado know that their interests were at one with the textile workers of Haverhill and Lawrence. His public addresses were reciprocal offerings of love, possible because the prospect of victory was so remote that Debs could settle for enlightening the people by stripping naked the abuses of American capitalism.

For Debs, a campaign year created a special fillip. In off years, he believed, capitalism functioned as the invisible system, nameless, faceless, ruthless. The hands of control moved invisibly behind the scenes, the charade of government a devious cover for the true brokers of power. But in election years, the ruling class threw off its silence and paraded its choice specimens, encouraged them to tell their most appealing lies, thus exposing them to the ridicule of socialist analysis. Furthermore, election years publicized the Socialists themselves, for when the major parties, largely identical groups competing for the right to fleece the people, tired of orating about the fragmentary differences between them, they abused the socialists as the common enemy, bringing to the public, in perverting but correctable form, socialist analysis and socialist solutions. Debs watched for every opportunity.

Debs saw no inconsistency in disdaining office and running for it, for, as he would tell Lincoln Steffens, then a roving correspondent for *Everybody's Magazine*, four years later: "When Socialism is on the verge of success, the party will nominate an able executive and a clear-headed administrator; not— not Debs."[11] Until victory became imminent, the party needed a dynamic orator like Debs. There may have been closer thinkers, like DeLeon; more astute infighters, like Hillquit; more successful politicians, like Berger. But in reaching the people with the force of fact and emotion, no one matched Debs.

With Debs at the head of the ticket in 1904, Socialists brought their 97,000 votes in 1900 up to more than 400,000. If they could maintain that pace, how many years away was victory?

For the next four years, Debs sorely tested his continuing viability. He fully endorsed the creation of the Industrial Workers of the World (IWW), a new organization with the goal, in the words of its founder Bill Haywood of the Western Federation of Miners, of putting "the working class in possession of the economic power, the means of life, in control of the machinery of production and distribution, without regard to capitalist masters."[12] In retaliation, Berger dropped Debs' column from the *Social Democratic Herald*. Hillquit joined in the attack. J. Mahlon Barnes, Hillquit's close ally and for many years national secretary of the party, viewed Debs as an outcast.

When Haywood and two other men were indicted in 1906 for the murder of former Governor Frank Steunenberg of Idaho, Debs plunged even more deeply. Instantly recognizing the stakes in the trial, Debs wrote an inflammatory article for *Appeal to Reason*, the influential Socialist weekly in Girard, Kansas, the publisher and the editor of which, J. A. Wayland and Fred Warren, had built up a national circulation of over 200,000 subscribers in rural and urban areas. Of the governors of Idaho and Colorado, who contrived the arrest and secret extradition of the accused from Colorado to Idaho, Debs said: "brazen falsifiers and venal villains, the miserable tools of the mine owners who, themselves, if anybody, deserve the gibbet." Of the accusation: "A ghastly lie, a criminal calumny... only an excuse to murder men who are too rigidly honest to betray their trust and too courageous to succumb to threat and intimidation." Of Moyer and Haywood: no more guilty of assassination than Debs himself; "our comrades, staunch and true, and if we do not stand by them to the shedding of the last drop of blood in our veins, we are disgraced forever and deserve the fate of cringing crowds."[13] Writing weekly in the *Appeal* and speaking from hundreds of platforms all over the country, Debs found that the labor movement, even the AFL, responded with support.

But the White House took the opposite line. President Roosevelt criticized "the so-called labor leader who clamorously strives to excite a foul class feeling on behalf of some other labor leader who is implicated in murder."[14] In a subsequent letter, Roosevelt linked Debs with the accused men as "undesirable" citizens.[15] As for *Appeal to Reason*, Roosevelt said it was a "vituperative organ of pornography, anarchy and bloodshed."[16] Debs responded in kind, eventually forcing the President to back away from his implied judgment that the two men were guilty—an impropriety that in another era could well have provoked a mistrial. The rancorous exchange served Debs's purpose well; it focused national attention on the trial and kept it there until the jury returned a verdict of not guilty.

The episode had its cost. Like all such political trials, it deprived the IWW of its leadership of the better part of a year, diverting the attention of labor leaders everywhere. The class in control chose the arena for battle, drawing on only a small part of its resources to tie up the main resources of the opposition. Even in defeat, the acquittal, there was victory. Haywood himself, imprisoned for fifteen months, lost control of his base, the Western Federation of Miners. Furthermore, the trial drove the IWW out of the political process. Though Haywood retained his membership in the Socialist Party, the IWW turned to syndicalism, the idea that unions should run the country. Debs allowed his membership in the IWW to expire.

Paradoxically, Debs' concentration on the Haywood trial and his persistent effort in favor of an industrial union like the IWW, a union he abandoned and probably should have repudiated, did not cripple his standing at the 1908 Socialist convention. The right wing made a furtive, and stupid, effort to deprive Debs of the nomination. When the Hillquit-Berger-Barnes coalition put forward doubts about Debs' health, pointing to his recent throat operation, Ben Hanford, Debs' running mate in 1904, drew out a letter from Debs that blew the coalition's ploy right out the window: "My general health is about all that could be desired. So far as strength is concerned, I have never had more to my credit, if as much. . . . My whole ambition—and I have a goodly stock of it—is to make myself as big and useful as I can, as much opposed to the enemy and as much loved by our comrades as any other private in the ranks. You need have no fear that I shall shirk my part in the coming campaign. I shall be in condition, and I hope there will be no good ground for complaint when the fight is over."[17]

As the anti-Debs forces squirmed, the convention gave Debs 90 percent of the votes on the first ballot, and Hanford was swiftly named as his running mate again.

The campaign of 1908 was probably the most notable Socialist effort, before or since. With contributions drawn in pittances from across the nation, the Socialists set off in the "Red Special," a train that traversed the country. Debs spoke as many as twenty times a day for seven consecutive weeks, his meetings filled with people who paid an admission charge—15 cents or 25 cents—to help sustain the costs of the campaign. The enthusiasm seemed to exceed anything that had ever occurred during a presidential race. The socialist press was confident of a million and a half votes.

When the tally came in, the Socialists had scored 420,000, up only 18,000 from 1904—a stunning disappointment. If the American worker could be seduced by the tepid radicalism of Bryan and deceived by the showy but vapid activity of Roosevelt, the future was further off than anyone in the party had dreamed.

Debs retreated to Terre Haute, exhausted, ill with rheumatism, lumbago, and headaches. He spent the next year on a restricted schedule: multiple articles for *Appeal to Reason* each month, frequent short trips, but no nation-wide lecture tour. Thereafter, he defended Fred Warren, editor of the *Appeal to Reason*, who was sentenced to six months in jail and fined $5,000 for sending scurrilous material through the mail ("Under capitalist misrule the judicial nets are so adjusted as to catch the minnows and let the whales slip through"[18]), and he argued for John and James McNamara, two officers of the AFL Structural Iron Workers, until the brothers confessed in a plea bargain that they had dynamited the Los Angeles *Times* building.

In the eighteen months prior to the convention of 1912, Debs carved out for himself a remarkably independent centrist position, setting himself apart from the major factions by offending their tenderest views without quite adopting the stands of their opponents.

In November 1910, he opened a new assault on the craft unions and their leaders. Samuel Gompers of the AFL, "who banquets with Belmont and Car-negie," and John Mitchell, head of the United Mineworkers of America, "who is paid and pampered by the plutocrats," were part of that leadership "more beneficial to the capitalist class than it is to the workers, seeing that it is the means of keeping them disunited and pitted against each other, and as an inevitable result, in wage slavery." These leaders were mere decoys used by the master class in the National Civic Federation. Only industrial unions on the economic front and the Socialist Party in political terms could express the determination to break the workers' fetters: "abolish the capitalist political state and clear the way for industrial and social democracy."[19]

When the Socialists made unparalleled gains in 1910, electing mayors in Milwaukee and elsewhere, putting numerous members into state legislatures, and even sending Berger to Congress, Debs, uneasy, threw out another challenge, warning of the "Danger Ahead" for the party: the spirit of bourgeois reform "that will practically destroy its virility and efficiency as a revolutionary organization." People who thought that vote-getting was of supreme importance and people who joined hands with trade unions to effect some specific purpose traded true progress for immediate political advantage, Debs believed. The Socialist Party might gain, but socialism would lose, for "Voting for socialism is not socialism any more than a menu is a meal." Debs had no tolerance for such expediency: "Socialism is a matter of growth, of evolution, which can be advanced by wise methods, but never by obtaining for it a fictitious vote. We should seek only to register the actual vote of socialism, no more and no less. In our propaganda we should state our principles clearly, speak the truth fearlessly, seeking neither to flatter nor to offend, but only to convince those who should be with us and win them to our cause through an intelligent understanding of its mission."[20]

A year later, just three months before the Socialist convention in May 1912, Debs sashayed a little closer to the center of the party by separating himself from Haywood, the IWW, and "direct action," what was known in the IWW as "the propaganda of the deed." In a significant article in the February 1912 *International Socialist Review*, entitled "Sound Socialist Tactics," Debs wrote: "For one, I hope to see the Socialist Party place itself squarely on record at the coming national convention against sabotage and every form of violence and destructiveness suggested by what is known as 'direct action.'" Sabotage was the tactic of anarchism, not socialism, he insisted. Given the law-abiding character of American workers, direct action would never appeal to them while they retained the ballot and the right to political and economic organization. Furthermore, acceptance of sabotage would entice police spies and *agents provocateurs* into the party to discredit it, leaving the party to take the rap for the deed of every spy or madman; "the seeds of strife would be subtly sown in the ranks, mutual suspicion would be aroused, and the party would soon be torn into warring factions to the despair of the betrayed workers and the delight of their triumphant masters." Debs made clear that his stand was tactical, not philosophical: "I am law-abiding under protest—not from scruple—and bide my time." Debs felt no scruple about violating capitalist property laws: they had been "enacted through chicanery, fraud and corruption, with the sole end in view of dispossessing, robbing and enslaving the working class." But in twentieth-century America, "butting my head against the stone wall of existing property laws...would be merely weakness and folly." There were times "where the frenzied deed of a glorious fanatic like old John Brown seems to have been inspired by Jehovah himself." But not here. Not now.

Having offended the radical left, Debs turned his attention back to the conservatives. Again he praised intellectuals as the service troops for the movement, not as its leaders: "An organization of intellectuals would not be officered and represented by wage earners; neither should an organization of wage earners be officered by intellectuals." So much for Hillquit and for Charles Edward Russell of New York, who would be the right-wing candidate for the presidential nomination. Debs repeated his stand against reactionary craft unions. So much for Berger and for those who sought to infiltrate the AFL. He praised rotation in office as an antidote to "officialism." So much for Barnes, Hillquit's ally who had been executive secretary of the party for many years.[21]

Still uneasy at conventions, Debs continued his customary lecture tour rather than attending the Socialist convention in Indianapolis as a delegate in 1912. He was ready to apply rotation in office to himself: he was promoting the candidacy of Fred Warren of *Appeal to Reason*. Nonetheless, the convention gave him no respite. First papering over the deep fissures within the party, the convention went on to record its certainty that only Eugene V. Debs had the national stature to carry the party through a national campaign.

The convention met with gravity and with ebullience. The "yellows" and the "reds" eyed each other with suspicion, as usual. The conservatives controlled the national executive committee and, therefore, committees and procedures, while the more radical wing appeared to have more votes. There were 293 delegates representing 47 or 48 states and 7 foreign-speaking organizations that held membership directly from the national office. In addition, fraternal delegates from socialist organizations overseas appeared; they were generally assumed to be a conservative force. The varied membership knew that it would have to deal with deep differences within its ranks. But first it had to get past a controversy about overalls.

The comrades from Indianapolis proposed to have the welcoming speaker, Carl Ott, appear before the convention in overalls, his dress a symbol of the party's proletarian character. John Spargo of New York, an intellectual and a conservative associate of Hillquit, protested that the costume would expose the convention to ridicule in the capitalist press. But the executive committee came down on the side of the overalls, adding the proviso that the speech be limited to five minutes. But Ott appeared the following day wearing bourgeois pants. He had brought his overalls to the hall that morning, but, in the words of the *International Socialist Review*, "the offending overalls had been removed from the convention's jurisdiction by interested parties."[22]

The key issue of the convention arose over the report of the Committee on Relation of Labor Organizations to the Socialist Party. The committee contained six members assumed to be friendly to craft unions, and three known to be hostile, the "three Toms": Tom Clifford of Ohio, Tom Hickey

from Texas, and Tom Lewis from Oregon. The convention, anticipating a free-
for-all, listened intently as the committee made its report. The declaration
began with standard boilerplate: Both political and economic organizations
are essential—the Socialist Party and the labor unions. Workers are "rapidly
developing an enlightened and militant class consciousness" as "attested by
the increasing virulence with which the organized capitalists wage their war
against the union." There follows a hint of what was to come: "Only those
actually engaged in the struggle in the various trades and industries can solve
the problems of form of organization." (Not just "trades," but "trades and
industries.") Therefore, the declaration goes on, the Socialist Party reaffirms
the position "it has always taken": The party does not interfere with forms
of organization or "technical methods of action in the industrial struggle,"
but leaves these questions to the unions themselves. At the same time, Socialists "call the attention of their brothers in the labor unions to the vital
importance of the task of organizing the unorganized, especially the immigrants and the unskilled laborers." It urges all labor organizations "to throw
their doors wide open to the workers of their respective trades and industries,
abolishing all onerous conditions of membership and artificial restrictions."
Meanwhile, it is the duty of all party members who are eligible "to join and
be active in their respective labor organizations."[23]

Labeled a compromise and written in a committee dominated by conservatives, the resolution was a victory for the radical wing. Though it fell far
short of Debs' condemnation of craft unions, it committed the party unequivocally to industrial unions and to unskilled workers who fell outside the
crafts. It even took a swipe at the National Civic Federation by name. When
the three Toms announced their support of the declaration, the convention
adopted it unanimously. Even Bill Haywood of the IWW called the declaration
"the greatest step ever taken by the Socialist party of this country."[24]

The conservatives also had their day, and Haywood was clearly their target.
The convention adopted, by more than a two-thirds majority, a statement on
political action and on violence: "Any member of the party who opposes
political action or advocates crime, sabotage, or other methods of violence
as a weapon of the working class to aid in its emancipation shall be expelled
from membership in the party."[25] It is time, one member from New Jersey
said, for the party to be on record as "opposed to jackass methods of fighting
capitalism."[26] Tom Clifford protested that "in no instance has the Socialist
party been or ever will be an organization for the suppression of crime."[27]

Once the issue had been raised, however, the convention had to deal with
it. To table a resolution condemning sabotage implied, or could readily be
made to imply, that the party condoned "direct action," that is, sabotage.
Berger, in an impassioned speech, insisted that the convention put itself on
record: "I for one do not believe in murder as a means of propaganda, I do
not believe in theft as a means of expropriation; nor in a continuous riot as

a free speech agitation. Every true Socialist will agree with me when I say that those who believe we should substitute Halleluja, I'm a Bum for the Marseillaise and for the Internationale should start a Bum Organization of their own."[28] Hillquit managed to have the last word on the resolution when he reported that the Committee on the Constitution was only one vote short of unanimous in favoring the sabotage amendment. "If there is one thing in this country that can now check or disrupt the Socialist movement," he warned, "it is not the capitalist class, it is not the Catholic Church; it is our own injudicious friends from within."[29] His view carried the day. A rollcall vote to delete the reference to sabotage lost, 90–191, and the convention accepted the ban as recommended.

A nod to the radicals with the recognition of industrial unionism, a nod to the conservatives through a repudiation of syndicalism and sabotage.

The Socialist platform played a similar balanced game, its introductory rhetoric sufficiently sharp to satisfy all but the most extreme left-wingers, its specific "Working Program" far-reaching yet reformist in tone.

The platform affirmed the existence of the class struggle, society "divided into warring groups and classes, based upon material interests," and the need to abolish the "incompetent and corrupt" capitalist system, "the source of unspeakable misery and suffering to the whole working class." The greedy hands of the plutocracy, already absolutely controlling the industrial equipment of the nation, was stretching its hands over undeveloped resources as well: lands, mines, forests, water power in every state. Workers received less of what they produced, their wages declining as the rich grew richer. Farmers were plundered by the price of tools and the costs of rents, freight rates, and storage charges. Small businessmen were reduced to propertyless wageworkers. Capitalism was "responsible for the increasing burden of armaments, the poverty, slums, child labor, most of the insanity, crime and prostitution, and much of the disease that afflicts mankind." The Republican and Democratic Parties remained the "faithful servants of the oppressors," their political conflicts "merely superficial rivalries between competing capitalist groups." The executive—whether Cleveland, McKinley, Roosevelt, or Taft—offered no check. Legislation like the antitrust laws and prosecutions based upon them "have proved to be utterly futile and ridiculous." The courts served as instruments to oppress the working class and to suppress free speech and free assembly.

All parties were expressions of class interests, the platform affirmed.

The Socialist party is the political expression of the economic interests of the workers. Its defeats have been their defeats and its victories their victories. It is a party founded on the science and laws of social development. It proposes that, since all social necessities to-day are socially produced, the means of their production and distribution shall be socially owned and democratically controlled.... Thus the Socialist party is the party of the present-day revolution which marks the transition from economic individualism to socialism, from wages slavery to free cooperation, from capitalist oligarchy to industrial democracy.

The "Working Program" then called for collective ownership of all means of transportation and communication and of all large-scale industry; for extension of the public domain; for collective ownership of land where practicable and, where not, "appropriation by taxation of the annual rental value of all land held for speculation or exploitation"; for collective ownership and democratic management of the banking and currency system. For the workers, the party wanted public works for the unemployed, and for the employed, shorter workdays, minimum wages, adequate insurance, effective safety rules, and an end to child labor. It sought progressive income, inheritance, and corporate taxes, the proceeds to be used for the socialization of industry. It favored votes for women; initiative, referendum, recall; proportional representation locally and nationally; and the direct election of the president and vice-president. It proposed to abolish the Senate and to deny the president veto power over legislation. It would deny the Supreme Court the power to declare laws unconstitutional, and it would abolish federal district and circuit courts entirely. (For these structural changes, it called for a constitutional convention to revise the existing arrangements.) These measures were merely a way station: "Such measures of relief as we may be able to force from capitalism are but a preparation of the workers to seize the whole powers of government, in order that they may thereby lay hold of the whole system of socialized industry and thus come to their rightful inheritance."[30]

The platform rightly regarded itself as revolutionary, aimed at changing the basic structure of American political and economic institutions. But the changes scheduled in the "Working Program" were to come as the result of victories at the ballot box. The final goal could satisfy Bill Haywood; the means to that goal contained nothing to jostle the sensibilities of Berger and Hillquit.

The divisive fight fought, the platform adopted, nothing remained for the convention other than the nomination of its standard-bearers. Hillquit and Berger would happily have put Debs out to pasture, and each came up with an alternate candidate: Charles Edward Russell from New York and Mayor Emil Seidel from Milwaukee. When Debs's name was put in nomination amid massive cheering, Berger raised the issue of Debs's availability: Debs was not at the convention, and again he had been ill. But the ploy went nowhere. Debs had made publicly explicit his willingness to run, and the convention would have no other. Debs won the nomination handily on the first ballot (165 for Debs, 56 for Seidel, 54 for Russell), and the convention gave Seidel the vice-presidential slot. Hillquit made one final maneuver for the right wing: he managed to have the convention accept his crony Barnes as campaign manager.

The convention ended, everyone savoring his victories and weighing his defeats. There was unity. "It is doubtful if either of the older parties can show an instance of equal partisan 'harmony' either as to platform or candidates," the *Independent* noted in an editorial.[31] But there was no solidarity. The differences were just below the surface.

PART IV

The 1912 Presidential Campaign

9

Setting the Wilson Image

The change was abrupt. Yesterday Woodrow Wilson was governor of a small northeastern state, perhaps near the end, not the beginning of his political career. The legislature in New Jersey having rebounded to full Republican control in the midterm election of 1911, Wilson could expect no new flurry of accomplishments. Even less could he stay alive politically for another crack at the presidency in 1916. He was in danger, as they used to say of frustrated presidential candidate Thomas E. Dewey in 1948, of moving from being a comer to being a has-been without ever having been an is. But in fact, Wilson did win his party's nomination. Win or lose in November, he would show up in history books that went beyond New Jersey residents and Princeton alumni.

The run for the nomination left Wilson a curiously contradictory legacy. He had projected himself as a public icon embodying a brilliant progressive vision; yet he owed his hairline victory more to political maneuver than to moral strength. Now with victory in hand, he faced a parallel anomaly: his model for America's future, a vista of grandeur, needed Democratic political machinery, a crazy quilt of shreds and patches in forty-eight states. The nominee understood the need to make Wilson the prophet and Wilson the organizer a single driving force.

For a moment the externals at Sea Girt remained remarkably the same. Mrs. Wilson managed the household. The children came and went as usual. Wilson found an hour for golf or for a walk on the shore and made quick gubernatorial trips to Trenton.

Then, quite insistently, his world took on new dimensions. Delegates from the convention came north to pay their respects. Oscar W. Underwood, whose ambitions never advanced far enough to create deep bitterness, arrived; the meeting was friendly, even warm. Champ Clark came and went, his dour countenance on page two of the *Times* the following day confirming that the hurt had not healed.[1] Fortunately for Wilson, Clark's real grievance was with William Jennings Bryan.[2] So when Clark returned to Sea Girt two weeks later at the head of the Democrats from the House of Representatives, he and Wilson publicly submerged past differences. Charles Bryan appeared, bringing the blessings of his more famous brother.

As the days passed, the Little White House became a marketplace, the house and porch overrun with reporters, tourists, villagers, and politicians. No protective barrier guarded the candidate against interruption, not even a policeman out front to ward off the curious and the insistent.

In addition, there was incoming mail that demanded attention. In early July, Wilson was opening each day's letters, scrutinizing every campaign contribution for an insidious connection. He tried manfully to deal with Princeton alumni, politicians, and other well-wishers, sweeping the tide back no more successfully than the sorcerer's apprentice.

When the pressure rose too high, Wilson fled to the University Club in New York. Reporters followed him across the Hudson River, but they kept their distance and let him walk the streets of Manhattan anonymously. On weekends Wilson stole off to nearby Atlantic Highlands for undisturbed reflection at the home of an old friend.

In meeting his new responsibilities, Wilson at first had little assistance beyond his own wits and instincts, not a bad endowment, but short of what was needed.

Control of the party was the first priority, authoritative command of the machinery for mounting a national campaign. Very promptly Wilson made clear that he would avoid the intrastate Democratic crossfire of bosses and reformers while he was engaged in the more important fight for the presidency. Then he dealt with the larger picture. When the Democratic National Committee met in Chicago July 15, his agents rammed through his definition of the campaign plan; there were mutterings in the corridor but no overt dissent. The committee also accepted his nominee for chairman, William F. McCombs, despite substantial sentiment that McCombs be sacked, for he was sick, cranky, jealous, anything but a team player. But dumping McCombs would have revived the familiar, and not unfounded, charge that Wilson was an ingrate. So he had McCombs named to the job with the understanding that William G. McAdoo, whose influence with Wilson McCombs deeply resented, would move in as vice-chairman. Three days later, Wilson, all but bypassing McCombs, named a campaign committee largely free of old party wheelhorses. McCombs acquiesced in the arrangements grudgingly, naming McAdoo as vice-chairman only after Wilson sent him a direct order by telegram. McAdoo also acquiesced. As events developed, McAdoo functioned as chairman for much of the campaign, for the sickly McCombs was absent for weeks at a time. Things moved more smoothly in his absence.

Financial management proved much easier. Henry Morgenthau of New York, Wilson's handpicked choice as chairman, set the initial budget for the campaign at $1,000,000. No contributions were to be accepted from corporations, no large contributions from men whose corporate interests made their money suspect. The idea was that with small contributions the American people would make Wilson's campaign their own. By the end of the campaign, almost 90,000 people contributed. As usual, however, the campaign rode on the donations of the wealthy; less then 2 percent of the contributors gave 66 percent of the total, and about half came from 155 individuals.[3]

The money supported a staff at headquarters in New York and a second office in what the Wilson people called "the West," that is, Chicago. Each location was a distribution point for buttons and posters, for Wilson's speeches and public statements, for movies of the candidate with phonograph records to match. The centers served primarily reporters from newspapers and magazines, for the press was the crucial link to voters who could not see the candidate in person, that is, to most of the people of the United States. These activities were new-style "educational politics," replacing nineteenth-century parades and rallies.[4]

The campaign committee was to ride herd on all these technical chores, letting the candidate make himself felt as a national figure, larger than his opponents, larger than party, larger than life itself.

Pious affirmations hastily adopted in Baltimore aside, the real platform of the Democrats was the issues that the candidate proposed for national debate. To create that agenda Wilson disappeared late in July, off to an unknown hideaway for a week with blank pads and a copy of the Democratic platform. For five days he sailed around Long Island Sound on the yacht of his classmate Cleveland Dodge, putting in at coves in the evening. Mrs. Wilson and their daughter Margaret were along. No mail. No visitors. No telephone or telegrams.

A week later, in preparation for the arrival of the Notification Committee, Wilson went over the speech with McAdoo and McCombs in New York, then spent an evening swapping yarns with his running mate Thomas Marshall, in from Indiana. Marshall had switched from chewing tobacco to cigars in acknowledgment of his new status, laying the groundwork for the statement that is almost all his countrymen remember him for: "What this country needs is a good five-cent cigar."

Finally, the important moment arrived, Wilson sharing headlines with Theodore Roosevelt, who was accepting his belated nomination on the same day. Wilson downplayed pomp. He invited no one. Everyone was welcome. Mrs. Wilson and the wives of other leaders sat on the veranda. On the lawn just beyond the porch, eight governors and scores of politicians great and small milled around with hundreds of other citizens: four hundred, including forty white-gloved policemen, from Jersey City alone.

After Senator Ollie James made the formal notification, a graceful tribute, Wilson accepted the nomination, his careful text a blend of the party's platform and the "faith that is in me."[5] He dutifully and explicitly rapped the Payne-Aldrich tariff. But every such specific criticism had to take a place subordinate to his vision for America. This is the sum of the matter, he said:[6]

There are two great things to do. One is to set up the rule of justice and of right in such matters as the tariff, the regulations of the trusts, and the prevention of monopoly, the adaptation of our banking and currency laws to the varied uses to which our people must put them, the treatment of those who do the daily labor in our factories and mines and throughout all our great industrial and commercial undertakings, and the political life of the people of the Philippines, for whom we hold governmental power in trust, for their service not our own. The other, the additional duty, is the great task of protecting our people and our resources and of keeping open to the whole people the doors of opportunity through which they must, generation by generation, pass if they are to make conquest of their fortune in health, in freedom, in peace, and in contentment. In the performance of the great second duty we are face to face with questions of conservation and of development, questions of forests and water powers and mines and waterways, of the building of an adequate merchant marine, and the opening of every highway and facility and the setting up of every safeguard needed by a great industrious, expanding nation.

The performance was formal, vague, awkward. His listeners grew restive standing for a full hour in the afternoon sun. Sensing their restlessness, he commented at one point: "Oh, I wish I didn't have to read this; it would be so much more interesting if I didn't have to."[7] But, not heeding his own impulse, he returned to his text. At the edges of the crowd, vendors sold hot dogs, popcorn, pink lemonade, and Wilson buttons, their sales pitch now and then drowning out Wilson's unamplified voice. Wilson went on at his own solemn pace, reaching for a new national consensus, an elemental commonality that spread across the nation, across classes, across parties. A partisan audience of Democrats could not hear. They did not perceive that Wilson was not talking to them, but to himself and to history.

For one part of his program, Wilson acquired an unexpected ally during the latter part of August. At Wilson's invitation, Louis D. Brandeis, a lawyer close to progressive causes and to Senator Robert M. La Follette, closeted himself with the candidate for three hours. Brandeis emerged from their conference with effusive delight: "I found Gov. Wilson a man capable of broad, constructive statesmanship, and I found him to be entirely in accord with my own views of what we need to do to accomplish industrial freedom."[8] In fact, Wilson brought Brandeis's position whole hog, filling a gap for which Wilson's previous experience offered scant preparation. For Brandeis and, subsequent to their time together, for Wilson as well, the central issue became the restoration of competition by law: "[M]onopoly is created by unregulated competition, by competition that overwhelms all other competitions," Wilson told the press, "and the only way to enjoy industrial freedom is to destroy that condition."[9]

As July and August slipped past, Wilson approached the opening of the campaign in September with his ducks in line. His campaign committee was functioning effectively. Money was coming in. Wilson felt comfortable with his choice of issues. The Republicans were wallowing in their disunity. President Taft was showing no will to fight. Roosevelt was apparently everywhere at once, but his organizational problems in forty-eight separate states showed no signs of abating. Lloyd's of London made Wilson a three-to-one favorite over Taft.[10]

A willing candidate, Wilson was a reluctant campaigner, for he wanted his campaign posture to attract voters by its obvious merit. The issues facing the nation were too serious, the solutions too complex, for the facile rhetoric of the stump; they required formal settings, careful thought, precise diction. Furthermore, he disliked asking for votes, for like Taft, he was sensitive to the dignity of the presidential office.

In a controlled setting, Wilson felt mastery. He had long experience as an academic, comfortable as an authority to be heeded in a structured lecture hall. With reporters he could even be informal, relaxed, and witty, since they understood who was in charge. When a *New York Times* reporter stepped out of line, Wilson used his contacts in New York to have the reporter pulled off the beat.[11] At Sea Girt and Princeton, he could do constructive work with visitors who evoked thoughtful public statements. These assets would be lost if Wilson rushed mindlessly to and fro, exposing himself to the unexpected, speaking from the top of his head instead of from the core of his being, consuming time needed for issues and for his own composure. Would careful statement yield to off-the-cuff responses and to awkward silences? Would he, offering leadership to the greatest nation, become a beggar for votes in an unseemly scramble? Would the process of election make him less worthy to be elected? Would Governor Woodrow Wilson become "Woody"?

Besides, there was New Jersey to govern. The nation would be watching the governorship in New Jersey for hints about the presidency in Washington. What better way to show his potential as president than to perform well as governor?

The argument for stability was impressive. But, of course, any such campaign plan in the republic of 1912 promised rhetorical triumph and political catastrophe.

Skillfully, McAdoo coaxed Wilson into the fray. There were important allies, people with entitlement like A. Mitchell Palmer in Pennsylvania, Bryan in Nebraska, Thomas Taggart in Indiana, William C. Sullivan in Illinois, whose claims could not be ignored, he said. There were old competitors, like Champ

Clark in Missouri and Judson Harmon in Ohio, whose sensitivities demanded overt courtesy. There were tense situations, like Charles E. Murphy's ostentatious control of the New York organization. The governor's fear of the stump could be addressed, too: He could be scheduled for formal occasions at which prepared statements drew on his best considered thought. Gradually, Wilson slid into a decision to make relatively short stabs into controverted electoral areas that Democrats had a chance of winning. McAdoo set up schedules piecemeal, never committing more than ten days on any single trip. Wilson came to acknowledge the need for local appearances, for Wilson in New Jersey was a newspaper item on the inside pages. Wilson in St. Paul before a wildly cheering audience would blanket Minnesota and create a stir throughout the Midwest.

Thus Governor Wilson became Candidate Wilson.

The abrupt introduction to campaigning started before Labor Day in southeastern Pennsylvania under the auspices of Palmer and the Democratic State Committee when Palmer got Wilson's agreement to make a "nonpolitical" speech to the Grange at Willow Grove. Then stops were added: Lancaster, Reading, two others. Arriving at the Grange, Wilson complained that America under the Republican administrations was in the hands of rich "self-constituted trustees" while the rest of the nation lived as wards. He noted that Roosevelt, a recent convert to the tariff, argued that the prize money of the tariff was legitimate booty, that the flaw in the tariff was that the prize money was not generally shared with the crew. Who supplies the plunder? Wilson asked. The answer: that great helpless class, the unbenefited consumer. Farmers, Wilson asserted, were fundamental to American prosperity; note that in the Lord's Prayer, the petition "Give us this day our daily bread" came before all other petitions. Yet when Congress offered Taft a "farmers' free list" to ease their burden of taxation, President Taft vetoed it because he "represents the trustees, not the people."[12]

At Reading, he told the Pennsylvania "Dutch" gathered there, "America can't be prosperous unless she is happy, and she can't be happy unless her people think the government is dealing justly by them. The Americans are just people. The only time they are dangerous is when you shut them out of the game."[13]

The day was an occasion for learning. Wilson went to Pennsylvania in a Pullman chair; no private car and no rear platform speeches: that was to be the formula. A steady stream of visitors overwhelmed him at his chair and even pursued him into the dining car. At Lancaster, Palmer insisted on a private car, assuring Wilson that it was "thoroughly democratic." The crowds amazed the candidate. At the Grange, he gave his speech in an auditorium, then repeated it for the thousands outside. A blacksmith shook his hand so firmly that it ached for the rest of the day. At Lancaster, the scene of his first unscheduled cartail speech, hundreds of people milled about the rear platform. Wilson registered his amazement at the "genuinely spontaneous" gathering with "no advance notice" where Wilson's portrait hung above the roadway and almost everyone waved "Win With Wilson" banners. His speeches were vague, rambling, diffident, self-conscious. Out of his element, buffeted by numbers, naive about where crowds came from, he left his Pennsylvania backers uneasy about the future.[14]

For Wilson, no matter. He had two speeches scheduled for Buffalo, New York, on Labor Day, and one of them was written out. "With these speeches," he said to his friend Mary Allen Hulbert (the former Mrs. Peck, recently divorced), "the campaign really begins."[15]

A better controlled format made Buffalo a more comfortable experience. He gave a scheduled talk to the United Trades and Labor Council of Buffalo, preparation of which having consumed much of a previous day. He had time to prepare notes for an evening address to a mass meeting. At an informal luncheon and on three other occasions, he just had to wing it. He spent three hours at the Lafayette Hotel, greeting the faithful and the curious. Though the day went on for more than ten hours, it had some measure of predictability.

As he spoke, Wilson started to take the measure of the crowd, injecting bits of humor—"I was a lawyer, I have repented"[16]—catching a murmur in the crowd when something he said was misunderstood, at once addressing a labor audience and assuring it that he was speaking to and for all Americans.

He had a double message: Democrats were ready, Republicans had failed. The Republican Party, with its standpat ideas, "is the very party which has got us into the difficulties we are now trying to get out of." He professed sympathy for the social goals of the Progressives, but those goals would founder if a Progressive president tried to deal with a mixed Congress: "I think we could all go fishing for the next two years." The Democrats were ready for leadership because sixteen years in the political wilderness had allowed them to be creative while the party in power had struck up an alliance with the special interests. Now the nation was ready to hear the Democratic message, and the Democratic Party was ready to lead the drive for popular rule and justice for all.[17]

A workman, leaving Braun Hall, told the *Times* that Wilson's talk left him feeling "very solemn, like coming out of church."[18]

Buffalo was a big step above Pennsylvania, but McAdoo was not satisfied. He urged Wilson to prepare his speeches ahead for the upcoming trip so that the Associated Press could have them in advance. "It is much better to repeat to large degree former speeches you have made, and to give out advance copies, than to make extemporary speeches and suffer their emasculation in print."[19] McAdoo had a point. The *Times* had reported that Wilson in Buffalo had called Taft "stupid"[20]—an extrapolation of what Wilson really did say that went wide of the mark. Roosevelt was explicitly raising the issue of bossism—Taggart, Sullivan, and Murphy—in St. Paul; both the *Times* and the New York *Evening Post* carried the story. Wilson had made a fetish of not dealing in personalities. Perhaps it was a luxury he could no longer afford.

From Buffalo, Wilson returned to New Jersey for an afternoon at the State House, then drove over to Sea Girt. The summer crowd had left the Jersey shore. The first nip of fall allowed a fire in the fireplace at the Little White House. Wilson hoped to stay at Sea Girt until the end of September, then set up his family in Princeton and his campaign in Trenton and New York.

There was time for speeches nearby. He gave his now-standard line on hardy, freedom-loving immigrants to one hundred foreign-language news-paper editors in New York City, and he used the occasion of a "dollar dinner" of the Woodrow Wilson Working Men's League in the German section of New York City to distance himself from the idea of absolute free trade: "Don't be afraid that you will meet a free trader in the dark anywhere, because there isn't any free trader who can get abroad in America at present." When Dem-ocrats spoke against the tariff, they spoke for "relative freedom in trade." He mocked the Republican article of faith that the tariff protected American jobs. In fact, the advantages of higher prices behind the tariff wall had never filtered down to workers; the industrial magnates kept the profits for themselves. Even more important, America needed to develop foreign markets—"if she doesn't get bigger foreign markets she will burst her jacket"—and no such trade could develop unless the United States opened its own markets as well.[21]

For the influential New York Press Club, he put together his soon-to-be familiar analysis of the elements in the third party: "those Republicans whose consciences and whose stomachs couldn't stand what the regular Republicans were doing," the largest element; high-spirited men and women of noble character, who see the party as the instrument to accomplish what their hearts have so long desired; and the third element "of which the less said the better." The program of the third party, "constructive regulation," was, Wilson said, an open alliance of the great interests and the government, not necessarily corrupt or dishonest, but scarcely disinterested. "And I say to those noble men and women who have allied themselves with that party because of the social programs: Who will guarantee to us that this matter will be just and pitiful? Do we conceive social betterment to lie in the pitiful use of irresistible power? . . . The history of liberty is a history of the limitation of governmental power, not the increase of it."[22] The journalists listened intently, withheld applause until Wilson had finished, then burst into cheers and songs.[23]

The work went out from Sea Girt that Wilson was abandoning the veranda and taking to the field with a will.

Before he won the nation, however, he had business to finish at home. In New Jersey, ex-Senator James Smith, Jr., was entering the September 24 pri-mary in a bid for the United States Senate. If Smith were to win, the message would be obvious: reform had staying power only for the duration of Wilson's incumbency in Trenton. Wilson felt that he had to act. Breaking custom on the sabbath, Wilson issued his manifesto: "Mr. Smith's selection as the Democratic candidate for the Senate would be the most fatal step backward that Democrats of the state could possibly take. It would mean his restoration to political leadership in New Jersey the moment my service as Governor ended, and with his restoration, a return to the machine rule which so long kept every active Democrat in the state in subordination to him and prevented every progressive program conceived in the interest of the people from being put into effect." Smith was entitled to run, of course, and if he won the primary, he was also entitled to the vote of every Democratic legislator. But Wilson, as governor of the state and as national leader of the party, had a "clear and imperative" duty "in conscience" to speak out. "We can indulge nothing when the stake is our country's welfare and prosperity and the honor of our party."[24]

In New York the situation was more delicate, for overt intervention in New York invited a whole gamut of risks: at the very least, resentment at the intrusion; at a more serious level, clumsy intrusion that meddled and lost; at the catastrophic level, intrusion that, regardless of success or failure, led the New York machine to retaliate by cutting a deal with the Republicans or Progressives: forty-five electoral votes for Taft or Roosevelt in exchange for an unobstructed Democratic shot at the governorship. Not intervening also had its risks. Both Roosevelt and ex-Senator Albert J. Beveridge of Indiana were making hay with the bossism issue. Murphy took the public posture of supporting Governor John A. Dix for reelection, and Dix's near total unpopularity within the party remained irrelevant as long as Murphy stood behind him. Reform Democrats, like Senator James A. O'Gorman and State Senator Franklin D. Roosevelt, were powerless to stop the "Juggernaut." When Wilson entered the state to fill an engagement at the New York State Fair at Syracuse, Murphy and Dix started a cat-and-mouse game with the candidate. After Wilson had agreed to speak, the Democratic organization had hastily summoned the state committee and the county chairman for the same time and place. After Wilson's speech, Dix's staff maneuvered a private meeting between Dix and Wilson to create the impression of gubernatorial rapport. But reporters nearby saw that when the door to the conference room opened, Wilson was sitting, unsmiling, as remote from Dix as he could. At lunch Murphy was seated one place away from Wilson. Wilson nibbled on some bread, then left the table. A photographer tried to catch a picture of the two; Wilson walked away before the camera could be focused. Finally Wilson returned as presidential candidate with impromptu remarks.[25] The assembled leaders of the New York Democratic Party listened. If they did not hear, it was only because Murphy controlled their attention.

Wilson said: "I'll tell you frankly, the people of the United States are tired of politics. They are sick of politics." The Democratic leaders of New York have "an extraordinary opportunity and an extraordinary duty" to equate public service with public duty. "The nation is waiting.... And I believe that nothing will be more inspiring, nothing will be more inspiriting, than to see the Democracy of New York lead the way."[26]

Having heard the speech, Murphy, never rattled, told the inquiring press that there had been nothing in Governor Wilson's remarks to take offense at. Dix, apparently unruffled by repeated rebuffs, affirmed his own progressive credentials: a pure food law, a limit on night work for women, and a commission to investigate the high cost of living.[27]

Two points for the Christians, two for the lions.

The next day Wilson whistled past reporters' questions. But he did explicitly reject Governor Dix's reported assertion that Wilson had promised that he would not interfere.[28]

The following day, Sunday, September 15, Wilson's private car, the Magnet, was attached to the Chicago train. Wilson motored from Sea Girt to Trenton and boarded with Dudley Field Malone, his secretary and Senator O'Gorman's son-in-law, and two stenographers. As the train neared Harrisburg, he emerged from his seclusion in his compartment to say: "You may state that I have nothing further to say about New York at present." He put special emphasis on "at present."[29]

Wilson's first "western" trip carried him through Chicago to Sioux City, Iowa. At the last minute the Democrats of South Dakota raised enough money to coax him into their state before his scheduled stop in St. Paul. He made a direct run back to Detroit, Michigan, and on to Columbus, Ohio, where Governor Harmon was waiting to greet him, then a return to home base.

Originally attached to the Chicago express, Wilson's car, an old wooden model, ended up at the rear of a slow freight train. At Columbus, the first city that Wilson went through after sunrise on the trip out, a crowd had already gathered. Wilson dressed hastily, moved to the back platform for give and take. He had plenty of time, for the train shuttled the increasingly angry candidate around the yards for an hour and a half. At Union City, Indiana, on the Ohio border, the train halted abruptly, and again Wilson went to the platform with what became a useful theme: the need for government free of the influences of special interests and devoted to the needs of the people. The theme was a happy choice, for if Wilson had only a minute, free government was a complete idea; if he had more, he could stretch out the implications for as long as his stop permitted. On this occasion he had barely started when the train pulled out. No matter, the crowd, accustomed to the traffic in the area, called out, we'll walk down the track and catch you at the next stop. Sure enough, the train chugged a short distance down the track, stopped again, gathering a new crowd to supplement the old. The dust was so thick that Wilson could not be seen at a distance of more than ten feet. "It makes me feel like a caged animal," Wilson said impatiently.[30]

At Logansport, Indiana, he turned Senator Beveridge's charge that Wilson would be controlled by bosses back on the Bull Moose Party. Beveridge's party talked of partnership between the monopolists and the government, he said. "Do you suppose his party is going to dispense with the bosses in that way, when the bosses are the agents of the monopolists, who see to it that the laws they do not want do not get on the statute books?"[31]

Unreconciled by a pro-Wilson engineer who pushed his throttle to seventy miles per hour to get Wilson to Chicago in time for his connection to Sioux City, Wilson abandoned his private car in Chicago: "Hereafter a common day coach will be plenty good enough for me. I want to be on a train that's going somewhere and has a chance to get there."[32] Unimpressed by his own effectiveness on the rear platform, Wilson, toward the end of the trip, telegraphed his Chicago office: positively no more rear-platform speeches. Returning home through Indiana, he told a crowd why: "I am tired of discussing the big questions of this campaign from the rear end of a train. It can't be done. The issues are too big. . . . I would a great deal rather shake hands with you and make your acquaintance than leave a compound fracture of an idea behind me."[33] And with that, he got off the train and started working the crowd.

Throughout the trip, Wilson kept coming back to what he called the "Abandoned Issues," the tariff and the trusts, abandoned because the Republicans and the third-party types seemed unwilling to deal with them.

A historically central Democratic issue, the tariff hurt consumers and farmers. But the issue carried risks for a campaigner. Too abrupt a decline in tariff rates would certainly disrupt American industry at all levels, and workers' fears for their jobs in the absence of high tariffs had been a potent factor in every campaign over the previous sixteen years and longer. President Taft warned that tariff reduction would force American workers to compete with cheap labor abroad. Protecting himself against the reasonableness of that charge, Wilson continually distanced himself from the notion of free trade, his own private inclination coinciding with his political sense.

Wilson wanted the tariff viewed in a new light. The inflated schedules of the Payne-Aldrich tariff melded the tariff issue into the trust issue, he argued, for the high level of import duties, providing great profits, encouraged the emergence of trusts. Once on the issue of trusts, Wilson felt surer ground. Trusts, controlling markets and labor, pushed prices to unconscionable levels, he said, hurting American consumers, suppressing American labor, and demolishing domestic competitors. Wilson proposed to lower the tariff in an orderly, gradual way and to regulate competition to preserve access to the market for all.[34]

Wilson distinguished between a big business and a trust: "A trust is an arrangement to get rid of competition, and a big business is a business that has survived competition by conquering in the field of intelligence and economy. I am for big business, and I am against trusts."[35]

The trick then, was to regulate competition in the marketplace. In Minneapolis, Minnesota, he made the process seem simple: "Everybody who has even read newspapers knows the means by which these men built up their power and created these monopolies. Any decently equipped lawyer can suggest to you statutes by which the whole business can be stopped, and after you have stopped the business you won't have to regulate it."[36]

Wilson carried his analysis one step further. He attacked Roosevelt's central notion that a commission of experts could regulate large corporations in the public interest: trusts would learn how to dominate the regulators, he said, just as they were, even then, dominating the Republican Party.[37]

Moving about the Midwest, Wilson pushed these issues vigorously, his restrained, conversational style winning him a hearing. In Sioux Falls, South Dakota, Bull Moose country where he met occasional moose "moos" and numerous Bull Moose banners, he won a special cheer for ruling Taft out of the race. Wilson was undoing Roosevelt's image of the prim schoolmaster. He felt his effectiveness with crowds, even telling his aides to wake him if crowds gathered.

WEST FINDS WILSON
IN TOUCH WITH LIFE

the *Times* reported.[38]

Seeing indications that Taft was no longer in the race, Wilson avoided criticizing him. At the parade grounds in Minneapolis, he paid an only slightly barbed "tribute of personal respect" to the President: "I do not believe that any man in the United States who knows the facts can question the patriotism, or the integrity, or the public purpose of the man who now presides at the Executive Office in Washington. If he has got into bad company, that is no fault of his, because he didn't choose the company; it was made beforehand. And if he has taken their advice, it was because they were nearest to him and he didn't hear anybody else."[39] A small bouquet for Taft. A prickly bramble for his predecessor.

Out in the West, Roosevelt was listening. Annoyed at Wilson's hint that the Progressive platform had been written by trust magnates like George Perkins, the Colonel insisted that the very same principles had shown up in his presidential messages. Odd, mused Wilson for his clutch of reporters, those were the very years when trusts had grown so abundantly. From San Francisco, Roosevelt demanded to know if Wilson was prepared to demolish the Interstate Commerce Commission, so fearful was he of governmental supervision. Roosevelt's industrial commission was simply an adaptation of the idea of the ICC, the Colonel said. In Columbus, Wilson replied: anyone who knew "the rudiments of our economic conditions" would not have raised the issue. The railroads of the nation were "of necessity a single unit," every one interlaced with all the others.[40]

By Columbus, on the trip back east, Wilson had his running legs. Arriving in the city at 8 AM, he slept until ten, then started on a round of five speeches and a parade. He shared the podium with Governor Harmon, with the prospective governor, James M. Cox, and with all the state Democratic candidates. He assured them that it was the first time he had seen a political organization in full panoply.[41] At the Chamber of Commerce building, he dipped into old memories to assure public school teachers that "after dealing with some college politicians, the men I am dealing with now seem like amateurs." He did not miss the old times at Princeton: "My own belief is that the side shows in college are swallowing up the circus."[42] Everywhere he went in Ohio, he heard extravagant claims of victory—in Taft's home state particularly, and in the nation generally. The *Times* reporter stepped aside from his reporting long enough to note that if Wilson returned to Sea Girt entirely overconfident, the steady diet of predictions was to blame; Wilson might even reach the conclusion that hard campaigning was a waste of time.[43]

The euphoria in Ohio ended abruptly because of the senatorial campaign back in New Jersey. Wilson attached his car to the fastest train he could find, touched base briefly at Sea Girt to greet his family and to receive a briefing from Joseph Tumulty, then went off to Jersey City to speak for Judge William Hughes of Paterson, the surviving reformist candidate who was standing up to Smith. Reporting on the enthusiasm for Democratic principles in the Midwest, he warned his audience in St. Mary's Hall that "Now there is no section of the Democracy in the Union that is more closely watched than that section that resides in New Jersey" (New Yorkers had to live with their demotion). A vote for Smith in the primary was a vote "to put the Democratic party out of business." He went on: "There are men connected with big business in this country who believe that big business is the necessary providence to take care of. And we know it is that kind of providence which God in his wisdom will sooner or later crown with a destroying disapproval. For there is a God in the heavens. There is justice in the souls of men. They are not going to be cheated. They are looking to us. Shall we cheat them? Is it possible that we should disappoint their confident hope?"[44] He offered Smith to Roosevelt and read him out of the party.

Satisfied, even confident, Wilson returned to Sea Girt for the sabbath, church in the morning and a long auto ride with Malone in the afternoon. The western trip had gone well, his strained voice a small price to pay for the routine of acclamation. New Jersey would shake down reasonably—Judge Hughes was a strong candidate. Six weeks until the election, and all the omens were favorable.

A new Wilson, breezy and jovial, made his second trip into Pennsylvania the next day. As he turned from side to side to address various parts of the crowd in Stroudsburg, he quipped: "I can't fire off on the swivel-gun principle." He wrung a few chuckles out of his appearance: "You know I'm not beautiful, and I don't know which side I'm best looking on." He even acquired some stock political blarney. When Palmer made his way up to the platform, Wilson greeted him warmly, then turned to the crowd: "I want to tell you people confidentially that I don't see how your district could have a better representative in Congress than Palmer. And for that matter I don't think any Congressional district in the United States has a better one"—an eminence that few others had detected. Wilson learned how to use his props. When a brakeman took the rear light off the train, Wilson noted: "You see, they realize there is no danger of a rear-end collision. Nobody else is running in our class." He backed off from diffidence: "I want a chance to fight for the liberation of America," adding with a snap of his jaw, "I know how to do it." The Pennsylvania party leaders were astonished at the performance, so much more confident than three weeks previously. As Wilson spoke, the crowds responded with "Hip, hip, hooray" and "Woody."[45]

Returning to Princeton for primary day, Wilson cast his vote for Hughes (who won handily) and greeted Princeton students who staged a P-rade ("the greatest of all college freaks," the *Times* said[46]) in his honor. He urged them to study up on currency reform, a bit of counsel as urgent for the candidate as for the undergraduates.

Then he went off to New York. McCombs needed stroking. Colonel Edward M. House had some ideas on how best to handle the tricky New York situation. Wilson's train arrived at Penn Station twelve minutes before Taft came in from another direction. "Well, isn't that enough?" Wilson asked his companions for the press to hear. "I don't care how far ahead we are just so we keep ahead."[47]

In the New York gubernatorial race, the stalemate continued. "The New York situation is acute," Colonel House wrote in his diary, "My idea is to have them decide upon some unobjectionable Tammany man for Governor of New York who would not bring discredit upon the party."[48] He drove Wilson up to Larchmont for a session with the ailing McCombs, and the three decided upon two possible compromise names. Murphy, meanwhile, continued to hang tough. For his part, Wilson held to his earlier decision: no overt moves that might cost him New York's forty-five electoral votes.

Wilson moved on to New England and to some fine tuning of his position on major issues. Opening the Connecticut state campaign in New Haven, he again responded to Roosevelt's taunts. Roosevelt had been ridiculing Wilson's definition of liberty as the limitation of governmental power. No statement had given Roosevelt more fuel, for it dated Wilson with Thomas Jefferson, belied the Democratic platform, and confined Wilson in the professorial closet. Roosevelt backed Wilson into a corner: If Wilson was afraid of special commissions, he was left to the unwieldy judicial process—slow, expensive, only marginally successful. If he favored special courts and commissions, he was capitulating to Roosevelt's ideas. Wilson had nailed restored competition to his mast: "the right use of competition will destroy monopoly."[49] But how was competition to be regulated effectively?

In New Haven, Wilson groped for new ground:[50]

The Democratic party does not stand for the limitation of the powers of government, either in the field of the state or in the field of the federal government. There is not a Democrat that I know who is afraid to have the powers of the government exercised to the utmost, but there are a great many of us who are afraid to see them exercised at the discretion of individuals. There are a great many of us who still adhere to that ancient principle that we prefer to be governed by the power of laws and not by the power of men. Therefore, we favor as much power as you choose, but power guided by knowledge, power extended in detail. Not power given out in the lump in a commission set up, as is proposed by the third party, unencumbered by the restrictions of law to set up a constructive regulation, as their platform calls it, of the trusts and monopolies, but a law which takes its searchlight and casts its illuminating rays down the secret corridors of all the processes by which monopoly has been established, and polices its corridors so that highway robbery is no longer committed on it, so that men are no longer waylaid upon it, so that the liberty of individuals to compete is no longer checked by the power of combinations stronger than any possible individual can be. We want to see the law administered; we are not afraid of com-missions. . . . Therefore, I am ready to admit that we may have to have special tribunals, special processes, and I am not afraid, for my part, of the creation of special processes and special tribunals. But I am absolutely opposed to leaving it to the choice of those tribunals what the processes of law shall be and the means to remedy.

Clearly, this statement was successful only in muddying the waters that Wilson's earlier statements had made too clear. Two days after New Haven, Wilson telegraphed Brandeis for help: "Please set forth as explicitly as possible the actual measures by which competition can be effectively regulated. The more explicit we are on this point, the more completely will the enemy guns be spiked."[51] Brandeis replied the next day with an extended set of notes; two days later he followed up with more detailed comments. Asked for a glass of water, Brandeis replied by turning on a hose. It was more than Wilson could absorb. Within the week he thanked Brandeis and told him to use the material himself.[52] Brandeis did so, framing his material into articles and editorials for *Collier's Weekly* that got the editor fired by the pro-Roosevelt publisher.[53]

At conservative Hartford, Wilson ran through the whole litany of issues with ease born of his recent trip—direct election of senators, removal of corrupt judges, bosses, tariff, trusts—before ending with an extempore par-agraph that may well have been his most effective statement thus far:[54]

The thought I wanted to leave with you is this: Here is the choice you have to make. The Democrats are proposing to intervene and, by lowering those duties which have protected special privilege, expose special privilege to a very wholesome, chastening kind of competition, and then to adopt a process of legislation by which competition will be so regulated that big business can't crush out little business, and that little business can grow instead of being built by private understanding into big business, and put every man who is manufacturing or engaged in commerce in this country on his mettle to beat, not the capital, but the brains of his competitors. Whereas, on the other hand, the leaders of the third party are proposing to you—I would say parenthetically that the leaders of the regular Republican party aren't proposing anything—but the leaders of the third party are proposing that you accept the established monopolies as inevitable, their control as permanent, and undertake to regulate them through a commission which will not itself be too carefully restricted by law, but will have the right to make rules by which they will accomplish what the platform calls constructive regulations. In short, it proposes to leave the government in the hands and under the influences which now control it and which, so long as they can control it, make it absolutely impossible that we should have a free instrument by which to restore the rule and the government of the people themselves.

Wilson proceeded to Boston and Fall River, Massachusetts. In Boston he called on President Taft at the Copley Plaza, a visit proper, informal, inconsequential. Had campaigning worn Governor Wilson out? Nearly. And is the presidential voice holding up? Oh, yes. And the gubernatorial voice? A bit husky now and then. Well, Roosevelt, Bryan, and I can sympathize with you.[55] End of historical moment, Wilson honoring the dignity of the presidential office that would soon be his, Taft treating Wilson with the respect to which his rank would soon entitle him.

Taft's prospects—and Wilson's—made politeness come easily. "I yield to no man in personal admiration of our present distinguished President," Wilson had said in Yale's New Haven.[56] La Follette, not quite an overt supporter but publicly hostile to both Roosevelt and Taft, deserved at least equal acclaim: "that sturdy little giant in Wisconsin, who is now such an indomitable, unconquerable champion of progressive ideas all along the line."[57] On the other hand, "Does anybody think it would be wise to have so extremely active a gentleman, so extremely aggressive and versatile a gentleman as is now leading the third party, put alone in Washington, an understudy to Providence?"[58]

Returning home through New York to speak at a testimonial dinner for McCombs, Wilson had a moment of terror. He heard that Elihu Root, now Republican senator from New York, had recently told a dinner companion that he understood that a judge in Pittsfield, Massachusetts, had or had seen a letter, perhaps from Wilson, that implicated Wilson in an action for divorce. Wilson's mind raced instantly to Mrs. Hulbert, the former Mrs. Peck, to see if she could cast any light on this potential catastrophe: "The mere breath of such a thing would, of course, put an end to my candidacy and to my career. It is too deep an iniquity for words."[59] Fortunately, the fears soon dissolved into gossip and hearsay, and nothing, not even gossip and hearsay, surfaced publicly.

The dinner for McCombs gave a chance to review the situation in New York. Wilson found his advisers still at odds with each other. McAdoo wanted Wilson to speak out openly against Dix and Murphy. McCombs and House urged caution: a statement, but no names. Caution won. From Sea Girt, Wilson issued a warning: the choice in New York must be "free and unbossed," as free and unbossed as the recent conventions of New York's Republican and Progressive Parties.[60]

When the convention met in Syracuse October 1, Murphy gave the convention its head and allowed it to nominate Congressman William Sulzer, a Tammany stalwart, for governor. Off again on the stump in Indiana, Wilson telegraphed his congratulations to Sulzer: "I am gratified by the action of the convention."[61] Later, when the New York *Evening Post* declined to back Sulzer because of his Tammany connections, Wilson snapped testily: "There's no use in being so damned ladylike."[62]

Back in Syracuse on the floor of the convention, Boss Murphy had just smiled.[63]

10

The Roosevelt Crusade

Theodore Roosevelt's posture differed strikingly from Woodrow Wilson's. Roosevelt did not have to identify himself to the voters, as Wilson did; he was probably the best known person, certainly the best known politician, in America. He ranked as First Citizen, not as President Roosevelt—that modern styling of ex-presidents came in with Harry S. Truman—but as Colonel Roosevelt, who had indeed been president. Furthermore, his reputation built on solid political experience, political in the cramped sense of party maneuver, political also in the ageless tradition of dealing with great issues of state, foreign and domestic. And finally, the message of the Progressive Party and the messenger were one; indeed, the identity between platform and candidate was so total that Roosevelt would have to batter down constantly the taunt that the Progressive Party had no reality beyond the ambitions of its standard-bearer. But Roosevelt enjoyed the advantage of that disadvantage: he could never be sideswiped, as Wilson could, by a demand that he square his public stance with the proclaimed goals of his party.

Yet reputation plus experience plus rapport with his party did not add up to bright prospects for victory. Roosevelt knew that. As he told a trusted friend in Great Britain, "We have almost all the money, almost all the trained political ability, and the great majority of the newspapers against us."[1] Money was not the problem; the Roosevelt campaign never faltered seriously for want of funds. The problem was more elemental. Even with the greatest political asset in the United States, Roosevelt himself, the Bull Moose could not put Progressive machinery in place in time for it to function effectively in forty-eight separate jurisdictions. A representative sample of Progressive leaders was, as a group, urban, white, upper middle class, native-born, Protestant, Republican males, frequently businessmen, lawyers, editors, and other professionals. With few exceptions, they worked for themselves rather than inside large institutions. They were uncomfortable with the conservatism of the dominant element in their party, but lacking, almost totally lacking, experience in national politics, they lacked the skill to help Roosevelt mount a national campaign.[2]

If in January Roosevelt could have foreseen the parade of events, perhaps he would have held off. But once committed, he had to play out his hand until the end.

He approached the campaign in good spirits:[3]

I am perfectly happy, for I have never in my life been in a movement into which I could enter as heartily as into this; and although I expect to lose I believe that we are founding what really is a new movement, and that we may be able to give the right trend to our democracy, a trend which will take it away from mere shortsighted greedy materialism. Our platform really does represent a pretty good mixture of idealism, of resolute purpose and of good plain common sense. My colleague, Hiram Johnson, is a trump, and the men I am with on an average represent a far higher moral type than the party leaders whom I have seen at the head of affairs during my lifetime.

Roosevelt called for a "sizzling" campaign, promptly heeding his own call by a tour through Rhode Island, Massachusetts, and Vermont. In Providence, he talked about the tariff on wool, and on the Boston Common he delighted a crowd of twenty thousand people by disarming hecklers who taunted him about Pennsylvania leader William Flinn. Toward the end of the month, he drove all over Vermont receiving the melancholy impression that his personal popularity did not rub off on other Progressive candidates. In reply to charges that some Republicans hoped would derail his campaign, he prepared a fully documented denial that his campaign committee in 1904 had exacted corporate contributions in exchange for the promise of future favors. He set up his staff in New York with George Perkins as head of the executive committee; Perkins' organizing skills and diligent commitment more than compensated for the snarling, though submerged, opposition he aroused within the party.

By the end of August, Roosevelt's blood was pumping faster. He had a message to deliver, and he was determined that every part of America would hear it.

Rising at 4:30 AM September 1, Roosevelt motored in from Oyster Bay to Grand Central Station to catch the 8:03 train north and east. His entourage was there ready: a press car, eight or so reporters from the *New York Times* and the press associations; and his own party—George Emlen Roosevelt, the Colonel's young cousin, in charge of "arrangements"; Colonel Cecil A. Lyon of Texas, security; Dr. Scurry L. Terrell, the physician from Colonel Lyon's regiment whose main responsibility was the candidate's voice and throat; and two stenographers. Through Stamford, Bridgeport, dour New Haven, and Hartford, Connecticut, on to Springfield, Massachusetts, before heading west in a dash to the Missouri Progressive state convention in St. Louis. In Terre Haute, Indiana, Eugene V. Debs's home town, the campaign managers hired a special train because the through express would not stop often enough for the Colonel to reach people in small towns. From St. Louis he moved north-west to Des Moines, Iowa, then directly north to Minneapolis and St. Paul, Minnesota, before turning west to Fargo, South Dakota. From there, the two cars—the Mayflower for the Colonel's party and the Sunbeam for the press—continued nonstop through Montana except for a major call at Helena; then on to Spokane in the state of Washington. Gone now a week from New York, Roosevelt had already covered more miles than Woodrow Wilson would in his first major trip. In a single overnight run from Fargo to Helena, Roosevelt covered about as many miles as President Taft would devote to his whole campaign. Only Debs had comparable energy, and though Debs was going everywhere, he was not going anywhere.

The pace held: after Spokane, the Washington state Progressive convention in Seattle and a stop at Tacoma; south to Portland, Oregon, then a dart across the whole state of Oregon to put a foot in Idaho long enough to try to needle Senator William E. Borah into overt support; south to touch base in north-western Utah, Taft country courtesy of Senator Reed Smoot and the Mormon Church, then west without a stop in Nevada, William Jennings Bryan silver country and only three electoral votes anyway, prior to a climactic arrival in San Francisco, California, the home state of Governor Johnson, the Bull Moose vice-presidential nominee, and a hotbed of progressivism. At San Francisco, Roosevelt scheduled a major address, the most important since his "Confession of Faith," and his first day of rest: church with Hiram Johnson, Jr., dinner with Gifford Pinchot. Before midnight, he was on his way down the coast to San Diego, then out into the barren lands: Albuquerque, New Mexico, and Tucson, Arizona. Now sixteen days out from his home base, he was bringing presidential politics to areas admitted to the Union just in time to vote in this election. The train moved almost straight north to Denver, Colorado, before turning east into the den of the Great Commoner for a brisk appear-ance at Omaha, Nebraska, and a relaxed weekend, church and palaver, with William Allen White in Topeka, Kansas, and a brief run into Champ Clark's Missouri. Then the brisk pace resumed. Roosevelt took a sharp turn southwest to address a gathering at Oklahoma City, where 20,000 people gathered to yell for the Colonel in a city that twenty years before had been an open waste.

Ebullient and determined, Roosevelt moved on to the South. There he stayed for about a week, preaching a new party alignment to white South-erners who abided with the Democratic Party even when they could not abide its candidates. A quick appearance in southwestern Tennessee was followed by a plunge to New Orleans, cordial beyond belief, then across the southern tier of states to Atlanta, hostile beyond expectation.

Then he was on the road home, an appointment with the congressional committee to investigate campaign financing (the Clapp committee) putting a terminal point to his barnstorming. A stop at Knoxville in eastern Tennessee was followed by a trip to Raleigh, North Carolina, and then, a month to the day after his departure, back to Pennsylvania Station in New York and a warm welcome from the local and national Progressive leaders.

The Colonel had traveled nine thousand miles—or ten, or eleven; the press's account grew as the trip matured—in a great circle around the United States, into some areas that had never seen a presidential candidate, much less felt that they knew one, through some areas that no Republican (or Republican labeled Progressive) could expect to win, among people for whom Washington, D.C., was as remote as the Lesser Antilles.

If Roosevelt could have collected the electoral votes of every state in which he had made a major presentation, he would have amassed 199 electoral votes. But subtract from that number the 67 votes of the Solid South, as dependable for conservative Alton B. Parker (except Oklahoma, which entered the Union in 1907) as for radical Bryan. So the trip seems rash, if not whimsical. Four and a half weeks vanished from a nine-week campaign. Roosevelt's managers in New York had told him not to make the trip; the big electoral votes were in the East and the upper Midwest, not on the Great Plains and in the raw Southwest and in the South. What does it profit a man to gain the whole electoral world of Arizona, California, Colorado, Oregon, South Dakota, Washington, Wisconsin, Wyoming (121 votes) if he suffer the loss of New York, Pennsylvania, and Illinois (112 votes)? The whole vote west of the Mississippi and north of Oklahoma (141 votes) could no more than match the 140 votes in the South that the Democrats took as a given—Wilson would not even campaign in those southern states. The industrial Northeast and the upper Middle West had the paydirt. Governor Johnson could take care of California; he might even pick up miscellaneous areas in the neighborhood. The Colonel was needed elsewhere.

So why the pilgrimage into the barrens?

Roosevelt gave his own answer to an appreciative crowd in Pocatello, Idaho. Yes, his manager had told him not to go west, he said. But two obligations pushed him: First, he owed much of his strength and character to the West, so the West deserved his attention as a presidential candidate. Second, the West had created progressivism and a Bull Mooser carrying the Progressive banner needed both to acknowledge that debt and to draw inspiration from the fount of good things. As the temporary voice for that reformist spirit, he belonged among his fellows, helping the West to keep its leadership in tripping up the bosses and in resisting the interests.[4]

Other impulses were at work as well, some that the Colonel would not avow in public and some that he could scarcely have acknowledged in private. He knew that he was running to lose. "My judgment is that Wilson will win, and that I will do better than Taft," he had told his friend abroad in strict confidence in August.[5] While Roosevelt was in Nebraska, some of his letters to friends in London leaked, revealing his expectation of defeat and recalling his son Kermit's remark that Daddy was praying for Champ Clark at the Baltimore convention.[6] Since Roosevelt could not win anyway, what was wrong with waging a campaign that he enjoyed rather than a campaign geared to the nice calculus of electoral returns?

The decision to run once made, a tame campaign was out of the question. The same restiveness that barely kept decision at bay through late 1911 now fueled a dramatic performance by the political stylist of his age. Roosevelt loved every minute of politics—the convolutions as well as the great decisive moments. The same Roosevelt that could say of the Spanish-American War— and say it on this trip—that "It was only a little war, but it was all the war there was"[7] that could say of the Panama Canal—and say it on this trip—that he had let Congress have its debate while the people, under his initiative, got their canal,[8] this Roosevelt was not going to relax at Sagamore Hill or emit editorial thunderbolts from the *Outlook* office when his nomination gave him a license to barnstorm the country, educating it to new thought and receiving in return the adulation that was his due. It was a question of doing what he did well: campaigning, being seen and heard, responding to the people in measure equal to their response to him.

And respond they did, each to the other. Midway through the trip, Charles Willis Thompson, the *New York Times'* reporter assigned to Roosevelt's train— a capable political observer with a good eye for detail and no discernible ax to grind—ran out of superlatives to describe the enthusiasm that Roosevelt evoked. In New Haven, the "dead town" added at the last minute, thousands gathered around, battled to shake hands, ran after the departing train. In St. Louis, the audience at the Missouri Progressive state convention was ebullient, giving off shrieks of approbation; even at the City Club, businessmen and professional men were respectful and attentive. Roosevelt knew how to play an audience: quiet and thoughtful for the City Club, boisterous and dramatic at the State Fair Grounds halfway between Minneapolis and St. Paul, where he spoke to a crowd of 25,000 by quadrants, moving from left to right, from front to back. When the left side protested his move to the right, he replied with a jovial "Square deal." Then to the right side: "Your five minutes are up"; smiling significantly, he added, "I'm coming back." The crowd roared with approval as it caught his double meaning. He moved center stage with the comment to right and left: "The center complains that I have been playing both ends against the middle." An old man fainted with excitement. Roosevelt pulled him up on the platform, turned him over to Dr. Terrell, went on with his speech. One overwrought admirer touched the Colonel's foot; "He had touched the hem of the garment of Moses," the astonished Thompson reported.[9] (The incident, the *New York Times* snorted on its editorial page, "typifies the unreasoning affection these people have come to bear for an audacious, emotional, self-contradictory, scarcely scrupulous but forcible and picturesque leader."[10]) Roosevelt was seen, and in part heard, by 100,000 to 150,000 people that day. At the Iowa state convention in Des Moines and in

Ottumwa, the audiences "went wild"; in Oskaloosa, with a population of 10,000, 10,000 turned out to listen to him lambasting the bosses.

In North Dakota, Robert M. La Follette territory, he became sober and grave in arguing for a Progressive victory without mentioning La Follette's name— in a no-win situation, he determined at least not to lose badly. But in Helena, he was a new man. Many of his old ranching buddies showed up, having moved to a newer West when the Dakotas became too crowded. Here he chatted, joked, exchanged anecdotes with language that made him one of them. He was "a middling old settler . . . just at the end of the buffalo days" and he had been "on the hurricane deck of a bronco" himself. He thought it would be "a good thing to have a President who knows an irrigation ditch from a dry farm, and who has seen alfalfa. I was always in the short grass country, and I worked among the cows."[11] "Short grass country" became a code word for his close ties to the West—would Wilson know the difference between short grass and alfalfa? In Spokane he took on two audiences of women and, after initial uneasiness, he found his voice as a "natural democrat" who wanted equality for all. (He fared less well with girls in Harvard, Nebraska. Befuddled by their age and sex, he gave them the same advice that he gave to boys: "Don't flinch, don't squeal, and hit the line hard.")[12]

By the time Roosevelt reached Los Angeles, Thompson topped his prior reports: "Wildest greetings . . . on this trip."[13] Three cars full of armed plainclothesmen guarded the Colonel's car, for the International Workers of the World, the "Wobblies," had threatened violence. Roosevelt, taking no notice of the threat, gave his planned talk, defending his break with the Republicans with the analogy of Abraham Lincoln's break with the Whigs. In Laguna, New Mexico, he lectured Indians on sign language. In Gallup, he recalled that half his regiment had come from New Mexico, as many as forty from Gallup itself. Then he arrived at "Roosevelt crazy" Oklahoma, where the crowd tore his suit and demolished his hat. Second only to Los Angeles in the level of enthusiasm, Thompson reported.

Roosevelt paced his style to the occasion. When he wanted to make substantive points, he waited for a set moment. In San Francisco he leveled a full attack on Wilson's fear of active government. In New Orleans he outlined a strategy for breaking the Solid South, his listeners absorbed as he spoke and cheering wildly when he finished. Even on the rare occasion when he created adverse tumult, he stayed in control. His Atlanta audience, annoyed at his putting Wilson into the Ananias Club—an assembly of liars—created an uproar that almost ended the speech. So Roosevelt jumped up on a table to continue; by the time the audience recovered from its astonishment, he had finished. With remarks from the rear platform of his train, he created the illusion that he was about to make a full speech, then he slid off into banter and conversation, finally waving his hat with a cheery "Goodbye and good luck" as the train pulled out. The Memphis *Commercial Appeal* spotted the secret of his success with crowds there: He spoke off-the-cuff, not saying much; in fact, nobody could remember what he said. Yet, when he finished, he left the impression that he was personally acquainted with every person in the crowd.

The Colonel had recently been on the stump in the primary campaign. He knew what to expect and, more important, he knew how substantial numbers of people would respond. He loved the throb of their adulation, his delight driving his voice up into a high falsetto that, in turn, fueled their enthusiasm. Roosevelt, like Bryan, played an audience, his alertness to his listeners as taut as their attention to him. Not many people avoid the adulation they know they deserve.

Furthermore, he had products of substance to sell: himself and his program. He was not simply a platform actor for whom attention was food and drink and applause was blissful music. He was a world leader, known abroad and knowledgeable about other continents. He knew enough to argue plausibly that Germany's high tariff underwrote its developing industrial growth while Britain frittered away its prosperity under an illusion of free trade. He knew enough of Denmark's social legislation to borrow from it for his own program. He wrote foreign policy into his platform, parochial, petty, jingoistic planks perhaps, but drawing on a knowledgeable view of what was at stake. He had changed the posture of America both here and abroad, not so much as he himself thought, but still in far-reaching, substantial, and, of course, controversial ways. In his years at the White House, as he saw them, he had set a movement on its way, only to see clumsy hands retard, if not reverse, the motion. Taft had let the banner fall. Wilson had no idea of how to pick it up. The process needed fresh thrust. Hiram Johnson sensed the mood: "half religious, half militant, wholly patriotic."[14] Roosevelt was Moses to lead the the way; he was, as his friend, the novelist Owen Wister, recalled in later years, the "preacher militant perpetual."[15]

Roosevelt's program, put forth as he circled the nation, had three parts for the nation, a fourth part specifically for the South. To the South he said: You need a real second party in order to protect your interests. The national Democratic Party, by opposing the development of the Panama Canal and the dredging of the Mississippi River and by lowering duties on sugar, directly affronts southern economic interests. The Republican Party in the South offers no alternative; it is a collection of political nonentities who hang around political clubs long enough to earn rewards from national Republican administrations. Tradition-bound and shackled by prejudice, the South cannot protect its economic interests. The Colonel never mentions blacks; his hearers understand his coded allusions. Now the South has its chance: The Progressive Party, ready to recognize existing custom in the South (read: keep blacks in their place) and to accommodate southern economic interests in the early twentieth century, offers a third way. His audience was attentive, roaring its approbation as he explored their "ancestral and traditionary opinions," then listening in thoughtful silence as he weaved his way through new ideas. "One of the most effective speeches he ever made," Thompson reported.[16]

Still, Roosevelt was working tricky ground, for his own record as president, both in appointments and in using Southern Republican delegations to maneuver the nominations in both 1904 and 1908, left him vulnerable.

When he got to Atlanta, where he made an ill-timed remark about Wilson's veracity, the Atlanta *Journal* pounced: "the eyes of this section have pierced your missionary makeup," the *Journal* said, and they see the "political adventurer you are." Roosevelt had belittled southern leaders and straddled the racial issue. "By turns you wear the lion's and the ass's skin." Roosevelt spoke of industrial justice, then urged a legalized monopoly; denounced bosses, then took them to his bosom; preached pure politics with "his own hands dripping with campaign fat from the interests." The loyal Democratic *Journal* did all the party could have hoped for, finishing off its attack with a final zinger: "In truth, you stand at Armageddon and you battle for the trusts."[17]

In truth, Roosevelt battled for a new political structure for America. With the racial issue isolated by way of the Progressive formula—inclusion in the North, exclusion in the South—he hoped to bring the South into the electoral competition, making the New South part of a new national coalition under the Progressive banner.

But there were flaws. The Republican Party could not be buried before it died, and Roosevelt's own prior record on racial and sectional issues was too extensive and too equivocal. When Herbert Hoover and Dwight D. Eisenhower finally broke the Solid South, they came with shorter and less discreditable records and with less battered hands.

Addressing the nation as a whole, Roosevelt focused on a central message, the need to regulate large industrial corporations through a national industrial commission modeled on the Interstate Commerce Commission. Roosevelt rejected the premise of the Sherman Antitrust Act, that combinations in restraint of trade were invariably undesirable. He regarded enforcement under the Sherman Act as capricious, ineffective, and destructive of the best economic interests of the nation. Size brought gains. If great size also brought problems, such as inadequate sharing of the prizes of bigness with industrial workers and with consumers, then a responsible national board could regulate corporate conduct, forcing managers to respond to workers and consumers.

The idea of a national industrial commission rejected three alternatives. The first would leave the corporation unregulated under principles of laissez-faire or in the name of property rights supposedly safeguarded by the Constitution. No one running for national office in 1912 could have gotten beyond the corner saloon by espousing entirely unregulated industry. The second would enforce existing law—the Sherman Act—in the face of all the ambiguities created by the Supreme Court about "reasonable" and "unreasonable" restraint of trade. Enforcing existing law satisfied President Taft. The third would restore competition to the market place by breaking up large firms that drove their competitors out by fair means and foul. Restoring competition was a principal theme for Governor Wilson.

Roosevelt argued across the nation that Taft's program had failed and that Wilson's alternative showed no insight. Taft's antitrust program, which in fact was the former Roosevelt antitrust program more vigorously pursued, hit malefactors and good businessmen alike, he insisted, and in any case trusts emerged essentially unscathed from their encounters with the courts. Restoring competition, Wilson's proposal, was to look back longingly to a world that had disappeared and that held no promise for the modern world where America had to compete with Germany and Great Britain, both too sophisticated to reject large corporations, the natural form of twentieth-century industry. The prizes of bigness were great. Why destroy them instead of sharing them? Why especially when an industrial commission, expert and politically responsible, could mitigate the evils while retaining the gains? As for the beauties of competition, Roosevelt used his stop at Pueblo to rebut Wilson's speech the previous day in St. Paul. Wilson had said that competition, not regulation, was the way to control trusts and that labor would suffer if government controlled corporations. Take a look at a local specimen, Roosevelt retorted: the Colorado Fuel and Iron Company. A competitor of the Steel Trust, it had recently been cited in a survey as having the worst working conditions of any plant in the country. Government regulation would retard monopoly; it would also mandate working conditions, minimum wages for women, for example.[18]

Roosevelt was recognizing the need to battle Wilson toe to toe; only by close engagement could the Colonel's superior experience and popularity score. His staff had prepared remarkably full files on Wilson's prior public statements, and they followed Wilson's current speeches closely in the newspapers, using telegraph lines even at remote whistle stops to keep their candidate up to date.[19]

The wires reported that Wilson was steadily attacking Roosevelt's formula for regulation of industry as a way of legalizing monopoly and of confirming the alliance of government and business. When Wilson went on to recall that "The history of liberty is a history of the limitation of governmental power, not the increase of it,"[20] Roosevelt used his appearance at the San Francisco Coliseum to retort. Plucking a favorite string—Wilson the cloistered professor out of touch with the real world—Roosevelt mocked this "bit of outworn academic doctrine" that survived in the professorial study for a generation after it had been abandoned by all who had experience of actual life. It was simply the laissez-faire doctrine of English political economists seventy-five years back. It applied to primitive conditions, maybe to the United States in the 1700s, before the days of Fulton, Morse, and Edison. "To apply it now in the United States at the beginning of the twentieth century, with its highly organized industries, with its railways, telegraphs, and telephones, means literally and absolutely to refuse to make a single effort to better any one of our social and industrial conditions." What was more, Wilson's knowledge of history was no good. Limitation of governmental power was a blow for liberty when kings possessed power exclusively. "But now the governmental power rests in the people, and the kings who enjoy privilege are the kings of the financial and industrial world; and what they clamor for is the limitation of governmental power, and what the people sorely need is the extension of governmental power."

Roosevelt wanted the issue clear between himself and Wilson:[21]

He is against using the power of the government to help the people to whom the government belongs.

We take flat issue with him. We propose to use the government as the most efficient instrument for the uplift of our people as a whole; we propose to give a fair chance to the workers and strengthen their rights. We propose to use the whole power of the government to protect those who, under Mr. Wilson's *laissez-faire* system, are trodden down in the ferocious, scrambling rush of an unregulated and purely individualistic industrialism.

Roosevelt's second major national issue, popular rule, lent itself to the kind of platform rhetoric that came so easily to him. Victor in the primaries, he respected the will of the people who had chosen so wisely, and he urged responsiveness to their voices through primaries everywhere, through the progressive trinity of initiative, referendum, and recall, through the direct election of senators, through popular recall of unpopular judicial decisions. Restoring popular rule would pinion the political bosses and would destroy forever the unholy alliance of bosses and special interests that dominated the two old parties.

As a starter, the theft in Chicago gave Roosevelt an apt illustration of machine rule. Roosevelt had a deft way of skirting a direct insult to Taft—it was risky to insult a sitting president—while making strong accusations. At Joplin, Missouri, he noted the yellow banners proclaiming Taft's candidacy: very appropriate, for "There never was a more yellow performance than that which gave Mr. Taft his renomination. Any man who supports that performance has a yellow streak in him."[22] At Pocatello, he argued that stealing a nomination was no better than and not much different from stealing a purse. As he made this argument, a pickpocket conveniently plied his trade; he was arrested on the spot.[23] Then at Boise, where Roosevelt was trying to lure or to squeeze play Senator Borah, who was right there on the platform visibly squirming, into an open endorsement of the Progressive ticket, Roosevelt intoned: "Any man who is acquainted with the facts [of the Chicago convention] and does not condemn them is blinded to the light and has a seared moral sense."[24]

Wilson did not fare much better. Privately Roosevelt might concede that

Wilson was "an able man and would make a creditable President."[25] But on the stump the Colonel portrayed the governor as amiable, sincere, and wise but inexperienced and remote from life as most men lived it. In Topeka, Roosevelt thought back to President James Buchanan. Buchanan believed that he ought to protect the Union, but could find no way; that secession was unconstitutional, but so were all the methods for putting it down. "Mr. Wilson says it is good to have fine purpose for helping labor and regulating the trusts, but he is against every practical expedient toward that end. Mr. Wilson is the Buchanan of the present industrial situation in the United States."[26] Roosevelt picked up Wilson's cautious remark in his acceptance speech, that the Democratic platform was not a program, and snapped a retort in Seattle: "If it is not a programme, it is a lying promise."[27] Even at the beginning of the tour, Roosevelt was taunting Wilson about the Democratic platform he was so reluctant to stand on: "I suppose there are intervals at which one leg is on it."[28] Wilson was posing as a progressive, Roosevelt said, but his platform was standpat or reactionary. His nomination was suspect. It occurred when the bosses at Baltimore realized that "his victory meant their victory." In Des Moines, Roosevelt recalled phrasing from "Confession of Faith" to tie Taft and Wilson in a bundle of bossism: "Nothing is gained by changing the whip of Barnes, Penrose, and Guggenheim for the scorpion of Murphy, Sullivan, and Taggart. All bosses look alike to us."[29]

All except, perhaps, William Flinn of Pennsylvania. In Tucson, a Democrat asked Roosevelt about Boss Flinn. Roosevelt replied with a tale calculated to bring a tear to gentle Progressive eyes:[30]

Flinn is as stout a champion of popular liberties as exists.... Flinn came to me last March, and I had never known him. He told me that he was going to support me because he believed that this country would not be a good place for his children to live in unless such social and economic justice was done as to make it a good place for other people's children to live in. [storm of delighted yells]... He told me that a long experience had taught him—and he said he had needed to learn it but that he had learned it—that the safety of our Government lay in making the people the real, and not the nominal, rulers of their governmental agencies. He fought squarely on that issue and carried Pennsylvania, and under his lead Pennsylvania adopted as progressive a platform as Arizona itself, a platform declaring in the most unequivocal terms for direct primaries, the initiative and referendum for every progressive measure.

Similarly, from Pueblo, Bryan taunted Roosevelt about Perkins' connection with the Progressive Party. Roosevelt gave a well-worn reply: Perkins wanted this country to be good for his child to live in; it could not be unless it was good for other people's children to live in as well.[31]

This impressive Progressive unanimity left unexplained the motives of childless Progressives. Still, Perkins' child could join Flinn's children in rejoicing at the brave new world being created for everyone's children. Roosevelt stuck doggedly to this apologia: his party leaders against his opponents' party bosses, his friends in industry against their special interests.

The Progressive platform's assortment of social legislation gave the Colonel his third major issue on the stump. Social legislation was a tricky topic, for under existing interpretations of the commerce clause of the Constitution by the Supreme Court, manufacturing fell within the province of the states. Therefore, a candidate for national office had limited room for maneuver, for the national government could do little. Even on the state level, the courts' reverence for property rights under the rubric of "freedom of contract" written into the Fourteenth Amendment discouraged major innovation. The Supreme Court's stand in *Muller v. Oregon* (1908) had tolerated a legislative mandate for minimum wages for women; but three years before, in *Lochner v. New York*, the court had struck down New York's attempt to limit working hours for male bakers. The Colonel moved cautiously, offering moral support for the narrow wedge of possible legislation, supporting the Progressive platform's stand on minimum wages for women, but adding (in *Outlook* and on the stump in Spokane): "We do not at the moment take up the question of minimum wage generally; we know that in all matters like this it is necessary to proceed slowly so that we may test each experiment, and then, if the test is successful, proceed further along the same line."[32] In Tucson, he promised to call a special session of Congress to make Washington, D.C., with the national government as employer, an "example city," an "experimental laboratory in social and industrial science through which we intend to bring up this Nation as a whole."[33]

For Wilson's statement of sympathy for the social goals of the Progressives, Roosevelt had only contempt: Like a sailor with a wife in every port but only one true love, Wilson liked to pose as sympathetic to every good cause, but then to support only inaction, or proposals so vague, so impractical, that Wilson was, in effect, making the straight jacket the national symbol. When Wilson expressed the fear that a legal minimum wage would draw other wages down to that level, Roosevelt snapped up the comment instantly: "The objection is purely academic; it is formed in the schoolroom; it will not have weight with men who know what life actually is."[34]

On social issues, Roosevelt had to deal warily with Debs. The Socialist platform offered more, far more, than the Progressives in the way of social reform, and Roosevelt's modest proposals paled before Debs's. On the other hand, both Debs and conservative Republicans complained that Roosevelt had pilfered from the Socialist platform. As he left Connecticut, Roosevelt tried to put space between himself and Debs: "I think that a will o' the wisp is too light a term to apply to Brother Debs. I think that no workingman will get what he seeks from the Socialists, and that he will be harmed rather than helped by such an association. Mr. Debs wishes to pull down in a spirit of hatred; I wish to build up in a spirit of brotherly love. Some of the Socialists want to go so far that they can't see where they're going, and I can't either.

If you try to take all the steps toward reform at once you'll find it quite a straddle. You'll probably split yourself and not get anywhere."[35] Within the same week, it became known that Robert W. Bruere, a prominent New York Socialist, had visited Sagamore Hill as part of a group that advised Roosevelt prior to the adoption of the Progressive platform and the delivery of Roosevelt's "Confession of Faith."[36] Some of his suggestions had been adopted.

With Wilson and Taft to deal with, Roosevelt did not need the additional burden of defending himself on the issue of socialism. So Debs did not figure prominently in his comments on the trip. An old man in Helena shook Roosevelt's hand after a speech and said: "I am for Teddy Roosevelt and Eugene V. Debs." "Thanks, but he's not running on the same ticket with me," Roosevelt replied dryly as his train pulled out. "Just fancy Debs's feelings if he could hear that," he said with a chuckle as he reentered his railway car.[37]

With opponents to left and right, Roosevelt ignored Debs and bunched Taft and Wilson into a single package. Both had been nominated by bosses with the backing of the special interests, Roosevelt argued, and both lacked a program for the future: nothing promising to say on the regulation of industry, the extension of popular rule, the issue of social justice. The "Wilson-Taft" platform," he said in Helena, had only "differences of declamation." With Taft faltering—Roosevelt heard that word everywhere except in Utah—the old Republican establishment figures, he said in Tucson, "know that there is nothing to be done with Mr. Taft, that he is a dead cock in the pit, and so that kind of people are turning to Mr. Wilson."[38]

The month on circuit left Roosevelt confident that he had given insight into the future by raising the essential issues for modern America. For hope in the future, he looked to the past, casting himself in heroic terms that, however inflated they seemed to his opponents—and to history—drew reverence and applause from his audiences.

The moment of decision paralleled the situation fifty years before, he had told his fervent supporters in Los Angeles. People who had voted for or fought for Lincoln now stood with the Progressives; those who denounced Progressives were the "copperheads of today":[39]

Lincoln, a life-long Whig, left the Whig Party when it proved false to the unionism of Henry Clay. So we in our day have left the Republican Party when it turns its back on the principles of Abraham Lincoln.

The men of '61 fought to give the black man and the black woman a fair chance in America. We fight to give every man and every woman a fair chance in this Republic. And it is curious how exactly this fight parallels that of fifty years ago. You remember, you older men here, when Lincoln was denounced as a radical; and yet the so-called conservatives would have wrecked the Union if it hadn't been for the radicals. It was the wise radicals who conserved the Union.

And now the men who call themselves conservatives, if they had their way, would bring destruction upon this Republic. It is the honest and sane radical who is the real conserver of our institutions. The favorite argument of the copperhead was that Lincoln was destroying the Constitution, and the copperheads of to-day are always saying that we are destroying the Constitution and damaging the courts.

The wearing trip finally came to an end. As a concession to fatigue, Roosevelt stayed in his stateroom across Virginia and up the east coast to New York, waving to a small group of admirers at Union Station in Washington, but resisting the invitation to speak. On home ground he still possessed high spirits and (thanks to Dr. Terrell) his voice. He was ready for a day of rest at Sagamore Hill, ready for a heady session in Washington with the Clapp committee, ready in 24-hours to meet with his managers to assess strategy— perhaps the trip through the upper Midwest that they wanted so badly.

So ended Theodore Roosevelt's first campaign foray. It was a triumph— not a victory, of course, but a triumph.

11

The Retiring Taft

President William Howard Taft's victory at Chicago ended his political combativeness. In battle with the greatest political titan of the era, affable Will Taft had won, not by a knockout to be sure, for he could never quite remove the taint of his stolen nomination, but by a decision so certain that all could see. He had won his battle, preserving the Republican Party from the demented extravagances of Theodore Roosevelt, indeed purging the party of its lunatic fringe. Within days after his nomination, he accurately defined reality: "[W]hatever happens we shall have preserved the party organization as a nucleus for conservative action in 1916."[1] Meanwhile, defeat was certain in November. When Charles D. Hilles, his campaign manager, worried about Mrs. Taft's reaction, Taft reassured him in strangely revealing words: Taft reported to his wife that he had told Hilles that "you [Mrs. Taft] had for a long time not expected to be reelected" and that "[you were] most gratified" in the "more important purpose of defeating Roosevelt in Chicago."[2] The President himself, having no taste for tilting at the inexorable, would observe the formalities of candidacy, but basically, he would remain a spectator, unabashedly presidential.

Still disdainful of Democrats generally, Taft made no exception for Woodrow Wilson. Out of power for so long, Democrats lacked "the training of governmental responsibility," and their platform, with its foolish naiveté on tariffs and its extravagant promises to one or another voting bloc, threatened to undermine American prosperity. Taft viewed Wilson himself as an "utter opportunist" who had changed his pitch recurrently to catch the fancy of passing audiences. Briefed on Wilson's experiences at Princeton, Taft foresaw a moment in Washington when Wilson's "know-it-all methods...his dictatorial manner and his inconsideration" would make it impossible for two

Democrats to speak cordially to each other. He applied a lawyer's scorn to Wilson's mellifluous speeches: "he is academic rather than soul-stirring, and what he says, though given in graceful form and pleasant to the ear, has not a great deal of substantial sediment that remains with those who hear him. They are conscious of a pleasurable sensation, but they don't carry away much."[3] Taft regarded Wilson's acceptance speech as "purring and ladylike."[4] It was "milk and water...a 'pink tea' message" that satisfied conservatives and angered Bryan.[5]

Roosevelt was, of course, far worse, Taft believed. Gone was even the pretense of the old friendship; too many things had been said and done on both sides. Privately to his wife Taft wrote off the Colonel as "the fakir, the juggler, the green good's [sic] man, the gold brick man." Avowing that he felt no hatred or emnity, Taft said of Roosevelt: "I look upon him as I look upon a freak, almost, in the zoological garden, a kind of animal not often found."[6]

Necessarily Taft faced up to routine campaign chores. Hilles moved on to the chairmanship of the Republican National Committee. With less than a third of the usual $3,000,000 budget, Hilles opened offices in New York, Chicago, and Portland, Oregon, but they functioned on a skeletal basis. Local parties that sought even minor financial help were turned away with little, or even nothing. The cabinet, for the most part, held aloof from the contest, pleading age, health, old ties to Roosevelt, distaste for the stump. Once past his masterful performance in Chicago, Elihu Root, to Taft's great annoyance, became "very timid."[7] Since Taft ruled out an active campaign for himself, his lassitude gave his principal associates just the excuse they needed to do what they wanted to do anyway. The shape of the campaign was defining Taft's role: with Roosevelt and Wilson (and Debs as well) taking the "radical" side, "I have no part to play but that of a conservative, and that I am going to play."[8]

The tag "conservative" did less than justice to the complexity of Taft's position. To be sure, he had surrounded himself with the standpat forces in his party: Root, Senators Nelson W. Aldrich of Rhode Island, W. Murray Crane of Massachusetts, even Boies Penrose of Pennsylvania, former Speaker Joseph G. Cannon. It was also true that he had made ill-formed remarks in favor of constitutional restraints that frustrated popular will, that is to say, popular passions. But to dismiss Taft as just a conservative was as wide of the mark as calling Roosevelt and Wilson radicals. The Taft of 1912 was still, in essence, the Taft of 1908, and Taft used the notification ceremony on August 1 to lay out his definition of self.

For Taft, the notification ceremony was the climactic occasion of the post-nomination season, the only major speech he made in four months from August to November. Five hundred invited guests filled the East Room of the White House. The Marine Band played martial airs before, during, and after the ceremony. Mrs. Taft and a handful of invited ladies sat on a raised platform. The President had all but closed his office for more than a week to prepare his declaration, and he arrived with a clutch of solidly typewritten pages to answer the call of his party. Root, acting in his function as permanent chairman of the convention, praised Taft's record. But first he assured his startled audience that Taft's title to the nomination was "as clear and unimpeachable as the title of any candidate of any party since political conventions began."[9] Taft, as uncomfortable as the audience that the gentleman protesteth too much, ignored the issue, accepted the nomination, and defined in detail what form of political figure the Republicans had recruited.

For those who wanted Taft to restate the gospel of individualism and the dangers of socialism, the President had reassuring words: "[T]he fruits of energy, courage, enterprise, attention to duty, hard work, thrift, providence, restraints of appetite and passion will continue to have their reward under our present system, and ... laziness, lack of attention, lack of industry, the yielding to appetite and passion, carelessness, dishonesty, and disloyalty will ultimately find their own punishment in the world here." Though Roosevelt and Wilson were not socialists, their clamor for change, a device to get elected, invited all sorts of panaceas, a "condition in which the rich are to be made reasonably poor and the poor reasonably rich by law." They were on a slippery path: "In the ultimate analysis, I fear, the equal opportunity which those seek who proclaim the coming of so-called social justice involves a forced division of property, and that means socialism."

But Taft also spoke some progressive hard truths. Rejoicing that at the convention "the Republican Party was saved for future usefulness," he reviewed the party's record of progress: "a successful crusade against the attempt of concentrated wealth to control the country's politics and its trade." As the result of the Interstate Commerce Act, the Sherman Act, the Pure Food and Drug Act, the Mann Act against interstate transportation of women for immoral purposes, and a host of other laws, he said, "Now the duty of Government by positive law to further equality of opportunity in respect of the weaker classes in their dealings with the stronger and more powerful is clearly recognized." Some spoke against so-called paternalism, he went on, as if it somehow violated the Constitution; "Nothing is further from the fact. The power of the Federal Government to tax and spend for the general welfare has long been exercised, and the admiration that one feels for our Constitution is increased when we perceive how readily that instrument lends itself to wider Governmental functions in the promotion of the comfort of the people."

The trouble with his opponents, Taft argued, was that they chased phantoms: the initiative did not supply employment, the referendum did not pay the rent, the recall did not furnish clothing. The steady, invariably constitutional process of the Republican Party was the only safe route to the general welfare. For Taft, the Constitution accommodated progressivism, and progressivism embraced constitutionalism. The old judge would not yield one for the other, and the reigning president found no conflict between them.[10]

The guests applauded politely as the President finished. Four hundred guests stayed for lunch, and, as the other hundred moved away from the White House, a steamroller passed between the White House and the Navy Department, reminding at least some of them that in political campaigns weighty words offer weak competition to symbols.

The notification speech effectively cleared Taft's campaign calendar. Congress dragged on in the Washington heat, and the President stayed around dutifully to sign a bill exempting American coastal vessels from Panama Canal tolls and to veto two Democrat-sponsored tariff reductions. Finally, Congress passed a deficiency budget, then adjourned. The President signed it, then departed.

Within an hour, Taft's private car was speeding north on the Federal Express. His wife and his brother Charles met his train in Boston and drove to Beverly, Massachusetts, for a day of golf before a presidential visit to the centennial at Columbus, Ohio. Passing through Springfield, Massachusetts, he waved off people who wanted a political speech: "I have given that up."[11] Returning to Beverly for four days, he then made one more trip to Washington, returning by train to New York and by yacht to New London. Hilles and the finance chairman joined him on the yacht for their first political conference in a month. On the way to Beverly, he gave an address to a convention of deepwater promoters. By the afternoon, he was on the Myopia golf course.

Thus, on September 1, President Taft was in place for the fall presidential race. For the nonce, he was the most distinguished summer guest on the north shore of Massachusetts, occasionally called away to attend to business, but essentially part of the affluent summer colony in Beverly. (According to a Roosevelt aide, Beverly was a community "principally noted for its baked beans and rheumatism."[12])

The presidential role was both ceremonial and substantive. At various times in the month, Taft returned to Washington briefly to greet conferences. He made an occasion of the fiftieth anniversary of the signing of the Emancipation Proclamation, using the moment to recall President Abraham Lincoln's limited action as a model of constitutional restraint: Lincoln, like Taft, had been urged to move more quickly and more dramatically. He maintained continual contact with the State Department by telephone and telegraph to stay alert to Nicaragua, where the United States had marines, and to Mexico, where revolutionary politics threatened trouble at the border. Aware of British criticism of the decision to exempt American coastwise vessels from tolls at the Panama Canal, he defended the American position in a statement to the London *Times*.

On one substantive issue, the President was resolute. He kept up his continuing fight for a stronger executive share in the construction of the federal budget. The difficulty lay in existing practice: executive departments made their own requests to Congress. Exercising control over his own appointees, Taft firmly ordered the budget process in each department to proceed in time for his prior review. Though Taft did not succeed in dismantling the old system, modern budgetary procedures in the national government date from his administration, for his successors built on what he started.

His official duties left the President with plenty of time for the vacation he treasured so highly. Occasionally rising at 6 AM to put routine work behind him, he turned freely to his morning golf game at the Myopia golf course, reputed locally to be the best and the most difficult in America. His game hovered at the one hundred mark, not good enough to threaten any of his constituents, not bad enough to suggest an area of incompetence. Golf was a good activity for Taft, as it was for Wilson: physical activity pursued at his own pace; essentially an individual sport—it was quite possible to play alone if there were no one else around—yet companionable if son Charlie, or others who were more than political friends, was available; remote from officialdom yet not distant in an emergency. On fair afternoons Taft bundled his ample bulk into the back of a touring car and enjoyed the Atlantic breezes and the friendly greetings of natives and summer visitors. His brother Charles had a summer place at Biddeford, Maine; the ninety-five-mile trip up the coast constituted an undertaking in the days of primitive roads. For his fifty-fifth birthday on September 15, he and his family went to Millbury, Massachusetts, to the home of his aunt, Delia Torrey, whose apple pies were a presidential favorite. Political interruptions were no more than incidents in a routine that had other goals.

Still, politics did intrude. There were occasional callers who sat on the front porch to report how the President was progressing in Indiana, or some other remote location. He went to Boston for a convention of mail clerks at Faneuil Hall; he favored civil service extension and decent pensions. He traveled to Maine to take a hand in the elections in early September and, returning home, stayed up until 1:30 the next morning to follow the returns that registered a solid victory for the combined forces of Republicans and Bull Moosers over the Democrats. The victory showed what Republicans could do when they worked together, he told the press the next day.[13] On his trips to Washington, he arranged to see Hilles, echoing for the press the optimistic reports that Hilles gave him on the Bull Moose failure to rally significant support nationally.

Hilles served as point man for the Republican effort. Lacking both a peripatetic candidate and a large stable of surrogates, he undertook an elaborate advertising campaign in newspapers and magazines, on billboards and streetcars.[14] He kept up a steady patter for the press. He complained of William Flinn's hold on Republican electors in Pennsylvania, and he showed special bitterness at the situation in California, where Governor Hiram W. Johnson's control of the state party meant that California's Republican electors would speak for Roosevelt. "The party of the third-term candidate professes through its leader many virtues," Hilles said, commenting specifically on California, "But the leader and the party openly condone stealing and cheating and make virtue of actions that are a stench in the nostrils of honest men." Hilles had a whole catalog of accusations: political depravity, personal cowardice, treachery, and plain stealing.[15] At the same time, Hilles was telling Taft and the press that conservative businessmen were coming to rally behind Taft: Taft had been a conscientious and successful administrator; whatever doubts may have developed about his trust policy paled before the more radical solutions that were being offered on Roosevelt's western tour.

Taft, in New London to speak in favor of deeper waterways, was more oblique on the subject of Colonel Roosevelt, but not noticeably more obscure. Seizing upon the figure of Benedict Arnold, Taft criticized those who sought to crawl into power over someone else. While deeply committed to deeper waterways, he felt regretful that love of self, self-absorption, and ambition for power had led Arnold onto the path that made him a great traitor.[16] Since Benedict Arnold was not running for office in 1912 and since Taft was not unveiling a statue of the Revolutionary scoundrel, his hearers were left to speculate on the contemporary significance of Taft's homily.

Toward the end of the month, Taft dallied with purely political affairs. In New York for a meeting with his campaign managers from around the nation, Taft spoke with confidence about the direction the election was taking. Setting up shop at the home of his brother Henry on West 48th Street, Taft was in good-natured form, amiably parrying reporters' trivial questions and teasing Nicholas Murray Butler, president of Columbia University, about running for the New York governorship. (Butler professed a preference for a job with the Brooklyn Rapid Transit, which paid more.) Taft predicted victory in November. Five or six weeks ago, he said, the general view was that the Republicans would hold a solid East, the Democrats a solid South, the third party a solid West, leaving only the Middle West as debatable ground. Today, he went on, with the elections about a month away, the Republican hold on the East had been strengthened, the Democrats having been routed in Maine and the third party routed in Vermont. Now even the third party conceded defeat in Utah, he said, and Hilles had assured him that Michigan, Washington, Idaho, and Wyoming were in good shape, and that "the proper kind of a campaign" would bring along Oregon, Kansas, and Minnesota "where the third-term strength has rapidly waned since the recent tour through that section by the party's candidate." A nearly solid West in combination with the "indisputable Republican hold on the Eastern states" would, he was sure, create sufficient strength to bring success to the party.[17]

The *Times* reporter found Taft serene, unworried, speaking "emphatically and apparently with the utmost confidence."[18] If Taft was seeing through a glass, darkly, he at least made sure that the glass had a roseate hue.

Returning to Beverly in the last week of September, Taft let his good-natured serenity disappear in an explicit attack on the Democrats and a wrathful denunciation of Theodore Roosevelt. The Republican clubs of Essex County assembled in his front yard to hear the President warn that Democratic promises "make certain the disturbance of business, the frightening of capital, the closing of factories, and the coming of hard times." No one could deny, he said, that a change in tariff policy would necessarily destroy a substantial part of the business now protected. Were the people "willing to assume the burden of the hard times that must necessarily accompany change?"

Then he went on to the third party. The more fundamental issue in the campaign, larger than the tariff or prosperity itself, was "the preservation of the institutions of civil liberty as they were handed down to us by our fore-fathers in the Constitution of the United States, and the state constitutions which were modeled after it." Without mentioning his predecessor by name, he assailed the new party and its leader: "A third party has split off from the Republican Party not for any one principle, or indeed on any principle at all, but merely to gratify personal ambition and vengeance, and in the gratification of that personal ambition and vengeance, every new fad and theory, some of them good, some of them utterly preposterous and impracticable, some of them as Socialistic as anything that has been proposed in the countries of Europe, many having no relation to National jurisdiction or policy, have been crowded into a platform in order to tempt the votes of enthusiastic supporters of each of these proposed reforms." Not united by principle, the party, he noted accurately, would go to pieces without the "remarkable personality of its leader." The "crazy-quilt character of the platform," many parts of it inconsistent with other parts, showed "a willingness to destroy every limitation of constitutional representative government in order that, by short cuts, these varied reforms . . . may be accomplished by the decrees of a benevolent despotism to be supported by the acclaim of hero-worshipping, emotional, undiscriminating, superficially minded, and non-thinking people."

It was Taft the conservative institutionalist who turned to the "most valuable lessons of experience in the past" to applaud "those limitations upon the majority contained in the Constitution, which have proven themselves to be of such inestimable service in the maintenance of the success of our democratic, constitutional, representative form of government." The claim of the Republican Party to continued power, he said, lay in its awareness of its limits: "A National Government cannot create good times. It cannot make the rain to fall, the sun to shine, or the crops to grow, but it can, by pursuing a meddlesome policy, attempting to change economic conditions, and frightening the investment of capital, prevent a prosperity and a revival of business which otherwise might have taken place. And, in view of the experience of the past in which we have seen efforts to bring about a change in monetary or economic policies, it can halt enterprise, paralyze investment, and throw out of employment hundreds of thousands of working men. The negative virtue of having taken no step to interfere with the coming of prosperity and the comfort of the people is one that ought highly to commend an administration, and the party responsible for it, as worthy of further continuance in power."[19]

The real Taft was speaking, making an authentic statement of a conservative alternative to activist government. If that position would not carry in the voting booths of America in 1912, he would accept defeat. He was not going to try to reverse his fate by making promises that went beyond what he believed, promises that he would be unwilling to keep. The certainty of defeat allowed him the luxury of setting forth his bluntest self. He would not solicit victory on any other terms.

Two days later, speaking first to the Republican Club of Beverly and then to Italian-Americans at City Hall, a little of the genuine anger he felt at Roosevelt's defection and spoiler role slipped out on the spur of the moment. Let the Progressives return to the Republican Party on their knees, he said; "in the not distant future these gentlemen who have deserted us in the hope of enjoying office on the one hand or a millennium on the other will find themselves without office, millennium, or party."[20]

The jovial William Howard Taft did not forget easily or forgive readily.

12

Debs's Critique

For Eugene Debs, campaigning was still not markedly different from not campaigning. Careening from one paying socialist meeting to another, coast to coast, filling socialist journals, most prominently *Appeal to Reason*, with sermons on the ills of capitalism were his occupation. A campaign simply gave his activity a special focus.

The focus was not victory. It was education in basic socialist principles. A tiny political victory, won on the votes of newly arrived reformist elements, led nowhere, Debs believed, for the reformers, ready to jump on the Socialist bandwagon in order to rebuke the ruling parties, were equally quick to desert once their own economic or political purposes were accomplished. Piecemeal reforms in the Socialist platform drew equal scorn; they were nothing more than the conservatives' bonus for controlling the party's apparatus. Offered scraps like these, he believed, workers characteristically stayed with Democratic or Republican (or breakaway Republican) candidates because Socialists had no chance of winning, and they bore the burden of capitalist denunciation as godless, foreign-inspired, and ridden with violence. Socialism had no future—unless Socialist orators and writers could bring voters to understand fully the capitalist system, its deceptive tricks, its ultimate indifference to its victims—indeed, its incapacity to have a human face.

With a confidence that a later generation regards as sentimental, Debs felt sure that when working people finally understood this message, they would turn on their masters and rally to the Socialist Party. Then, as the capitalist parties collapsed in their internecine warfare and the economy collapsed in its own contradictions, the stage would be set for true revolutionary change, not in 1912, but down the road. He was confident that a campaign of education brought closer the day when true socialism would win on the votes of true socialists.

The *International Socialist Review*, in its August issue, featured a boxed quotation from Debs that sent forth exactly this stern message: "To my mind the working class character and revolutionary integrity of the Socialist p[ar]ty are of first importance. All the votes of the people would do us no good if our party ceased to be a revolutionary party, or came to be only incidentally so, while yielding more and more to the pressure to modify the principles and program of the party for the sake of swelling the vote and hastening the days of its expected triumph."[1]

For those Socialists who shared Debs's view, Debs remained the heroic voice, energetic and fearless. Those with more centrist ideas—successful politicians like Victor L. Berger or Emil Seidel, intellectuals like Morris Hillquit or Charles E. Russell—accepted Debs as a front man, useful for his skill on the stump, for his national reputation, and for his availability. Victory was not so imminent that his radicalism carried intolerable costs.

Yet the tugging and hauling between the yellows and the reds never let up. Responding to pressure from the membership, Debs attempted to get rid of Hillquit's nominee, J. Mahlon Barnes, as campaign manager. But when Debs was unwilling to force a showdown, Hillquit, controlling the votes on the party's executive committee, won by hanging tough. Barnes stayed on. Debs snarled about Hillquit in a letter to Barnes: "It is a pity that a man who is so skilled in the trickery of capitalist politics was not a delegate at Chicago or Baltimore instead of Indianapolis."[2] Berger's newspaper in Washington riposted for the moderates: "Many intelligent Socialists have long known that Gene suffers from an unduly exaggerated ego."[3]

The Socialists' habit of heady rhetoric, fueled both by conviction and by powerlessness, did surprisingly little to retard planning for the fall campaign. In June, a joint meeting of the campaign committee and the executive committee called for publication of 25,000,000 copies of a sixteen-page pamphlet on socialism and for distribution to all local organizations for postage only. It authorized a "one-day wage fund" to be collected on July 20 to finance the campaign. (In fact, the campaign budget never went above about $66,000.) It set Labor Day as the formal occasion for opening the campaign, and it called for a show of workers' power through simultaneous meetings all over the United States on Socialist Day, the first Sunday of October. Debs and Seidel were urged to make recordings with greetings that could be used at these demonstrations. Debs was authorized to travel with two companions and a stenographer, Seidel with one companion and a stenographer. The campaign speakers were allowed $5 a day plus expenses, not more than $3 a day for hotels and incidentals. A sliding scale of fees was set for the candidates' appearances: $100 for cities with populations of more than 100,000 down to $25 for cities of 25,000 or fewer. For the joint appearance of Debs and Seidel in New York City, the rate went up to $350. It was agreed that 30 percent of all profits from an appearance would go to the local state party. Mindful of the breakneck pace of the 1908 campaign, Debs insisted that he have time off to rest every three weeks.[4]

Almost immediately, Debs, and Seidel too, were off and running. On June 16, a crowd of 100,000 or more poured into Riverview amusement park in Chicago to hear Debs set the issue for the campaign: "In this campaign there are but two parties and one issue. There is no longer even the pretense of difference between the so-called Republican and Democratic parties. They are opposed to each other...purely in a contest for the spoils of office." Piddling variations in the platforms were gestures to accommodate party factions or lures to deceive voters. Taft and Roosevelt were mere puppets of the ruling class, literally bought, paid for, and owned, body and soul, by the powers that were exploiting the nation and enslaving and robbing its workers, Debs said. "The emblem of a capitalist party on a working man is the badge of his ignorance, his servility and shame." Debs responded to the contagion of his own enthusiasm: "We are united, militant, aggressive, enthusiastic as never before. From the Eastern coast to the Pacific shore and from the Canadian line to the Mexican gulf the red banner of the proletarian revolution floats unchallenged and the exultant shouts of the advancing hosts of labor are borne on all the breezes. There is but one issue that appeals to this conquering army—the unconditional surrender of the capitalist class."[5]

As Debs spoke, the major parties had not yet acted. Roosevelt and Taft were still competing for control of the Republican convention, and Debs noted gleefully that they were doing some excellent campaigning for him: "They are telling the truth about each other."[6] When the Democrats finally nominated Wilson, Debs hooted: "Wilson is entering this campaign as a 'progressive,' a great friend of the workers. He has as rotten a labor record as any man possibly could have."[7] Even before Roosevelt went back to Chicago for the Bull Moose convention, Debs wrote him off: "A more servile functionary to the trusts than Theodore Roosevelt never sat in the presidential chair.... Roosevelt must stand upon the record he made when he was president and had the power, not upon his empty promises as a ranting demagogue and a vote-seeking politician."[8]

Still, when Roosevelt's candidacy became a reality, Debs knew he was being upstaged. Responding to the *New York Times*, which had asked for a comment, he said: "The really progressive planks in the Progressive platform were taken bodily from the Socialist platform, and even the red flag of socialism was appropriated, or at least imitated, by the red bandanna of the Roosevelt followers."[9] But do not be deceived, he told the New York *World* in response to a similar request: Though Socialists agree with much that was in the Progressive platform, the Bull Moose platform "does not contain any of the vital and fundamental principles of Socialism and is [in] no sense a Socialist platform." While aiming at "some of the flagrant evils and abuses of capitalism," in its central thrust it "supports and strengthens the existing system."[10] Roosevelt would have agreed totally.

During the summer months, while Seidel canvassed Wisconsin, then moved south and southwest, Debs met a large crowd in St. Louis, then came as far east as Maine. Wherever possible, both campaigners made their visits coincide with local socialist lyceums—day-long gatherings that were part carnival and family outing, part political jamboree and emotional catharsis. Debs thrived on his frenetic schedule. Bearing up with hoarseness and the fatigue of travel was an old habit. When he arrived anywhere, there were crowds, and more often than not, old comrades, to listen and, in turn, to be listened to. He had his message so clearly in mind that the pieces fell into place as soon as he uncrossed his legs to stand up. The vigor of his speech and the warmth of his personality bent the audience toward him, and he in turn leaned out to them, his tall lanky body and extended bony finger reaching out over them. Since his task was educational, he could speak, and in his judgment did speak, the unvarnished truth. His strong voice reached all sides of even large gatherings, and his sustained optimism, finding special justification in the political chaos of 1912, brushed off on those who listened.

The year 1912 was a special year for optimism, Debs believed. Of course Roosevelt, by stealing socialist ideas, would confuse issues; and of course Wilson, capitalizing on Republican disarray, would make gains for the more reactionary of the two parties. As a result, however, the Socialist vote would be a true Socialist vote: the trimmers and reformists would be siphoned off by the phony promises of Wilson and Roosevelt; the hearty residue would be Socialists committed for the long haul, brothers and sisters committed to genuine revolution.

In Washington, another Socialist voice spoke up. Early in July, Victor L. Berger, the most prominent elected Socialist in America, representing the fifth congressional district of Wisconsin, rose in the House of Representatives to lambaste the old parties. Champ Clark, fresh from his humiliation in Baltimore, was in the chair. Taft had beaten the progressives in Chicago; Roosevelt had bolted, but the Bull Moose had not yet issued its shrill call.

Berger paid his respects to the members of the old parties: they were often "very cultured and accomplished gentlemen . . . personally honest." The Republicans were "the favorite organization of the big capitalists" (applause on the Democratic side); the Democrats, though becoming capitalist in the South, drew their strength in the North from corrupt machines and the liquor interests (applause on the Republican side). With elections coming, he said, the Democrats had discovered the workingman (laughter on the Republican side). But neither party could be a vehicle for the workingman: "If you want to ride horseback, you will not take a donkey."

And what of the candidates that these parties offered? All personally honest. Taft had done no wrong "other than 'stealing convention delegates' willing and ready to be stolen." In any case, "political graft is the very application of business principles to politics." All three enjoyed the support of trusts, bosses, and political machines. All stood for rule by the wealthy class. Their platforms were interchangeable. Wilson, whose stands on immigrants and labor were well known, would bring in a new "era of reaction and 'high finance' " such as the nation had suffered under Grover Cleveland. Taft, who knew that the Republican Party was "the favorite organization of the big capitalists," wanted it to remain so. And Roosevelt, "with his brilliant but very erratic mind," might change his principles by tomorrow afternoon (laughter and applause); he was "the pathfinder of a new organization which is on its way to nowhere in particular." His support included Flinn of Pittsburgh, "a reactionary from head to heel, soaked and saturated in the municipal corruption of that smoky inferno."

The real issue, Berger went on, was the class issue. Workers created surplus value only to have it stolen by their capitalist masters as profit, rent, interest, insurance. "Social freedom, complete justice, can be accomplished only by the collective ownership and democratic management of the social means of production and distribution," he said, and only the Socialist Party moved in that direction. Because Socialists knew that the goal could not be reached in a day, they favored reforms along the way: they were pro-initiative, but they cared more about old-age pensions; they supported referenda, but fought for unemployment insurance. They knew revising the existing Constitution to be essential, but economic reform—social control of the trusts—was more important. Still, while the Socialist Party was revolutionary in its final aim, Socialist reformers would support the "peaceful, lawful, orderly transformation of society," welcoming all real reforms that were not "political bait."[11]

Berger's speech and responses to inquiries went on for seventy minutes, one hour allotted by the chair, ten more minutes awarded by unanimous consent of the House. Not once did Berger hint that his party had a presidential candidate named Eugene V. Debs.

The candidate could be similarly selective in definitively outlining Socialist objectives. In his "speech of acceptance"—actually a statement released to the press from Terre Haute August 26—Debs ignored the platform's reforms and concentrated on the Socialist analysis of economic and political realities. Like Berger, but even more than Berger, he heaped contempt on the reformist pretensions of the Democratic, Republican, and Progressive Parties (by this time, of course, Roosevelt had officially joined in the fray). The three parties, he said, were "essentially one and the same. They differ according to the conflicting interests of the privileged classes, but at bottom they are alike and stand for capitalist class rule and working class slavery." They all "stand for the private ownership by the capitalists of the productive machinery used by the workers, so that the capitalists can continue to filch the wealth produced by the workers." Only the Socialist party asserted that the wealth produced by the working class belonged to the working class.

Fortunately, Debs asserted, the workers, seeing that "the class of privilege and pelf has had the world by the throat and the working class beneath its iron-shod hoofs long enough," were gaining in vision and in the sense of their own power; they were ready "to destroy all despotism, topple over all thrones, seize all sceptres of authority...tear up all privilege by the roots, and consecrate the earth and all its fullness to the joy and service of all humanity." The capitalist class survived only on the votes of the workers; let those votes once be withdrawn, "all ruling classes disappear and all slavery vanishes forever." Every vote for a capitalist party was to be a vote for wage slavery, and poverty, degradation; every vote for Socialists, a vote for emancipation. The Socialists proposed "to abolish this monstrous system and the misery and crime which flow from it in a direful and threatening stream." Their mission was "not only to destroy capitalist despotism but to establish industrial and social democracy."[12]

Not for Debs were Berger's soothing words about the respectability of the party, or Berger's reassuring promises of orderly, incremental, legal progress toward the cooperative commonwealth. Debs retreated not an iota from his statement to Ray Stannard Baker four years before: "We would have the government take the trusts and remove the men who own or control them: the Morgans and Rockefellers, who exploit; and the stockholders who draw dividends from them."[13]

Debs formally accepted the Socialist nomination for president on his own terms. If Berger and Hillquit and Barnes and Seidel and even the Socialist platform put forth different views, those statements did not bind Debs.

Both Debs's acceptance speech and Berger's analysis of Socialist principles appeared in the official *Socialist Campaign Handbook* for 1912. Thus the Socialist Party entered the fall campaign with its inner conflicts over revolutionary tactics unresolved, its fragile unity sustained only by the party label and by shared distaste for capitalist institutions.

Throughout September, Debs and Seidel continued their arduous selling of the Socialist message, putting up with dreary travel via the railroad system of America, North to South, east coast to west coast. Their variant messages, different without quite becoming contradictory, never clashed because they appeared together only once, and on that occasion Seidel took proper second billing, leaving Debs center stage to appeal to the future.

The release of Debs's acceptance statement gave him fresh momentum. With a new campaign kickoff, Debs went north to Fergus Falls, Minnesota, and then took off for the West where Populist antecedents, aggrieved miners, and reckless independence created an apt setting for the Socialist message. He appeared in Butte, Montana, went on to the state of Washington, came down the coast to the cities of California, and then started back home through the southwest: Phoenix, Arizona; El Paso, San Antonio, Galviston, and Houston, Texas; then on to Oklahoma, which, with Nevada, was to give him the highest proportion of the vote (16.61 percent) anywhere in the nation. He went on to Kansas, then eastward to Kentucky before finding his way back to Terre Haute for a short rest. His brother Theodore and Ellis B. Harris of Wisconsin, a publicity man assigned by the national campaign committee, were with him, Theodore, as usual, the candidate's man of all chores, Harris handling what little publicity showed up in the press. Four days of rest allowed Debs to recover his voice and his vigor. He doubled back to Davenport in eastern Iowa, toured central Wisconsin, then headed east through Indianapolis, Cleveland, and Philadelphia on his way to the miniclimax on Sunday evening, September 29, at Madison Square Garden in New York City.

Meanwhile, Seidel kept himself equally busy. Having canvassed his home state of Wisconsin quite thoroughly and Minnesota as well, Seidel took off for the East through Indiana and Ohio, stopping in Pennsylvania, veering north through Vermont, on to Maine, then south again for several stops in Wilson's New Jersey. While Seidel was in Trenton, his brother Debs was in San Francisco. Seidel followed the trail south: to Delaware, Maryland, Virginia, North and South Carolina, Georgia, Florida, briefly west to Alabama, north to Tennessee and West Virginia; then two days in Ohio before traveling to Buffalo and Rochester, New York; Massachusetts and New Hampshire, then short stops: south through Boston, Rhode Island, and Connecticut, on his way to the joint appearance in New York City.

Unlike the candidates of the major parties, Debs and Seidel did little campaigning from the back end of their trains, for campaign appearances had to pay their own way. Lacking angels with large bankrolls, the Socialists counted on small contributions and on admissions fees: 15 cents to 50 cents, $1 for the gala event in New York, $10 for a box. Local party members organized each appearance of the candidates as a way to rally support for local candidates and to draw crowds for the Socialist message. A hall was rented, a local park engaged, perhaps a permit to parade solicited. If local authorities balked at giving Socialists a hearing, as they did in Manchester, New Hampshire, the local party had to clear the way prior to the arrival of the guest of honor. The local groups used whatever techniques they had mastered, whatever they could afford. The meeting in Sioux Falls, South Dakota, was advertised by a single sandwich man walking the streets of the town. The registered membership of the party served as the starting point. Then the party drew on its considerable experience with lyceums to create rallies around family outings in order to disarm the direst fears of conservative folk conditioned to detect anarchy behind every socialist smile. Once the crowd was in place, young supporters circulated among the people, selling pamphlets, banners, and red scarves. A good meeting might bring in $300 to $700, enough to pay the speaker the going rate and still leave a surplus for the state organization and for other local activities.

The Socialist organization, though small, formed a remarkable network throughout the nation. All, or perhaps one short of all, the states were represented at the Indianapolis convention. The delegates spoke on behalf of

125,826 paid-up members—the number larger than usual because of active recruitment by state secretaries in anticipation of the convention. The party claimed accurate information about its ranks. In the *Socialist Party Handbook* issued for the 1912 race,[14] 71 percent of the members were listed as American born. The Germans had the largest foreign contingent (about 9.5 percent), followed by Scandinavians (5 percent), English (4 percent), and the noisy and radical Finns (2 percent); all others accounted for the remaining 9.5 percent. The Lyceum department of the national party was especially attentive to the foreign element: there were organizations for the Bohemians, Finns, Italian, Poles, Scandinavians, and "south Slavics." For most foreign groups, central headquarters translated the party's messages into the particular languages; indeed, much of the money collected in dues from these groups returned to them in the form of this specific service. The tie to the party among these Socialists was most likely to be exclusively with the central office; the moderate wing of the party was glad to keep them thus isolated, their presumed radicalism confined within their own language groups, not infecting the state organizations.

The *Handbook* recorded that 41 percent of the members were craftsmen, more than twice the number of laborers (20 percent). Farmers accounted for 17 percent, "commerce" for 9 percent, and transportation for 5 percent. Five percent were "professionals"—including Debs and Seidel, Hillquit, and Berger—and 3 percent housewives. The listing suggests that women played only a minor role in the party. Yet the 1912 convention had twenty-five women delegates, about 10 percent, and the National Executive Committee included one woman, the National Committee had two, and one of the international secretaries was a woman. The party boasted that eight prominent national lecturers were women.

With a passion for figures that seem more precise than accurate, the party logged its essential statistics. Prior party attachment was credible: 40 percent were converted Democrats, 35 percent born-again Republicans, 15 percent prior Populists, 4 percent fall-away Prohibitionists, and 6 percent independent. What had converted them? Periodicals converted 39 percent, discussion, 19 percent; books, 13 percent; study, 10 percent; street meetings, 8 percent; lectures, 7 percent; leaflets, 4 percent. The total added up to a neat 100 percent, and no one seemed concerned with overlap. Did "study" ever include "books," did "discussions" ever emerge out of "periodicals"? Did a "lecture" ever occur at a "street meeting"? Of periodicals, the party claimed an abundance: 13 daily papers, 5 in English and 8 in foreign languages; 262 weeklies in English, 36 more in foreign tongues; and 10 English and two foreign monthlies. The year 1912 was the era of the printed (and spoken or orated) word, and the Socialists desperately needed their own vehicles to reach the people. The multitude of papers served local or specialized audiences, for no other periodical commanded the national circulation of *Appeal to Reason*.

The national reach of *Appeal to Reason* contributed to the standing that

Debs, one of its most regular writers, continued to hold with most elements of the party. When put together with his indefatigable commitment to the lecture circuit and his readiness to discuss socialism at any moment of the day or night, his journalism kept him constantly, or at least continually, at the center of party affairs.

Important as a journalist, Debs was preeminent as an orator. A fellow fighter in the IWW, Elizabeth Gurley Flynn, caught his appeal: unforgettable experience, matchless orator, torrent of burning eloquence.[15]

Debs paced back and forth on the platform, like a lion ready to spring, then leaned far over the edge, his gaunt tall frame bending like a reed, his long bony finger pointing—his favorite gesture. His deep blue eyes appeared to look searchingly at each one in the audience, he seemed to be speaking directly to each individual. Such intimate eloquence is hardly possible in this era of mechanized speech. Debs' voice was strong and clear and could be heard in the largest hall and outside places. He spoke with imagery and poetry of expression, drew word pictures of the lives of the workers, of child labor, of men in prison, or at war. He was full of loving kindness of those who are heavily laden, and had a searing contempt for "gory-beaked vultures" who fatten on their exploitation. His strong sense of labor solidarity never wavered.

Heywood Broun, a great newspaperman who never met Debs, recalled in a lament after Debs's death what a "hard-bitten Socialist" had told him:[16]

Gene Debs is the only one who can get away with the sentimental flummery that's been tied onto Socialism in this country. Pretty nearly always it gives me a swift pain to go around to meetings and have people call me "comrade". That's a lot of bunk. But the funny part of it is that when Debs says "comrade" it's all right. He means it. The old man with the burning eyes actually believes that there can be such a thing as the brotherhood of man. And that's not the funniest part of it. As long as he's around I believe it myself.

Conscious of his skill on the platform, Debs would have loved to face his opponents man to man. Indeed, he challenged each of them to meet him in Philadelphia. Taft's executive clerk replied courteously by telegram: "President regrets that he cannot accept invitation extended, as he is taking no active part in the campaign."[17] Taft was not Debs's primary target in any case; Debs's tour left him convinced that Taft was "entirely out of the race."[18] As for Theodore Roosevelt, busy in Spokane with his own campaign, a face-to-face confrontation with Debs would only have highlighted the resemblances between his own platform and specific Socialist reforms. Roosevelt preferred to dismiss Debs as a "will-of-the-wisp."[19] Wilson's failure to respond promptly to Debs's challenge gave rise to a report in the socialist press that he might be willing to debate. But the silence continued. Circumspect, if also slightly patronizing, Wilson told an audience in Buffalo: "I have a great respect for the Socialist party because I know how many honest and serious men are in it." But since none of the "minor parties" was going to win, Wilson said, he was going to confine his attention to the serious contenders.[20]

With no one willing to fight him directly, Debs fought on by himself, his eye on the horizon beyond. To the extent that those "deceived by the bellowing of the Bull Moose" cut down the vote of the Socialist Party, he told the workers in Los Angeles, "the results will be of advantage to the workers, as it will separate the sheep from the goats and consolidate the militant revolutionary power of the working class under the banner of Socialism."[21]

The goal across the nation was to reach the sheep and to hold them. At each stop, the audience—three thousand was not exceptional—appeared, cheered, contributed to a modest pot that sent Debs to the next stop, and finally propelled his campaign in September to its climax at the great gathering in New York City.

Fifteen thousand men and women, in about equal proportions, gathered inside Madison Square Garden, with three thousand more outside pressing on police lines. The other candidates, Seidel for the vice-presidency, Charles E. Russell for the governorship of New York, warmed up the audience. Then Debs's appearance brought the proceedings to a halt for twenty-nine minutes, according to the *New York Times*, with such wild applause that even Debs succumbed to the tribute. With experienced tact, he turned the ovation back to his audience with his first words: "There could be no more eloquent tribute than this to the genius of socialism. What I see here is infinitely more important than anything I can say here."[22] The gathering foretold the victory that would come, he said. More interruptions and shouting, the red flags, red scarfs, red banners, red aprons, red neckties creating just the right atmosphere for repeated outbursts of the Marseillaise and the Internationale. Debs tossed two threats out to the capitalist class: 30,000 shirt-waist workers would soon strike against their capitalist masters in New York—a local threat; and then, the kind of threat that confirmed the nation's worst fear of the Socialist movement: if two Lawrence strike leaders were convicted of murder, Debs said, there would follow an uprising of the whole working class. His revolutionary anger voiced, released, Debs settled into a threnody on his opponents. Having been at all three conventions as an observer and reporter, he had not seen a single workingman present as a delegate. "The Republican, Democratic, and Progressive Parties are but branches of the same capitalist tree. They all stand for wage slavery."

He had a peg on which to hang each of his opponents:[23]

William Howard Taft is a former more or less celebrated jurist who was a specialist when it came to issuing injunctions to keep workingmen in subjugation.

Wilson is a mild-mannered gentleman, ladylike in his utterances, and I have nothing to say against him personally, and politically he had nothing to say for himself. He is the kid glove on the paw of the Tammany tiger.

Now for Theodore Roosevelt. He is to-day the champion of the oppressed and the downtrodden of the Nation. A new role for him . . . a mystic Moses . . . Just think of it! Theodore Roosevelt, who in all his life never had any use for the working class except to use them as a means to further his own selfish, sordid ambition! Theodore Roosevelt, who to-day stands on a platform that four years ago he denounced as anarchistic!

Take all three of these candidates, and not one of them has ever had to look for a job. Not one of them has ever been on strike. Not one of them has ever been slugged by a capitalistic policeman, and not one of them has ever been in jail. Not one of them—yes, all of them together—ever produced enough to fee[d] a gallinipper.

The crowd loved the performance, and Debs loved them for loving it. The moderates might squirm at his extremism—uprisings by the workers were not in the lexicon of Hillquit and Berger, or of Seidel, for that matter—but Debs was the candidate, and the audience cheered at his biting scorn and his blunt threats. The party emerged from the meeting some $10,000 richer.

When Debs returned to Terre Haute for a brief rest, he knew that the cause of education had been well served.

13

Campaign Roundup

As October began, with five weeks left until election day, the three principal candidates had settled into final postures, theirs to hold until the voters chose among them. Woodrow Wilson, frontrunner, certain of victory, had only to avoid disaster. Neither President William Howard Taft nor Theodore Roosevelt could win on his own, but Wilson could lose through a catastrophe—an as-yet-undisclosed scandal, a careless act or statement, a disabling illness like the seizures, which may have been strokes, that he had suffered at least twice before. Roosevelt understood the national picture shrewdly: "My judgment is that [Wilson] will win, and that I will do better than Taft. There is of course a chance that my movement may gain strength enough to enable me to beat Wilson, but I think this very improbable."[1] In those states, like Pennsylvania and California, where the Bull Moose had taken over the machinery of the regular party, its success was assured against Taft, most likely against Wilson as well; in states where Taft's forces retained control of the party—the principal Republican goal—Roosevelt's inroads would allow Wilson, more often than not, to slip past the two of them. As for Taft, comfortable at Beverly, moseying on the golf course of Massachusetts with an occasional sidetrip into neighboring states, the certainty of defeat and the obligation of presidential dignity shaped his conduct. Official remarks now and again would show that his party still lived, but he had no intention of romping around.

Debs was on the outside with little money and less political machinery. Even with as much nomadic energy as Roosevelt and with more oratorical skill than Wilson, he got his only competitive edge from his breakneck pace of travel. While Emil Seidel went off to the plains and to the Northwest and West, Debs moved north from New York City to New England, back through western New York to the middle states and across the industrial tier out to

Illinois. Victory, never even a remote possibility, seemed less urgent than ridiculing the flummery of his capitalist foes.

So the campaign opened its second month on an even keel, the players clear on their courses, all without illusions about its future direction.

Just back from his national trip around the circle, Roosevelt hurried down to Washington to testify under oath before the Clapp committee. The inquiry explored two charges: that Roosevelt had received large corporate contributions in 1904 and that those gifts had bought preferential treatment. The first charge was obvious, the second unprovable. Roosevelt's $1,535,000 in contributions from corporations in 1904 were a matter of public record; they did not violate the law at the time they were received. Mild and self-contained, Roosevelt mocked the notion that dollars bought subsequent favors. "If ever I find that my virtue is so frail that it won't stand being brought in contact with either a trust magnate or a Socialist or a labor leader, I will get out of public life," he said.[2]

In practice, Roosevelt kept his distance from money matters. In both 1908 and 1912, he learned about contributions only by reading the newspapers. If money came from the rich, their generosity did them no discredit: "I am proud of the fact that there are at least a few men of wealth who possess the farsightedness and the generous understanding of the needs of the times which make them powerful champions of the American people."[3]

Debs, in Paterson, New Jersey for a rousing speech to four thousand of Wilson's constituents, hooted at Roosevelt's posture: "Teddy will pass into the political history of the country . . . as Teddy the Innocent. Eight years have passed since J. P. Morgan dropped $150,000 into his campaign fund, but he never found it out until yesterday. I have been somewhat anxious about my own possessions in this campaign after reading Teddy's experiences as recited by himself. I am in dread that J. P. Morgan will drop $150,000 into my campaign fund when I am not looking and then about eight years from now I will have to swear I did not know about it."[4]

Debs's sniping aside, the Colonel's explanation did bespeak a vexing innocence. Outright bribery—the exchange of money for a specific official act—was scarcely the issue. The issue was comity of interest between wealth and political policy. At the Progressive convention, for example, George W. Perkins had induced Roosevelt to reshape the platform's handling of the Sherman Act. Perkins prevailed because of his credibility, and his credibility rested on prior usefulness, at least some of which rested on his prior financial support of Roosevelt's activities. The process was too uncomfortable for Roosevelt to sort out when he himself was the beneficiary, especially when clumsy charges before the Clapp committee allowed him to face only crude intimations of extortion and bribery.

Not surprisingly, T. R. understood money and influence more readily when he dealt with his opponents. International Harvester and U.S. Steel (except for Perkins) were supporting Taft and Wilson, he noted, and the implications of that support were easy enough to imagine.[5] He never hinted that any direct deal had been struck. But alert voters would not misunderstand.

Wilson, already back on the campaign trail in Gary, Indiana, a U.S. Steel town, revived the argument by saying quite explicitly that steel monopolists favored the Bull Moose Party because that party intended to maintain monopoly.[6] At Pueblo, Colorado, he restated the issue for the voters: "You, therefore, have to choose now a government such as the United States Steel Corporation thinks the United States ought to have, or a government such as we used to have before these gentlemen succeeded in setting up private monopoly."[7]

Roosevelt, furious, demanded that Wilson prove or retract the charge that the trusts were behind his program.[8]

When Wilson reached Kansas City, Missouri, he backed off; he was unprepared to prove or to retract. He did not mean that Roosevelt had received money from U.S. Steel—it makes no difference where Roosevelt had gotten his money, Wilson said. "I meant, and I say again, that the kind of control which he proposes is the kind of control that the United States Steel Corporation wants."[9] Roosevelt called Wilson's dissembling "sheer nonsense,"[10] and even the *New York Times*, which the day before had reveled in the acclaim of Woodrow Wilson as "Woody," "Doc," and "Kid,"[11] thought Wilson had gone too far. Its reproof, however, was not scalding: "Unless the proofs are accessible, it is probably better not to say these things."[12]

Despite the gaffe, Wilson's second trip roused enormous enthusiasm. In Indianapolis, the starting point, Thomas Taggart staged a wild demonstration that left the press certain that the prim schoolmaster now had the manner of a winner. It was here that the phrase "new freedom" appeared for the first time; it came out almost conversationally, certainly not as the label for the Wilson program that it eventually became.[13] Moving north toward Chicago, Wilson scheduled hour-long stops in Peru, Kokomo, and Plymouth, Indiana, as alternatives to rear-platform appearances. He passed through Chicago, then proceeded to Nebraska. At Cedar Rapids, Iowa, a passing freight train sideswiped his railroad car; Wilson was unscratched. When he arrived at Lincoln, his long session with William Jennings Bryan was a love feast. "Let me ask you to do twice as much for Wilson as you ever did for Bryan," the Great Commoner told his loyal supporters. "For I have as much at stake in this fight as he has, and you have as much as I have."[14] Then Wilson and Bryan took Sunday off for church and dinner.

Overnight Wilson went on to Denver, Colorado, memorable for his triumphant appearance during the campaign for the nomination, then back to Kansas City for fence-mending with Champ Clark. Indeed, warming Clark's ego was Wilson's principal accomplishment at this stop, for after Clark introduced him, Wilson's voice was all but gone. His audience took the occasion to see the candidate, then simply departed during his inaudible remarks. Returning through Chicago, he found 100,000 standing in the rain to greet him. Former Vice-President Adlai E. Stevenson was on the platform, Sullivan still nowhere to be seen. Returning east through Cleveland, Wilson used his presence in Ohio to remind the voters in a hoarse, troubled voice that Taft "was an amiable gentleman surrounded by gentlemen who know exactly what they wanted."[15] Finally, back to New York, on to Princeton, the first Sunday spent uninterruptedly with his family since the nomination.

Taft, meanwhile, had little to occupy him except his daily routine. Ensconced in the President's Cottage in Beverly, he played golf most mornings and took a drive most afternoons, occasionally visiting the Beverly Republican Club, greeting visiting war veterans, going off to Boston or, more rarely, to other New England states. He talked world peace with Pierre Loti, the French naval officer, novelist, and peace activist, opened the new YMCA on St. James Street in Boston, visited friends and vacationing cabinet members, as busy with their summer holidays as he was with his.

In a statement issued the first Sunday of October, he voiced satisfaction with the progress of the campaign. There was a trend to the Republicans, he had heard from Charles D. Hilles, especially in the Northwest, where farmers knew better than to let Wilson tell them they had no need for tariffs. The country was prosperous, business was expanding. There was no need for a standstill that would be caused by reduction of the tariff or by anarchistic assaults on institutions—a nod each to Wilson and to the Colonel. Harmonious relations were growing between employers and employees: "The Golden Rule is getting to be more and more a guide in business as well as in religion. Social and economic conditions are growing better, not worse, and Republican policies, fostering and stimulating National prosperity, undoubtedly tend toward this betterment." The cost of living was high, to be sure, but wages were two to seven times better than in Europe, he said; Wilson could not have picked a more unfortunate time to suggest tariff for revenue only. "[T]he American people are in no need of quack nostrums, and too busy to listen to their vendors." He acknowledged the potential of a national incorporation law, a reasonable change that fell short of the idiocies that his opponents were calling for, but he was "utterly opposed to the proposal to have an Inter-State Trade Commission fixing prices and otherwise exercising control over business affairs. Such a control, because not guided by law, but by personal discretion, would be both despotic and socialistic, and no reader of history needs to be told that the two terms have a very close relation."[16]

Taft was off on a six-day tour as he uttered these pronouncements. He went through western Massachusetts to see retiring Senator W. Murray Crane, then on to Vermont: lunch in Brattleboro, and dinner in Manchester as the guest of Robert T. Lincoln, the Great Emancipator's son. He found time to stop off in West Townshend to visit his own father's birthplace. His western tour completed, Taft went to New York to review the fleet drawn up in full array in New York harbor, addressed his "lads" in blue, defended naval expansion and strong fortification of the Panama Canal, dined with his brothers, and returned to Beverly for a vacation.

Hilles ran the campaign from New York. His responsibility clearly had more to do with collecting and disbursing funds, maintaining contact with Republican leaders nationally and complaining about Wilson and Roosevelt than with scheduling the time of his principal.

Standpatter or not, his opponents had no doubt, Taft jumped out in front on at least one issue. Drawing on a staff report based on the experience of the Raiffelsen banks and Landschafter societies in Germany, Taft proposed to state governors that states charter cooperative credit plans and establish land-mortgage banks as a foundation for cooperative mortgage-bond societies. Later on, he said, Congress should pass legislation permitting creation of national land-mortgage banks, strictly supervised by the government, to market and guarantee debenture bonds of the state land-mortgage banks. True to his principles, Taft saw the federal government's role as simply that of monitor: "the proper field of imposing restrictional legislation for the purpose of preventing speculation."[17] Still, for all the institutional restrictions in Taft's proposal, it offered a more substantial suggestion for the farmer than either of his major rivals had undertaken.

Roosevelt's overall posture was clearly more aggressive. He paused on Long Island for a day or two after his success with the Clapp committee, then started again to round up votes in the crucial northern industrial tier of states. Saving four days toward the end of the campaign for the contest in New York, he drew up secret plans to go to Michigan, Minnesota, and Wisconsin, then work his way back east through Illinois, Indiana, Kentucky, Ohio, Pennsylvania, Maryland, and even Wilson's New Jersey. There were 226 electoral votes in those states. He kept his plans under wraps as much as possible to confound the Taft rebuttal team that followed wherever he went. Openly he had nothing but contempt for the trailing "truth tellers." In fact, they got under his skin.

Arriving in Saginaw and Detroit, Michigan, Roosevelt clarified his intent on the proposed industrial commission. Clearly Wilson's challenge had some bite. To a generation that had lived with the exposures of the muckrakers and with the anti-trust activity of three administrations, accepting monopolies looked like surrender to the forces of evil. Wilson burlesqued the idea of a regulatory commission that accepted monopolies. He had the industrial commission saying to the trusts: " 'Now, go easy, don't hurt anybody. We believe that when you are reminded of your moral duties you are not malevolent, you are beneficent. You are big, but you are not cruel, and when you show an inclination to be cruel, here is a government agency that will remind you what are the laws of Christianity and good conscience.' "[18] Recognizing the anxiety that Wilson and Taft could evoke, Roosevelt made clear on the stump in lower Michigan that he intended specific legislative definition of the terms under which corporations could function.[19]

Fascinatingly, Roosevelt and Wilson were approaching each other, moving in from the extremes. While Roosevelt was narrowing the discretion of his proposed industrial commission by promising to define by law the standards under which it would act, Wilson had been led to acknowledge that effective legal action against the trusts required "the creation of special processes and special tribunals" to supplement slow expensive action through the courts.[20]

If Roosevelt was vulnerable on the trust commission, Wilson was vulnerable on labor. When Wilson defended the Democratic platform's commitment to labor's right to organize, Roosevelt asked the workers of Michigan, just how recent and dependable was Wilson's conversion to that stand? As little as three years before, at a Princeton commencement, the Colonel reported accurately, Wilson had told his new graduates that workers did as little work as possible for their wages, that they were held back by their unions, that America grew ever more full of "unprofitable servants" (this last reference was both biblical and domestic).[21] Indeed, Wilson seemed to have held these views until he went into public life. "I am not questioning the sincerity of Mr. Wilson's change," the Colonel said with ironic politeness, "but I wish to call attention to the fact that the extreme lateness of his conversion and its very imperfect nature do not warrant him in making any comment whatever on the Progressive platform in this matter."[22]

In the industrial Midwest, full of first- and second-generation citizens, Roosevelt tossed a collection of Wilson's embarrassing remarks on immigrants into the campaign. Drawing from books and articles that appeared over Wilson's name, Roosevelt savored the quotations for an audience in Duluth, Michigan: "our own temperate blood, schooled to self-possession, and to the measured conduct of self-government, is receiving constant confusion and yearly experiencing a partial corruption of foreign blood"; "multitudes of men of the lowest classes from the South of Italy and men of the meaner sort out of Hungary and Poland, men out of the ranks where there is neither skill, nor energy, nor any initiative or intelligence"; the Chinese, "more to be desired as workers, if not as citizens, than most of the coarse crew that came crowding in every year at the Eastern ports."[23] To these reminders of his imprudent past, Wilson responded with silence, or with fluffy admiration for those immigrants who came freely in quest of the American dream. Wilson never undid the damage of these early statements. By ignoring them or replacing them with balm for the moment, he left the issue as a canker rather than a cancer on his presidential hopes.

Roosevelt did not dwell on Wilson's notions on immigrants. He did dwell on the tariff, a more complex issue, even more complex as a battleground. The simple fact was that Roosevelt as president had left the tariff alone because it was fraught with political peril. He favored a protective tariff in principle, both as president and as candidate, though not the Payne-Aldrich tariff. He had to distance himself from both Wilson and Taft, from Wilson by mocking free trade and even "relatively free trade," from Taft by aligning himself with those for whom Payne-Aldrich demonstrated Taft's subservience to special interests. During the campaign, Taft renewed his explicit defense of Payne-Aldrich: it was apparent to a close observer, especially if that observer happened to be Taft, that Payne-Aldrich had reduced overall schedules by 10 to 21 percent.[24] To hold both Taft and Wilson at bay, Roosevelt with one hand had to defend the protective tariff without saddling himself with the special interests and with the other hand attack Democratic notions of tariff for revenue only and of tariff as the mother of the abusive trusts. His own proposal for a "scientific" expert tariff commission avoided the purported errors of both and fit right in with the political economy underlying his campaign.

Roosevelt carved out a deft argument. In Oshkosh, Wisconsin, Roosevelt, answering Wilson, explained why he had not tackled the tariff during his nearly eight years in office: There had been two sweeping revisions in the previous eight years (presumably Wilson-Gorman, 1894, and Dingley, 1897), and the tariff could not claim priority until the very end of his administration. In fact, Roosevelt went on in a neat swipe at Wilson, railroad and trust magnates had used agitation for tariff reform in his administration as a red herring when they felt their own interests threatened. "Mr. Wilson is obligingly trying to play their game at this moment."[25]

Later on, Roosevelt found Wilson equally vulnerable on the issue of trusts. New Jersey was the home base of many of the largest trusts in America, and Governor Wilson had assaulted them in his inaugural message in 1911. Why had nothing occurred thereafter? Easy, Wilson replied, the Republicans controlled the upper house of the legislature. Not so easy, Roosevelt retorted, for the Republicans held only a only a one-seat margin in the Senate and at least one Republican senator had introduced legislation to alter the incorporation laws of New Jersey. Why had Wilson not used the same kind of executive initiative that Roosevelt had shown against a sometimes hostile congressional majority to ram through regulation that was needed?

Roosevelt was in high form, his audiences frequently responding with frenzy well beyond the warmth that Wilson evoked. At Oshkosh, Roosevelt felt confident enough to reply to Robert M. La Follette, without quite mentioning his name. He felt momentum. At times it felt more real than the logic of electoral votes.

He took a day off to nurse a raspy throat. Then, on October 14, he went to Milwaukee, where he was shot.

As Roosevelt was leaving the Hotel Gilpatrick to go to the municipal auditorium with Colonel Cecil Lyon and Elbert E. Martin, a stenographer, he climbed into an open roadster, then rose to acknowledge the cheers of a small crowd. John Schrank was waiting for just such an opportunity, as he had waited previously in Atlanta and Chattanooga and perhaps other cities as well. Drawing a revolver, Schrank fired one shot at the Colonel. A Milwaukee policeman, standing nearby, watched. But Martin, a former New Hampshire farm boy, coal stoker, and football player, leaped across the hood of the car and wrestled Schrank to the ground, immobilizing his shooting hand. Roosevelt sank back into the car with surprise and shock, still unaware that a bullet had entered his body. The crowd surged forward, intent on dealing with the assassin in its own way. "Stop, stop. Stand back. Don't hurt him. Bring him to me," Roosevelt commanded. Martin dragged Schrank to his feet and brought him over to the Colonel for inspection. "Why did you do it? What was your reason?" the Colonel asked sadly, and, without waiting for an answer, told Martin to hand Schrank over to the waiting policeman and his supervising captain.[26] (The popular story that Roosevelt sank into the arms of an aide and said: "Take me to Murphy at the Mercy. I need the Catholic vote" is, unfortunately, apocryphal.)

The group entered the car to go on to the auditorium. Roosevelt's staff insisted that he be checked. Roosevelt refused. Only then did he notice red spots surrounding a hole in his overcoat. Looking further, he saw that his manuscript had been pierced and his glasses case had been nicked. Realizing that the Colonel had indeed been wounded, his companions wanted to return to the hotel for immediate medical attention. But Roosevelt would have none of that retreat. He ordered the automobile to proceed to the auditorium. "You get me to that speech. It may be the last one I shall ever deliver, but I am going to deliver this one," he said in a voice that experience had taught his staff was the last word.[27] Arriving at his destination, where no word of the incident had been reported, he allowed a team of doctors to inspect the damage. A bullet had entered the Colonel's chest just below the right nipple. Blood was seeping, not flowing. The doctors uniformly demanded that he remove himself to a hospital for surgical care. Roosevelt remained adamant. The party moved onto the stage, the crowd greeting the Bull Moose leader with the enthusiasm that by this time had become routine. A hush was restored when the chairman warned the audience that the Colonel had just been shot, but that he wished to continue with the program as scheduled.

"Friends," Roosevelt began, "I shall ask you to be as quiet as possible. I don't know whether you fully understand that I have just been shot; but it takes more than that to kill a Bull Moose. But fortunately I had my manuscript, so you see I was going to make a long speech, and there is a bullet—there is where the bullet went through—and it probably saved me from it going into my heart. The bullet is in me now, so that I cannot make a very long speech, but I will try my best."

The audience held its breath as the Colonel continued, his perforated manuscript discarded as he reflected on his situation, rambled, disregarded the repeated attempts of his friends to have him call a halt.

First, some things about myself: "I have altogether too many important things to think of to feel any concern over my own death...my concern is for many other things.... I can tell you with absolute truthfulness that I am very much uninterested in whether I am shot or not. It was just as when I was colonel of my regiment... I cannot understand a man fit to be a colonel who can pay any heed to his personal safety when he is occupied as he ought to be occupied with the absorbing desire to do his duty."

He was absorbed, he said, with the Progressive movement. He wanted to say something to the people, and especially to the newspapers. He knew nothing about the "coward" who shot him "but it is a very natural thing that weak and vicious minds should be inflamed to acts of violence by the kind of awful mendacity and abuse that have been heaped upon me for the last three months by the papers in the interest of not only Mr. Debs but of Mr. Wilson and Mr. Taft.

"Now, my friends, I am not speaking for myself at all. I give you my word, I do not care a rap about being shot; not a rap."

He had said nothing on the stump that he could not substantiate, he went on.

His friends tried to intervene at a pause, but he objected, "I am not sick at all. I am all right."

The attempted assassination pointed up the urgency of avoiding in America the fight between the haves and the havenots, he continued. Another pause and another intervention to which Roosevelt replied, "My friends are a little more nervous than I am. Don't waste any sympathy on me. I have had an A–1 time in life and I am having it now."

On and on the speech went for forty-five minutes, maybe fifty. Progressives believed in all the people regardless of creed or birthplace, he asserted. Henry Cochems, who had introduced him—his family had come from Germany; his father and his father's seven brothers had served in the army four years after they had come from Germany.

"I am all right—I am a little sore. Anybody has a right to be sore with a bullet in him. You would find that if I was in battle now I would be leading my men just the same. Just the way I am going to make this speech."

Roosevelt defended the right of labor to organize and demanded that laborers take the lead in denouncing crime and violence.

"I know these doctors, when they get hold of me, will never let me go back, and there are just a few things more that I want to say to you."

Wilson had attacked him on the trust issue, he continued. Compare the records. Roosevelt had revived the antitrust act and amended the Interstate Commerce Act, and now he was proposing an industrial interstate commission that would make court decrees effective. By contrast, let Wilson or Wilson's friends point out one thing he had done about the trusts in New Jersey.

Comfortable back on campaign issues, Roosevelt added one final appeal. The Republican bosses, the Barneses and the Penroses, "would rather see the Republican Party wrecked than see it come under the control of the people themselves." The Democratic party "has distinctly committed itself to the old flintlock, muzzle-loaded doctrine of States' rights." The people could vote progressive or reactionary. If they voted Democratic or Republican, they voted reactionary. Roosevelt offered the alternative: "I ask you to look at our declaration and hear and read our platform about social and industrial justice and then, friends, vote for the Progressive ticket without regard to me, without regard to my personality, for only by voting for that platform can you be true to the cause of progress throughout this Union."[28]

The speech ended, Roosevelt allowed himself to be hustled off to the Milwaukee Hospital for inspection. A bullet had entered his right breast, caught itself in the tough chest muscles that years of fitness had given the Colonel, then came to rest along the fifth rib, less than an inch from his heart. A train was ordered to take the Colonel to Chicago. Mrs. Roosevelt, at the theater in New York, was notified; she waited overnight, then went west on the fastest train. In Chicago, her husband was taken to Mercy Hospital.

The nation responded to the attempted assassination with attentive concern. President Taft, for himself and for the nation, offered regrets for the injury and satisfaction about the chances for complete recovery. Mrs. Wilson told Mrs. Roosevelt of the Wilsons' shock and solicitude. Wilson telegraphed his rival. (Roosevelt was touched: "Bully. Wilson is of the right American blood, notwithstanding the fact that he and I are opposed in a political sense."[29]) Debs lamented the "most regrettable" incident. "No one could more sincerely regret such a thing than I do and I am glad he is recovering."[30]

The nation followed daily bulletins. There was to be no attempt to remove the bullet. Rest, total rest, was necessary for recovery. The doctors did nothing to conceal their professional dismay that Roosevelt had spoken to a large crowd for forty-five minutes. The London *Standard* might view the performance as a "display of cool and stoical courage," but the doctors judged it the "height of imprudence."[31] They attempted to keep the hospital room unencumbered with visitors and excitement, but they failed utterly until Mrs. Roosevelt arrived and took command. Roosevelt yielded with amiable truculence: "I never was so boss-ruled in my life as I am at this moment."[32]

Meanwhile, back in Milwaukee, the police were trying to make sense of their prisoner. A thirty-six-year-old immigrant from Bavaria, in this country for twenty-six years, Schrank had stalked Roosevelt as a "traitor to the American cause" for violating the third-term tradition, he said. He was not an anarchist, a Socialist, a Democrat, or a Republican. Eventually, Schrank was indicted for assault with intent to kill. He was committed to the Northern Hospital for the Insane.

Assassination attempt aside, the election was still scheduled for November 5, twenty-two days after the shooting. The London *Times*, until then confident of Wilson's victory, saw the need for new prophecies, and an early visitor to Mercy Hospital predicted that the shot aimed at killing Roosevelt would in fact elect him. Both Senator Joseph M. Dixon and Gifford Pinchot, who presumably were not in shock as Roosevelt had been, picked up Roosevelt's charge that the assassin had been inspired by the vilification from the Colonel's opponents; Pinchot in New York said that the unstable were fired up by charges against Roosevelt unmatched since the days of Lincoln and Washington: coward, drunkard, charlatan, demagogue.[33] From the other side of the political spectrum, the Socialists demonstrated that tastelessness was not

a Republican monopoly. Charles Edward Russell called the assassination attempt "individualism at work." His remark paled before the more extended
comment of the socialist New York *Call*:[34]

There is not a Socialist who does not deplore the assault made on Mr. Theodore
Roosevelt, even though it is just such an action as he himself has time and again
advocated. It was an individual, strongman attempt to set right the problems of humanity. It was thoroughly Rooseveltian, thoroughly in keeping with Rooseveltian
teachings, thoroughly in keeping with Rooseveltian ideas.
    These many years Socialists have struggled valiantly to combat the idea of killing.
They knew all along Roosevelt was and is in favor of killing. He has been a hunter,
a ranchman, a "soldier" in a most limited way, assistant in the Department of the
Navy, Governor, President. When and where and how was his voice ever lifted against
killing? In all his writings, when and where and how did he oppose individual action?
Never at any time, and he never opposed it in any way. We deplore sincerely the fact
that he has fallen a victim to his own preachings.

By contrast, Roosevelt's principal opponents remained models of decorum.
Taft, scarcely campaigning anyway, simply remained silent. The Democratic
high command was in turmoil. Most of the Democratic leadership at national
headquarters wanted Wilson to carry on. Colonel Edward M. House, who had
no official role, possessed the shrewdest sense of the situation: "My thought
was that if he [Wilson] continued to speak after T. R. had been shot, it would
create sympathy for T. R. and would do Wilson infinite harm. The situation
is a dangerous one and needs to be handled with care. The generous, the
chivalrous, and the wise thing to do, so it seems to me, is to discontinue
speaking until his antagonist is also able to speak."[35] Wilson, uncertain, suggested delay. But House muscled the committee members as much as he
dared, pulled an end run around them by dealing directly with Wilson, won
the only vote that mattered. Wilson announced that he was suspending the
campaign as soon as he fulfilled three days of commitments in Delaware,
West Virginia, and Pennsylvania. He also imposed on himself the further
resolve not to discuss the Bull Moose platform or Roosevelt's position on
issues until the Colonel was back in the fight.[36]
    Chivalrous and wise, as House said, the decision was clever as well, for
Roosevelt's clearly articulated positions on a formidable triad of issues—tariff,
trust regulation, and social legislation—had left the governor on the defensive.
Among the three major contestants, Roosevelt's positions stood out most
clearly: on the tariff, an expert commission to make "scientific" recommen-
dations; on trusts, an industrial commission to regulate; on social legislation,
an ad hoc experimental approach with prompter action where the federal
government had clear jurisdiction. Taft stood pat on the essentials of Payne-
Aldrich; he looked to the courts to bear the main burden on regulating trusts,
especially after court decisions in 1911 created some flexibility under the "rule
of reason"; he deemphasized even the scant social legislation that appeared

in the Republican platform. Wilson held to the goal of a reduced tariff, always careful to retain emphasis on protecting jobs from foreign competition; on trusts, he looked for legislative remedies even as he allowed for special processes and special tribunals; he had little to say about social legislation. Now Roosevelt's silence through necessity and Wilson's through choice removed these key issues from the campaign debate, leaving Wilson with a free ride in the final days. In the name of good sportsmanship, Wilson gained virtual immunity.

Sick as he was, Roosevelt understood. He quickly seized upon Bryan's "manly and proper statement" that discussion of the issues should go on. From his hospital bed in Chicago three days after he was shot, Roosevelt spoke for himself and his friends: "[W]e emphatically demand that the discussion be carried on precisely as if I had not been shot. I shall be sorry if Mr. Wilson does not keep on the stump, and I feel that he owes it to himself and the American people to continue on the stump." Then moving against the familiar hint that the Bull Moose campaign was no more than an extension of his overextended ego, Roosevelt noted that the principles of the party were even then being expounded by Governor Johnson, Senator Albert S. Beveridge, Jane Addams, Gifford Pinchot, hundreds of others, all standing for the same just cause. Finally, he made an oblique crack at Wilson's courtesy: "So far as my opponents are concerned, whatever could with truth and propriety have been said against me and my cause before I was shot can be with equal truth and equal propriety be said against me, and it now should be so said; and the things that cannot be said now are merely the things that ought not to have been said before. This is not a contest about any man; it is a contest concerning principles."[37]

Eager for a brawl, he sent Beveridge to Louisville, Kentucky, to deliver the speech that Roosevelt had written for the occasion. The highlight of the speech was the demand that Wilson explain publicly why he had not amended New Jersey's incorporation law to control Standard Oil and "similar monopolies" that functioned under New Jersey's benevolence.[38]

On other fronts, the Bull Moose campaign staff recruited Elbert Martin to make political grand rounds showing off the hands that had throttled Schrank's neck.[39] In New York, Perkins added his bit: While Mr. Wilson was refraining from personal attacks on Mr. Roosevelt, perhaps he could find time to say where he stood on the Democratic platform.[40]

From Wilson came no response. His staff beefed up security around him, plainclothesmen and Captain Bill McDonald, a former Texas Ranger whom Colonel House summoned by wire from Texas: "Come immediately. Important. Bring artillery."[41] When the governor went off to Delaware, he noted the national sadness provoked by "that atrocious assault" upon "that gallant gentleman lying in the hospital at Chicago."[42]

With Roosevelt and the third party off limits, Wilson redirected his attention to President Taft: "The most that can be said of the President is that he is sitting on the lid. He has sat very successfully on the lid, and nothing has got away."[43] At Wilmington, he changed the metaphor and extended his analysis to the whole Republican Party: "And the Republican party sits like a complacent grandmother and twirls its thumbs and says, 'My dears, so long as you sit perfectly still, you are perfectly safe and you won't be sorry.'" It might be better to be safe than to be sorry, Wilson said; "It is also safer to hug your base than to steal a base."[44] (The Boston Red Socks had just beaten the New York Giants in the world series.) The Republicans were offering nothing more than the program already in place, the very program that had led to the nation's present misfortune, he said, even as the Democratic Party made its commitment to the present and future—and to victory.[45]

The imminence of victory made Wilson insistent that he be given a Democratic Congress. The House of Representatives was already Democratic, and safe, but the Senate was harder to win. Assuming that the presidency was also safe, Wilson focused on the need for a Democratic sweep. A Republican victory would be a decision to stand pat, a Bull Moose victory would postpone reform because the President and Congress would be constantly at odds. Toward the end of the campaign, Wilson, talking to his own Jerseyites, put the matter in dramatic terms, stark but safe: "[I]f you are not going to vote to support me in Washington, don't vote to send me to Washington.... If I get men back of me who think as I do, we shall in God's Providence bring about a prosperity and an open door for all the men coming on in this country, such as they have not known in a generation."[46]

As Wilson made final rounds in the eastern states, his statements became less concrete, less detailed. It was more a time for political orotundity than for aggressive statements that might cost at the polls. He defined bosses in such lurid terms that no one could disagree just as no one would acknowledge any kinship with the scoundrels being described. On the tariff issue, he took advantage of the rich opportunities his opponents, up to and including President Taft, persisted in giving him by regularly charging him with favoring free trade. Just at the end of the campaign, Wilson again responded with a show of weariness: "I have not heard any thoughtful Democrat declare for free trade. I have heard every Democrat declare for what I have—going through the tariff with as fine a tooth comb as is necessary to find all concealed and illegitimate special privileges and cut every one of them out, and leave absolutely safe every sound and healthy fiber of American business." He would be a surgeon cutting "with such a nice and discriminating skill that no healthy fiber will be touched or damaged."[47] The statement was safe—even Republicans were unlikely to cheer for diseased "foreign growths upon the body politic." It avoided specifics. Was he talking about wool, sugar, steel? Any one of those items involved votes. Ironically, Republican misstatement of Wilson's position allowed him to make an aggrieved retort that still avoided a specific and costly stand.

His handling of trusts became similarly general. In response to counsel from antitrust experts at Columbia,[48] he moved away from emphasis on competition as the ultimate solution and took refuge in a formula of non-commitment. He concentrated on the horror of the trusts, but he blurred his remedy simply by omitting it.

Roosevelt's running mate, Hiram Johnson, sputtered with frustration: beautiful speeches and charming metaphors said nothing about real governmental problems; Wilson was merely marking time to avoid raising issues that would cost him votes.[49]

Other issues, previously fenced out of the campaign, did not disrupt Wilson's latter days. His stand in favor of local option kept prohibition in its place. Maud Malone, an active suffragist, interrupted a speech in Brooklyn with a demand that he state his position on votes for women. He refused, then protested mildly when the police dragged her out of the hall under arrest.[50] He never made striking inroads on the hyphenate vote, but he used the presence of Hermann Ridder, publisher of the *New-Yorker Staats-Zeitung*, as chairman of a Democratic meeting in Carnegie Hall in New York to oppose "any niggardly immigration policy" and to praise one of "the great solid, energetic elements of our people"—not German-Americans, but "those Americans who proudly look back to a lineage that finds its beginnings in the Fatherland."[51] Bishop Alexander Walters of the African Methodist Episcopal Zion Church wanted Wilson to speak to a Negro Democratic gathering; the candidate put Walters off with a letter that assured him that Negroes "may count upon me for absolute fair dealing and for everything by which I could assist in advancing the interests of their race in the United States."[52] Finally, the Catholic issue surfaced when Thomas E. Watson, populist, prominent anti-black leader and antisemite, withdrew his support from Wilson because of a report that Wilson had joined the Knights of Columbus, a Catholic fraternal order. The head of the K of C noted that Wilson, as a non-Catholic, was ineligible for even honorary membership.[53] All these subsidiary issues remained contained, fenced about with careful distinctions and smothered with rhetorical bunting.

They did not jar his expectations of victory. Wilson felt no misgivings as he discussed major appointments—should McAdoo be Secretary of the Treasury? should Bryan be ambassador to Great Britain?—with Colonel House.[54]

Out at Oyster Bay, Colonel Roosevelt was gradually seizing authority back from Mrs. Roosevelt. Shot on October 14, Roosevelt had stayed at Mercy Hospital in Chicago for about a week. His activities curtailed, he still managed to see reporters, Jane Addams, and high ranking Bull Moose leaders like Hiram Johnson. Roosevelt was itchy to get home. He left the hospital under heavy police guard, walked to the ambulance wearing the same overcoat, then boarded a special train east. Through Indiana and Ohio, crowds appeared along the track, silent, bareheaded, reverent. The train arrived at Grand Central in New York, slipped away to Oyster Bay, stopping just before the town to avoid the crowd gathered to welcome him back. For less than a week, he behaved on command. Then, less well than he thought, he started activities again: a jolly visit with the "old guard" of reporters who had traveled with him, an unscheduled appearance in khaki downstairs, a walk in anticipation of his fifty-fourth birthday (October 27), an optimistic prediction for election day following the final campaign appearance at Madison Square Garden October 30, a climax and a valedictory.

President Taft continued to watch both opponents from Beverly. Roused to intervene, he characteristically released a statement. He wrote off the Bull Moose Party: it was "an open secret on every street corner" that the third party did not expect success. The only question remaining was: "[H]ow many Republicans are willing to assist in completing the demoralization of the Republican Party, and handing the reins of government over to the Democrats to gratify mere desire for revenge." The Democrats fared only slightly better. Stung by Wilson's charge of drift during the past four years, he recalled that Lincoln was accused of letting the nation drift too: "It drifted—yes—with Lincoln at the helm, from the reefs of secession and slavery into the placid waters of union and liberty. Under Lincoln's successors it has sailed on, propelled by the winds of prosperity, save when its voyage has been halted by just such a visitation of storm and stress, of torn protection sails and broken business bulkheads, as we are now threatened with should Baltimore supplant Chicago, which it did not in 1860 and will not in 1912." Fortunately, "Democratic workingmen refuse to be led from the factory and good wages of 1912 back to the Democratic hard times of 1893–1897. They prefer independence and money in the savings bank to loss of employment and dependence on charity." American businessmen, manufacturers, and farmers could similarly see their true interest. The net result he stated with confidence: "in every State in which the Republican Party is not disfranchised old-time majorities will be rolled up for the Republican candidates."[55]

There was still time for travel, even as his vacation was coming to an end. He drove as far as Portland, Maine, made the one hundred-mile journey back to Boston in a leisurely eight hours, returned to Beverly for a final day or so. It was time to take off for Washington, passing through Massachusetts, stopping at Jamestown, New York, and at three Pennsylvania locations for quick speeches. *Harper's Weekly* was publishing his summary of the issues. He had administered existing laws regulating the trusts, not made his own judgments on what the laws should have said, and as a result, the nation had received effective trust regulation: finances revealed, parent companies dissolved, competition restored, business left uninjured. Tariffs under Payne-Aldrich were down 10 percent. He had secured one new battleship a year, and he had created the army reserve. The nation was prosperous.[56]

Back in Washington, he issued his final appeal, almost certainly not intended as parody: "The choice for the voters is not obscure; on the contrary it is as plain and clean an issue as was ever presented in our political history—it is between actual and assured prosperity, active industries, good wages, a flourishing market and rapidly growing foreign trade, on the one hand, and depression of business, paralysis of industry, loss of employment for wage earners, and general demoralization of trade at home and abroad, on the other hand. On one side prosperity and real progress; on the other a leap in the dark. The American people have more than once surprised those who thought the people was being successfully fooled, and I believe that a similar surprise awaits our opponents on the coming 5th of November."[57]

Returning to New York to launch a battleship, USS *New York*, he passed unnoticed through Pennsylvania Station. That evening he dined with political and financial leaders. The following day he launched the battleship, then returned to Penn Station for the trip back to Washington, his train four tracks away from the car that was bringing his old friend Roosevelt into the city for his appearance at Madison Square Garden.

That night, Vice-President James S. Sherman, Taft's running mate, died in Utica, New York, after an illness that stretched back into the summer. The symbolism was striking, but everyone had too much good taste to comment on it in public.

A careful ear could detect comparable symbolism in Colonel Roosevelt's address at Madison Square Garden October 30, less than a week before election day. Roosevelt's first public performance since Milwaukee, it tested his physical strength even as it revealed his judgement on the cause.

The crowd was tense and enormous, inside and outside. Scalpers had a field day, but even at inflated prices for tickets, more people wanted admission than the Garden's 16,000-capacity could accommodate. When Roosevelt entered, neither he nor his hosts could still the crowd for forty-five minutes. Roosevelt watched, bemused, a little impatient because of his limited strength, but not without appreciation of the outpouring of loyalty and affection. They wanted to hear him, but they could not resist reminding him of their debt to him. They could see that the occasion required solicitude for his weakness, but their hysteria might give him strength. Repeatedly, his gestures for silence showed signs of success only to be buried beneath a new wave of cheering, and Roosevelt, in turn, could not deny his supporters their occasion for homage. When he finally got their attention, his carefully crafted remarks were apt for the moment. The time for aggressive attack had slipped away, and Roosevelt could not recover in a charismatic speech the momentum he had lost in the fortnight since his injury. Entitled "The Purpose of the Progressive Party," the speech had the tone of a lament for a career now closing.

Our task, not so great as Washington's and Lincoln's but "well-nigh as important," Roosevelt began, is to intervene in a timely fashion to prevent the division of America between the haves and the havenots, to insist on the rights and duties of every man and woman in America. "We war against the forces of evil, and the weapons we use are the weapons of right." We do not propose to substitute law for character; "yet the individual character cannot avail unless in addition thereto there lie ready at hand the social weapons which can be forged only by law and by public opinion operating through and operated upon by law." We apply the principles of Sinai, the Golden Rule, and the Sermon on the Mount to the living issues of our day; we reject "the dead dogmas of a vanished past," appeals to formulas of states' rights, or the history of liberty being the history of the limitation of governmental power, or the duty of the courts to determine the meaning of the constitution. We seek to lift burdens from the oppressed, to stand for the sacred rights of women and children, to protect the labor of men from excessive hours, underpayment, injustice, and oppression. "It is idle to ask us not to exercise the power of the government when only by the power of the government can we curb the greed that sits in high places, when only by the exercise of the government can we exalt the lowly and give heart to the humble and the down-trodden." The Progressive platform sets forth our faith on every point: machinery for securing popular government, methods for meeting the needs of farmers, businessmen, laborers. "There is not a promise we have made which cannot be kept. There is not a promise we have made that will not be kept. Our platform is a covenant with the people of the United States, and if we are given the power we will live up to that covenant in letter and in spirit."

He recalled words from his prenomination campaign in New York, and their poignancy in his present weakened condition had special force. "The leader for the time being, whoever he may be, is but an instrument, to be used until broken and then to be cast aside; and if he is worth his salt he will care no more when he is broken than a soldier cares when he is sent where his life is forfeit in order that the victory may be won. In the long fight for righteousness the watchword for all of us is spend and be spent. It is of little matter whether any one man fails or succeeds; but the cause shall not fail, for it is the cause of mankind."

"Friends," he concluded, "what I said then I say now. Surely there never was a greater opportunity than ours. Surely there never was a fight better worth making than this. I believe we shall win, but win or lose I am glad beyond measure that I am one of the many who in this fight have stood ready to spend and be spent, pledged to fight while life lasts the great fight for righteousness and for brotherhood and for the welfare of mankind."[58]

The audience cheered, hearing and not hearing what their leader had said. If he were never to speak again, he could ride into eternity on these final words.

For the Democrats, Roosevelt's was a hard act to follow. Attentive to the externals, they made sure that the ovation for Wilson stretched past an hour, a third again as long as the cheers for the Colonel. Similarly "whole-lunged," "whole-souled," and "utterly ungovernable,"[59] the cheers unnerved Wilson sufficiently to have him discard his fully prepared speech—perhaps the second such since the acceptance speech—and to speak man to man, person to person. From the conditioning of many appearances, the familiar ideas came forth, enriched by the drama of the occasion: "There is no cause half so sacred as the cause of the people. There is no idea so uplifting as the idea of service of humanity. There is nothing that touches the springs of conscience like the cause of the oppressed, the cause of those who suffer and need not only our sympathy, but our justice, our righteous action, our action for them as well as for ourselves. And so, when I look about upon this great company, the thought that moves me is that government is an enterprise of mankind, not an enterprise of parties, that parties are but the poor servants of the cause of mankind."

The Republicans, it developed, were particularly poor servants. Though they started this campaign with a clear vision of great reforms to accomplish, "they drew back from their own purposes . . . and hesitated to act at all." The other branch of the Republican Party housed adventurers who proposed to change "all the centers of energy and organization in the Government of the United States from the combined organs of the government to the discretionary action of the executive."

The Democrats, by contrast, sought simply to crush monopoly, to punish those who broke the law, to restore government to the people. The goal is right, justice, not benevolence. The goal can be met only with a united government, and the only party that can provide that unity is the Democrats. "Your only chance for immediate action is to vote for the single, united, cohesive, clear-sighted power that is within your reach—that great combined, rejuvenated, absolutely confident body of men who are now going to take charge of your government at Washington. You know what they propose to do, and you know what they don't propose to do."

The goal was unity in purpose for the whole American people, he said in a peroration that had more music than meaning: "And when the American people have thus joined together in the great enterprise of their common life, they will wonder how it ever happened that they permitted the great special interests to grow up and overshadow and smother the wholesome growths of the garden. Then they shall wonder that it was ever necessary to summon them to the conclusions of the ballot. I propose that men now forget their individual likes and dislikes, their individual sympathies and antipathies, and, drawing together in the solemn act of a sovereign people, determine what the Government of the United States shall be."[60]

Wilson's speech was hollow. The sentences parsed, but the ideas did not scan. He ambled from phrase to familiar phrase and poured in every line that had evoked response during the campaign, even the tired jokes about his failing voice. The campaign complete, the verdict all but certain, Wilson reverted to a long American tradition of bombast that made orating a form of public entertainment. He was not imparting information, or even attempting to convince. He was establishing a presence, a mythic Wilson beyond politics. For such a message, content is accident. Aura is all. Fatigue, even to the point of exhaustion, joined with political prudence to corrupt the fantasy of a lifetime, the orator as statesman, making sonority the surrogate for meaning.[61]

Yet Wilson's speech, even in garbled and inaccurate form, was enough to revive Roosevelt for one more appeal to the voters. In a striking final statement given at Oyster Bay, with almost no one still listening, with the campaign too far along for impact, Roosevelt gave final definition to his stand on the tariff and, especially on the trusts: on the tariff, protection, reduction of excessive duties, a tariff commission based on the experience of Germany; on trusts, a full statement that explicitly resurrected the specifics that Perkins had expunged in Chicago: "The anti-trust law will remain on the books, and it will be strengthened by prohibiting agreements to divide territory or limit output, by prohibiting a refusal to sell to customers who buy from business rivals, by prohibiting the custom of selling below cost in certain areas while maintaining higher prices in other areas, by prohibiting the use of the power of transportation to aid or injure special business concerns—in short, by prohibiting these and all other unfair trade practices. The Inter-State Industrial Commission will give us an efficient instrument for seeing that the law is carried out in letter and in spirit, and for effectively punishing not only every corporation, but every individual who violates the provisions of the law."[62]

The statement was definitive beyond previous versions, light years from the generalities of Wilson. It appeared in Sunday's papers. The election was Tuesday. Who could hear above the background noise created by last-minute hustle, bombast, and boisterous twaddle?

In the Midwest, Debs was making his final appeals, spirited valedictories to five months of campaigning. In Grand Rapids, Michigan, he recalled that Emerson had said that when God turns a thinker loose on the world, the earth trembles. "The Socialist Party ... is turning thinkers loose, capitalism is beginning to tremble and well it may for its end and the final triumph of the people is as sure as that the sun shall rise tomorrow."[63] In Minneapolis, Minnesota, one meeting overflowed into a second meeting, which also overflowed, as Debs predicted that the Socialist vote would be "a surprise to the country," for workers recognized the true issue, workers' ownership of the tools of industry. He praised his running mate Seidel, and he assured his followers that "Never was the promise of Socialism so cheering as it is now. The workers of the nation are awakened and aroused as never before in the history of the country."[64] On the Saturday before election day, three large assemblies in Chicago heard Debs make his confident and defiant plea.

The final days were rather still. The President paid his respect at Sherman's funeral, swung back through New York City to lunch with his brother Charles and to ride through Central Park and along Riverside Drive prior to catching a train that would allow him to make a dozen stops in Ohio on his way home to Cincinnati. On election day, he voted, played golf, waited for the results before returning to Washington on Wednesday.

The Colonel returned to Madison Square Garden to plug for the Bull Moose candidates for New York state offices. With contempt, he spurned the suggestion of leapfrogging Wilson's sixty-three-minute ovation at the Garden; he had no taste for manufactured demonstrations. He holed up at Oyster Bay, argued with his wife about whether to wear a coat (he lost), ridiculed his old friend Elihu Root who had had the ground cut out from under him by a New York Court of Appeals decision, voted at town hall, and settled in at Sagamore Hill to watch victory and defeat.

Debs went back to Terre Haute, responding to his neighbors' demand for a few remarks. On election day, he had no reason to rise early, for, not having been in Terre Haute to register, he was ineligible to vote. Instead, he celebrated his fifty-seventh birthday.

Wilson circulated in New Jersey, campaigning to the end for Democratic candidates for Congress and for Democratic state legislators who would vote Judge Hughes into the Senate. He drove to the coast for speeches at Long Branch, Freehold, and Red Bank. Returning through Hightstown, his car struck a mound. The governor was thrown against the supports in the roof, the jolt producing a four-inch bloody scalp wound. "Only a scratch—and private property," he told reporters to whom he refused a snapshot of the unwonted and unwanted bald spot.[65] He continued his rounds to Paterson and Passaic, half a farewell, half a bid for support in Washington. He offered congratulations to his secretary, Joe Tumulty, on the birth of his sixth child; Tumulty resisted a suggestion (not from Wilson) that the boy be named Thomas Woodrow Wilson Tumulty. On election day, Wilson voted in turn, amiably assuring election officials that as governor he would enforce the law against reporters who loitered too close to the polling booths. He walked around Princeton, showing Captain McDonald where he had eaten as a freshman, returned to Cleveland Lane to join his extended family, a few friends, and a scant dozen expectant reporters. By early evening, the election returns were coming in by a telegraph receiver set up in the library, the same instrument that had brought Grover Cleveland news of victory twenty years before. The governor waited, calm, interested, not uncertain.

At exactly 10 PM, Mrs. Wilson got the word from the telegraph operator that all doubt was passed. Approaching her husband, she placed her hands on his shoulders and kissed him. "My dear," she said, "I want to be the first to congratulate you."[66] The word spread to the nearby campus. Soon the bell in Nassau Hall proclaimed Princeton's victory over both Yale and Harvard. When the undergraduates proceeded from the campus to Cleveland Lane, President-elect Wilson greeted them affectionately, then called them to his crusade—and theirs:[67]

I have no feeling of triumph tonight, but a feeling of solemn responsibility. I know the great task ahead of me and the men associated with myself. I look almost with pleading to you, the young men of America, to stand behind me in the administration. The purest impulses are needed. Wrongs have been done, but they have not been done malevolently. We must have the quietest temper in what we are going to do. We must not let any man divert us. We must have quiet tempers and yet be resolute of purpose. But let us hear them all patiently, and yet, hearing all, let us not be diverted.

You men must play a great part. I plead with you again to look constantly forward. I summon you for the rest of your lives to support the men who like myself want to carry the nation forward to its highest destiny and greatness.

PART V

Postmortem and Aftermath

14

Understanding Victory and Defeat

The Democratic victory in 1912 suggested a landslide: Governor Woodrow Wilson carried 40 states and 435 electoral votes, leaving the remainder for Theodore Roosevelt and President William Howard Taft to divide: Roosevelt with 6 states and 88 electoral votes, Taft with 2 states (Vermont and Utah) and 8 electoral votes. Eugene V. Debs tallied 6 percent of the vote, but, as expected, carried no state. Two minor parties, Prohibitionist and Socialist Labor, polled just over 1 percent of the vote, the bulk going to the Prohibitionists. Furthermore, the Democrats controlled the Congress decisively. Having won the House of Representatives in the election of 1910, the Democrats now possessed over two-thirds of the seats of the lower house: 291/435, their Republican foes reduced to 127, 17 others divided among Progressives and other minor parties. The Senate also went Democratic for the first time in 20 years: 51 senators (10 more than in the previous Congress), leaving the Republicans with 44 seats, the Progressives with 1. Nevertheless, Wilson's electoral victory, however decisive, was deceptive. Republicans, regulars and Progressives, had polled 50.5 percent of the popular vote, Wilson less than 42 percent. The Republicans had beaten themselves, beaten each other, making the New Jersey governor the beneficiary of their fratricide.

Wilson, indeed, had little to show for his campaign except victory. In 25 states with an electoral total of 278 (12 more than needed for a majority), the combined Republican and Progressive vote swamped Wilson, though the Republican division allowed Wilson to sail between them and claim all 278 votes. To these he added the 2 new states, Arizona and New Mexico, as well as the perennial 13 Democratic southern and border states. Still, his popular achievement was unremarkable. Though the total number of voters had increased about 1 percent since 1908, fewer citizens voted for Wilson in 1912 than had voted for William Jennings Bryan in 1908. In the 17 states that both Bryan in 1908 and Wilson in 1912 won, Wilson's proportion of the vote dropped below Bryan's in 12.[1]

Nonetheless, Wilson's 6,293, 019 votes gave him a plurality over Roosevelt's 4,119,507 and Taft's 3,484, 956, and his victory in the electoral college was the most substantial since Ulysses S. Grant had crushed Horace Greeley forty years before.

The anatomy of the voting pattern invites interpretation.

Suppose that the Taft machine had allowed its attention to flag for a moment, permitting progressive Republicans to block Taft's nomination by depriving his managers of control of the convention. Any number of slips were possible: a moment of inadvertence by Elihu Root, the permanent chairman; a revolt by quixotic black delegates from the South who would have preferred victory and patronage with Roosevelt to defeat and loyalty with Taft; a defection within other Republican state delegations with similar ambitions or with more lofty ideological preferences for the future; a direct bribe by someone to a key leader, not a likely occurrence, but not so remote from the reality of politics as to lie beyond belief. Suppose also that Roosevelt could not have controlled the convention either—a legitimate supposition, for even if Roosevelt had won fifty of the contested delegates, a fair figure beyond the nineteen that the Taft forces let him have and short of the seventy-four that he alleged were stolen, he still fell short of a majority. He could have expected no help from Senator Robert M. La Follette, and even stray votes—the seventeen that belonged to Senator Albert A. Cummins, for example—could not have put him over the top. Then a deadlocked convention, not unlike the Democrats' in Baltimore, would have had to seek a compromise candidate. Neither Taft nor Roosevelt would have considered La Follette. Taft had been willing to go with Root or with Supreme Court Justice Charles Evans Hughes. Roosevelt would have held out against Root until the winds blew Chicago into Lake Michigan, and anyway, Root, sixty-seven years old, had little interest in the job—if he were going to make his play, he would have done so five to eight years earlier. Hughes could have been coaxed, as he was four years later; but he needed a direct request from Taft and the prospect of a decently united party. Hughes, as governor of New York for four years, had reasonably progressive credentials—if not a La Follette, he was certainly miles ahead of his successor, John A. Dix. Cummins and Governor Herbert S. Hadley of Missouri were possibilities from Roosevelt's camp, Hadley much more than Cummins, for he was moderate in his views, and he conducted himself with aplomb in the frenzy of the convention. In fact, both, and again especially Hadley, were the subject of intrigue even in the convention that Taft dominated. If a true and prolonged deadlock had developed, the alternative to perpetual deadlock was compromise; both Taft and Roosevelt delegates would eventually have forced the issue; they wanted a winner, and they wanted to go home. Taft himself could not have foreseen a victory in November, and

Roosevelt was vulnerable to reminders that the issue was progressivism and not himself. If the convention had agreed on Hughes or Hadley, with the show of unity characteristic of major party conventions even after a moderate flow of blood in the streets, the pattern of the November vote suggests clearly that a predominantly Republican nation would have returned a Republican candidate to the White House. To be sure, there was a Democratic trend in the nation: the Democratic majority in the House of Representatives in 1910 and the astonishing gain of ten seats in the Senate in the election of 1912 attest to that. But the changes in the Senate occurred even as Wilson fell below Bryan's total vote in 1908. The nation was quite capable of making Congress Democratic while it elected a Republican president. Competing with a candidate with progressive credentials approximately equal to his own, Wilson could not have pulled a substantial number of votes away from his Republican opponent. If Wilson had tilted right to gain more conservative votes, he would have had to separate himself from his progressive protestations and from the legacy of Bryan. The Republican majority in the nation would have no reason to entrust its future to such a Democratic chameleon.

The result of Taft's control of the convention was that compromise never became an option: Taft's bull-headed victory led to Roosevelt's bolt and to ultimate defeat for both men. Compromise would have given the nation a Republican candidate almost sure to win—against Wilson, against Speaker Champ Clark, against any obscure compromise candidate the Democrats could have dredged up from their inexperienced ranks.

Suppose the impossible: that Roosevelt had won at the Republican convention, won marginally, the only way conceivable as long as Taft's wrath guided the Republican organization. Defections from the party's campaign would certainly have followed. Though it is hard to imagine Taft speaking publicly for a Democrat, or even giving covert support from his sulking tent, as La Follette did during the campaign, Taft's inactivity in a Wilson-Roosevelt battle would have made his indolent fall campaign in the Wilson-Roosevelt-Taft battle look like a cyclone. Root actually threatened to bolt if Roosevelt were nominated; but Root was a personage of no political consequence once his function at the convention ended. Republican financial support would have followed Root out of the party; but it did anyway, as Charles D. Hilles had occasion to lament all too frequently. Still, the bulk of the party faithful, and certainly the party leadership, had no place to go. The same pressures that kept most of Roosevelt's governors from joining his Bull Moose party, that is, the institutional bonds that tied their futures to the Republican Party apparatus, would have kept the party's organization intact for Roosevelt too if he had been the candidate. An experienced hand at reconciling or sidetracking political dissidents, Roosevelt would also have known how to moderate his radical stances—as he did during the campaign in any case—to meet the needs of the occasion. He could have battled successfully for middle ground if Wilson had tried to flank him either to the left or to the right. Wilson could not have been more progressive, more radical, than Osawatomie and Columbus had made Roosevelt; and if Wilson had swerved sharply right, Roosevelt could have waved the name of William Jennings Bryan as a taunt to Wilson's pretensions. If Roosevelt and Wilson had both scrambled for moderation, Debs would have gained some support. But no one regarded the Socialist Party as a serious threat; even in Oklahoma, where Debs did not have to compete with Roosevelt as the radical voice, Debs took under 17 percent of the vote. If Roosevelt had been nominated as a Republican, the party's national status as the majority party and his own campaigning dynamism would have carried him to victory. Even massive defections would not have crippled him. If he had retained a mere 52 percent of Taft's Republican vote in nine states outside the South with ten or more electoral votes, those states plus the six states that he won would have given him more than enough to win. Some of those states would have been tough: in Missouri, he would have needed 99 percent of Taft's votes. Some would have been very easy: in Massachusetts and Iowa, 20 percent would have been enough. If Missouri, or any other individual state, let him down, there were at least fifteen more states outside the South where he could have recouped his losses. In the North, the Midwest, and the West, he could have counted on the self-interest of the party organizations and the long-standing voting habits of the American people to reinforce his own campaigning and to carry him to a third term as president.

The most plausible alternate scenario is vastly more complex. Suppose that Roosevelt, having lost in Chicago, declined to summon the Bull Moose, leaving Wilson and Taft to fight out their differences. Even as a noncandidate, Roosevelt would have been the uninvited guest at the banquet that followed: his posture would have been the crucial variable in the election.

It is inconceivable that Roosevelt would have campaigned for Taft, so angry, even corrosively bitter, had their differences become. But if the inconceivable had come to pass, Roosevelt swallowing his hurt to protect the party that had nurtured his career for three decades, Taft with Roosevelt's help would undoubtedly have romped to victory on the strength of the Republican national majority that functioned almost everywhere but in the South.

Conversely, it is almost as inconceivable that Roosevelt would have campaigned for Wilson. A lifetime distrust of Democrats, reinforced by what he viewed as a stale and reactionary Democratic platform in 1912 and by Wilson's evasive and opportunistic espousal of progressive causes, would have made Roosevelt choke on words of praise for Wilson's candidacy, especially since such words would have been vulnerable to the charge that Roosevelt was being vengeful and spiteful. But, again, if the inconceivable had come to pass, if Roosevelt had supported Wilson against Taft, then Roosevelt would have wrested enough votes from people who regarded themselves as Republicans to assure Wilson of victory. Roosevelt polled over four million votes. If only a fourth of his supporters followed him into Wilson's camp, the Democrats could have turned their minority into a majority: New York, Ohio, Missouri, Indiana, New Jersey, Wisconsin, and California, together with the states invariably Democratic, would have given Wilson his majority in the electoral college. To turn these votes, Roosevelt would have had to be active; sub rosa support of Wilson, like La Follette's, would not have been enough.

In all probability, a Roosevelt who lost in Chicago and who shunned a third party would have gone hunting during the campaign, avoiding a race to which he could see no good end. In that case, the election of 1912 would have followed a different line. President Taft, protected from the certainty of failure that Roosevelt's presence foretold, might well have thrown off his lethargic indifference in order to capitalize on the national Republican majority. But his efforts would have been in vain. The sullenness born in the prenomination campaign and in the convention would have dogged his travels, and the national thrust of progressivism would have needed a more convincing outlet. Even without a cue from Roosevelt, progressives and, even more, the masses of people who felt the need to get a leash on unrestrained power that was shaping their lives without their consent would have sought such a spokesman. Wilson the campaigner would have given voice to their needs with a dynamism that Taft could never have matched. Between the perceived extremes, Taft at one end and Debs at the other, Wilson, something of a conservative who had acquired the vocabulary of a progressive, would have made himself the popular tribune for the future. There was flair in his vision, yet sobriety in his speech.

Speculations aside, the election produced its winners and losers. Wilson was the clear winner in a triumphant personal victory reinforced by a Democratic Congress that gave promise for the years ahead. Taft, though suffering a humiliating defeat, was also a winner: the Republican Party remained a stolid agent for traditional constitutional values, and the recent rebels would have to grovel on their way back to its sheltering arms. Debs, having doubled the Socialist vote in four years, appeared to be a winner, but within months after the election, gross internal strains in the party revealed that 1912 was a climax rather than a milestone for the Socialists.

The biggest loser of all was Theodore Roosevelt. He lost the election, but that was to be expected. Even more serious, his crusade apparently led nowhere, and his army turned on itself, bickering so remorselessly that he had to cooperate in disbanding it, letting its tattered remnants find refuge where they could—in the old discredited parties and with the Socialists. Root was right—Root was often right—when he warned Roosevelt not to tempt fate in 1912: "the consequences to your future, to your power of leadership in the interests of the causes which you have at heart, and to your position in history, would be so injurious that no friend and no number of friends have any right to ask such a sacrifice."[2] Roosevelt understood Root's argument, and he acknowledged the perils of his course "from my own personal standpoint."[3] But his combative nature drove him; once in motion, he realized that combat built its own momentum. Defeated in Chicago, he felt he had no option but to go on. As he told the French ambassador, "I would rather take a thrashing than be quiet under such a licking."[4] So he took his thrashing, and he paid the price that Root had predicted.

15

The Progressive Legacy

The accession of Woodrow Wilson to the presidency on March 4, 1913, gave a spurt to progressivism that lasted for more than sixty years. In that process Wilson's role was central, as much in the ambiguities he created as in the certainties he imposed. The herald of a new era, coming into power in a yeasty environment for change, he both shaped and was shaped by the political realities around him. By the end of his two terms, the thrusts of progressivism, the dynamics of elections, and the pressures of war had created new, and enduring, relations between the national government and both the American people and the American economy.

The changes occurred both in the Constitution and in the statutes.

Two amendments, the first since post–Civil War days, were ratified without action by the Wilson administration. The Sixteenth Amendment, authorizing a federal income tax, went through Congress with President William Howard Taft's endorsement; it was declared ratified a week before Taft left office. The Seventeenth Amendment, providing for the direct election of senators, became a part of the Constitution in May 1913, less than thirteen months after Congress had submitted it to the states. The first provided revenues for federal projects beyond current imagination; the second brought the voting population one step closer to the wheels of power. Together they reflected the two prongs of progressivism: more popular rule and a larger role for the government in manipulating the economy.

The legislative program of the Wilson years—both acts that Wilson initiated and those that he supported or tolerated—ranked with the first administration of George Washington and the first three years of Abraham Lincoln's tenure. Faithful to his campaign stand, Wilson, on the very day of his inauguration, called Congress into special session to reduce the tariff. Breaking a 113-year precedent, Wilson appeared in person before a joint assembly of senators and representatives in April, insisting that they remove the abuses that Republican Congresses had left in their wake. When the congressmen faced the usual difficulty of reconciling their constituents' needs with the overall national interest and when lobbyists, more numerous than congressmen, poured into Washington to keep their individual oxen from getting gored, Wilson went over all their heads to the American people, denouncing the special interests represented by the lobbyists, holding the feet of Democratic congressmen to the flame of public opinion until Congress gave him the Underwood tariff, which reduced duties an average of 20 percent.

Already Wilson was active on another front. For over four years, a National Monetary Commission, authorized in the Roosevelt administration and headed for much of its life by the conservative Senator Nelson W. Aldrich of Rhode Island, had studied ways to coordinate national banks in a system that could even out the dips and swells in the banking and currency systems. Far from expert on the topic, Wilson knew, even as a candidate for the presidency, that control of such a system could not be left in private hands. In proposals for the Democratic platform that he wrote in June 1912, he had insisted that control rest with the government or "some public instrumentality which the banks cannot manipulate or dominate."[1] When a bill for a central bank dominated by the private member banks themselves emerged from the House Banking Committee, Wilson, on the advice of Louis D. Brandeis and under pressure from progressives in both parties, held firm for public control. The Federal Reserve System, created by Congress in December 1913, six months to the day after Wilson had laid down the law, allowed for private ownership of and substantial private control of twelve regional federal reserves banks, but vested in a central body, the Federal Reserve Board, the authority to set policy for the system.

The following year, Congress, in response to Wilson's recommendation, set up the Federal Trade Commission (FTC), a Democratic version of Theodore Roosevelt's most notable political proposal, the interstate industrial commission. Wilson's support for the FTC showed how far he had come from the soft generalities of his acceptance speech in August 1912. In the campaign, he had sidled toward Roosevelt's position, all the while obfuscating his movement. Now in power, he had no further need to dissemble. The FTC, replacing the Bureau of Corporations, collected information on businesses and, more important, it received authority to issue cease-and-desist orders against unfair business practices, subject to review by the federal courts. Less than a month later, Congress also passed the Clayton Antitrust Act, which restricted antitrust action against labor unions and farm organizations and strengthened the Sherman Act by specifying acts that offended the national intent to preserve competition. Though the Clayton Act appeared to embody changes consistent with Wilson's campaign rhetoric, Wilson did next to nothing to aid its passage. Having reduced the tariff, gotten a hold on the banking and currency systems through the Federal Reserve System, and set up the Federal Trade Commission as the government's agent for dealing with most interstate businesses, he believed that the essentials were in place.

Compared with progressive pretensions, Wilson's position was minimal. He was holding to his preelection stand that no deep antagonism separated business and the rest of society; that national harmony rested on consulting everyone's interest, including businessmen's; that wrongdoing needed to be punished personally, that is, that wrongdoers needed to be punished, but that they were few and far between. Wilson carried his sense of harmony even into the regulatory agencies: he staffed both the Federal Trade Commission and the Federal Reserve System with men so well disposed to the interest they were meant to regulate that progressives in Congress and in the intellectual and social service communities screamed their derision. Even Brandeis, close as he was to Wilson, was dismayed.[2]

Wilson's sense of self as the harmonizer of the national interest cut two ways: just as he refused to put on the hostile face against businessmen, he also refused to kowtow to other special interests, like farmers or workers, who most progressives thought needed the special solicitude of the people's government. Even so disadvantaged a group as the eight million largely disfranchised blacks did not excite his empathy. Black rights were not high on most progressives' agendas, to be sure, but under Wilson black Americans fell back as segregated facilities became the norm in governmental offices in the nation's capital. In creating national harmony, Wilson was not disposed to accost dominant white sentiment in the South. President of all the people at a time when the European war from 1914 onward demanded strong diplomatic postures, he disdained special interests as divisive.

The approach of the election of 1916, however, propelled Wilson to a new stance. Roosevelt's Bull Moose coalition, abandoned by its leader, was dissolving, and a united Republican Party under a moderately progressive and utterly respectable leader, Justice Charles Evans Hughes of the Supreme Court, seemed likely to ride the national majority to victory in November 1916. Anticipating the danger, Wilson once again unfurled progressive banners. Early in the year he nominated Brandeis to the Supreme Court, and he stood behind his choice until the Senate rebuffed the determined—and vicious—attack that the business and legal communities mounted against the Jewish reformer. Shortly thereafter, Wilson, reversing his stand in the previous two years, signed into law the Federal Farm Loan Act, a sort of Federal Reserve System for farmers that made credit more readily available through farmers' cooperative loan associations, and the Warehouse Act, which permitted licensed warehouses to issue receipts on farmers' products that could serve as collateral for loans. Swallowing constitutional scruples, he threw his full weight behind the Keating-Owen Child Labor Act, which forbade the shipment of the products of child labor in interstate commerce. (Both Keating-Owen and its successor, passed in 1919, were later declared unconstitutional by the

Supreme Court.[3]) Wilson also allowed Congress to create the tariff commission that had figured so prominently in Roosevelt's thinking, and he supported exemption from antitrust action for businesses that combined to promote exports (though the Webb-Pomerene Act did not pass until early in 1918).

Wilson's march to renewed progressivism—a maneuver as much forced upon him as initiated by him—revealed much about the nature of presidential leadership in the post-Roosevelt years. The President himself occupied a crucial role: the capacity to initiate and the power to veto granted him unmatched prominence. But the shape of policy owed much to congressional blocs, which sensed their constituents' needs at the local level, and to the recent prominence being gained by the intellectual community: the universities; the nationally organized professional groups, like social workers and consumer advocates; and the reforming press, most prominently in this period, the brilliant array of publicists, like Walter Lippmann and Herbert Croly, assembled at the recently founded *New Republic*. Struggling to maintain its tenuous hold on national power, the Democratic Party, and Wilson at its head, could ignore pressures from below only with great peril; Wilson's support for the first child-labor bill was in responce to an explicit warning that social workers regarded it as the litmus test for progressivism.[4] By propelling himself to the front of progressives who were running well ahead of him, Wilson in the election of 1916 held his own progressive supporters from 1912, acquired many of Roosevelt's followers, and drew thousands of votes away from the Socialists.

Even so, Wilson's victory in 1916 was marginal. In addition to his progressive posture, Wilson had both the issue of peace and war and Hughes's striking ineptitude as a campaigner going for him. Nevertheless, his majority in the electoral college, 277 of 531, down from 435 of 531 in 1912, finally rested on California's 13 electoral votes; and California's swing to the Democrats hinged on less than 4,000 out of almost a million. Discounting the South and border states that always voted Democratic, the rest of the nation was still not prepared to give a majority to Democrats.

Nonetheless, the war years provided a stimulus for both prongs of progressivism. The dominant male electorate made female voting a national right through the Nineteenth Amendment. And the imperatives of war led to deep federal intrusions into the American economy: the Shipping Board to build, purchase, or lease a fleet for transport, the War Industries Board to convert industrial facilities to war needs, fuel and food administrators to allocate those essentials, the Railroad Administration to draw the nation's tracks into a single system, and a bountiful War Revenue Act to pay part of the cost. A nation at war with the single goal of victory acquired the skills and devices that made laissez-faire a hollow memory and established for the future the conviction that government, regulating—even controlling—the economy in the public interest within the rubrics of private ownership in a capitalist system, could play an effective role in meeting its constitutional obligation "to promote the general welfare."

That conviction persisted for decades. In the twelve Republican years from Wilson to Franklin D. Roosevelt, it took a perverse form: close collaboration, indeed mutual support, between business and government. From the Commerce Department and then from the presidency, Herbert C. Hoover interlocked Washington and business's quest for profits. Probusiness appointments to regulatory agencies so drained the tradition of vigorous governmental supervision that even as early as 1925 Senator George W. Norris suggested abolishing the Federal Trade Commission "to save the money of the people."[5] But in the Great Depression, the mood of 1912 came alive again as a new President Roosevelt, also a onetime Assistant Secretary of the Navy, revived the traditions of his former chief and of his deceased cousin. The New Deal revived the notion of government serving individual constituencies: the National Industrial Recovery Act (NRA) for industry, its section 7a and then the Wagner Act for labor, the Agricultural Adjustment Administration for farmers, the Social Security Act for the elderly, the Civilian Conservation Corps for the young (and for conservation), the Home Owners Loan Corporation for householders, the Tennessee Valley Authority for the total life of a region.

Even in detail, the parallels were striking. Just as outsiders had pushed Wilson to new measures in 1916, it was Congress that pushed FDR into some "second New Deal" measures like the Wagner Act. Just as the Wilson administration had passed both the Federal Trade Commission Act and the Clayton Antitrust Act, the Roosevelt administration, through the NRA, encouraged businesses to write industry-wide codes that restrained trade in quite dramatic form; then, with the demise of the NRA in 1935, the antitrust tradition revived, finding its most dramatic expression in the 1938 report of the joint executive-legislative Temporary National Economic Committee (TNEC). In turn, the TNEC's thrust collapsed under the impact of World War II. Just as Eugene V. Debs had complained in 1912 that Theodore Roosevelt had just stolen twenty-one Socialist planks, his successor Norman Thomas, as perennial a Socialist candidate for president as Debs had been, accused both Democrats in the 1930s and Republicans in the 1950s of stealing his thunder.[6]

In succeeding administrations, Harry S. Truman kept the progressive tradition alive even in the face of congressional determination to halt or to reverse it. His successor, Dwight D. Eisenhower, left the entire structure of reform intact: the most important domestic accomplishment of his eight years was to place beyond partisan debate the structure that Democratic progressives had built. After John F. Kennedy's one thousand days, Lyndon B. Johnson revived both thrusts of progressivism: in his program for the "Great Society" he exercised the taxing and regulatory powers of the national government in an attempt to "abolish poverty" so rampant in the "other America," the millions of invisible poor who had fallen between the cracks of previous reforms; and in the Civil Rights Act of 1964 and the Voting Rights Act of 1965, he sought to extend the benefits of citizenship to the black minority slighted by Wilson and largely unattended by the administrations since. His successor, Richard M. Nixon, rerouted federal tax dollars to states and cities—bloc grants for housing and employment—and he pushed, unsuccessfully, for a family assistance package that, through negative income taxes, would transfer federal tax money to the poor. Furthermore, the late 1960s and the 1970s witnessed a whole new era of "social regulation," laws and federal regulatory agencies to enforce them, that sought to avert physical harm to the public: occupational safety and health, environmental protection, strip mining—ten in all from 1964 to 1977. Environmental legislation, placing an enormous burden on corporate decision making and increasing the role of bureaucrats responsive to "public interest" lobbies, forced American industry to multiply its attention to federal regulation and made legal and accounting firms in Washington, D.C., a major growth industry.[7] The momentum of protective legislation carried even into the years of Gerald R. Ford, a transitional figure certainly not seeking out new tasks for the national government.

The Nixon/Ford years may well have played the progressive string right out to its very end. Thereafter, the leadership of the national government backed off. The next two presidents, Jimmy Carter and Ronald Reagan, ran for the presidency against Washington and its bureaucratic establishments. Caught up in commitments that two generations had locked in place, they nevertheless made opening moves toward deregulation, restoring to what they spoke of as a "free economy" the power to control its own destiny.[8] A new congressional generation, variously known as "neoliberals" and "Atari Democrats," pursued the argument that the old progressivism had had its day.[9]

That day, if indeed it is ending, lasted sixty to seventy years. Its dawn in the election of 1912 had embraced all four protagonists: President Taft at one end had pressed antitrust suits with vigor beyond his predecessors. He had pushed along the income tax amendment. He had made a modest proposal for farm loans. At the other end, the Socialist platform, rather more than Eugene V. Debs himself, had proposed a panoply of reforms deemed radical at the time, many of which are now the law of the land. In the center, Theodore Roosevelt and Woodrow Wilson went their variant ways, then became a single strand as Wilson absorbed substantial chunks of Roosevelt's ideas and as Roosevelt himself was edged off political stage center. The legacy of the presidential election of 1912 gave meaning to an era, and only now may it be supposed that that era has ended.

Notes

BIBLIOGRAPHIC ABBREVIATIONS

WWP	Arthur S. Link, ed., *The Papers of Woodrow Wilson*, 58 vol., Princeton, 1966–1988.
TRL	Elting E. Morison, et al., eds., *The Letters of Theodore Roosevelt*, 8 vol. Cambridge, Mass., 1951–1954
TRW	*The Works of Theodore Roosevelt*, 24 vol., New York, 1923–1926.
WHT/LC	William Howard Taft Papers, Library of Congress
EVDF	Eugene V. Debs Foundation, Terre Haute, Indiana.
C.C.A.	Circuit Court of Appeals.

INTRODUCTION

1. Henry David Thoreau, "Civil Disobedience," *Miscellanies*, Boston, 1894, 131.

2. Grant McConnell, *Private Power and American Democracy*, New York, 1967, 30–50, 358–359.

3. Herbert Spencer, *The Man Versus the State*, Caldwell, Ohio, 1940, 183–184, 202. Originally written in 1884.

4. Martin J. Sklar, *The Corporate Reconstruction of American Capitalism, 1890–1916*, Cambridge, Mass., 1988, 4–5, and passim.

5. Richard L. McCormick, "The Discovery That Business Corrupts Politics: A Reappraisal of the Origins of Progressivism," *American Historical Review*, February 1981, 247–274.

6. Richard Hofstadter, "The Meaning of the Progressive Movement," in Hofstadter, ed., *The Progressive Movement 1900–1915*, Englewood Cliffs, N.J., 1963, 2–3. For an

influential view that the "movement" was a "mirage," see Peter G. Filene, "An Obituary for 'The Progressive Movement,'" *American Quarterly*, 1970, 20–34.

7. Robert H. Wiebe, *The Search for Order, 1877–1920*, New York, 1967; Samuel P. Hays, *The Response to Industrialism, 1885–1914*, Chicago, 1957; Alfred D. Chandler, Jr., *The Visible Hand*, Cambridge, Mass., 1977, 1–12, 484–500; Thomas K. McGraw, "Rethinking the Trust Question," in McGraw, ed., *Regulation in Perspective*, Cambridge, Mass., 1981, 1–24; Hofstadter, *The Age of Reform*, New York, 1955, 131–269.

8. William Ashley, *Surveys Historical and Economic*, New York, 1900, 409, quoted in Louis Hartz, *The Liberal Tradition in America*, New York, 1955, 222. See also Gabriel Kolko, *The Triumph of Conservatism*, Chicago, 1967. Wiebe's earlier article, "Business Disunity and the Progressive Movement, 1901–1914," gave a brief early account of businessmen who divided over urban-rural, East-West/South, large-small, and functional (shipper/carrier) lines. *Mississippi Valley Historical Review*, March 1958, 664–685.

9. J. Joseph Huthmacher, "Urban Liberalism and the Age of Reform," *Mississippi Valley Historical Review*, September 1962, 231–241; John D. Buenker, *Urban Liberalism and Progressive Reform*, New York, 1973.

CHAPTER 1

1. Richard Hofstadter, *The American Political Tradition and the Men Who Made It*, New York, 1948, 233.

2. Robert Coles, *Privileged Ones: The Well-Off and the Rich in America (Children of Crisis*, vol. 5), Boston, 1977, 369, 361–409 passim.

3. Edmund Morris, *The Rise of Theodore Roosevelt*, New York, 1979, 143.

4. Ibid., 161–162.

5. Ibid., 162.

6. Quoted in John M. Blum, "Theodore Roosevelt: The Years of Decision," *TRL*, vol. 2, 1485.

7. Morris, *Roosevelt*, 475.

8. Lincoln Steffens, *The Autobiography of Lincoln Steffens*, New York, 1931, 259–260.

9. Theodore Roosevelt to Henry Cabot Lodge, January 19, 1896, in Lodge, ed., *Selections from the Correspondence of Theodore Roosevelt and Henry Cabot Lodge*, vol. 1, New York, 1925, 210 (hereafter, *Roosevelt-Lodge Correspondence*).

10. *New York Times*, January 23, 1896.

11. Roosevelt to Lodge, January 19, 1896, *Roosevelt-Lodge Correspondence*, vol. 1, 210.

12. Morris, *Roosevelt*, 537.

13. Ibid., 569–571; *New York Times*, June 3, 1897.

14. Morris, *Roosevelt*, 611.

15. Ibid., 664.

16. Ibid., 668.

17. "Note on Roosevelt's Nomination for the Governorship," *TRL*, vol. 2, 1474–1478.

18. Philip C. Jessup, *Elihu Root*, vol. 1, New York, 1938, 200.

19. Morris, *Roosevelt*, 686.

20. William Allen White, *The Autobiography of William Allen White*, New York, 1946, 297–298.

21. James David Barker has shrewd comments on Roosevelt's use of the press in *The Pulse of Politics*, New York, 1980, 29–46.

22. Morris, *Roosevelt*, 734.

23. Ibid., 724.

24. The whole exchange is contained in Roosevelt to Lodge, May 27, 1903, *TRL*, vol. 3, 481–482. John M. Blum has a spirited account of the new president's political maneuvers in *The Republican Roosevelt*, Cambridge, Mass., 1967, 37–54.

25. Theodore Roosevelt, "First Annual Message," December 3, 1901, *TRW*, vol. 17, 100–107.

26. Hofstadter has a deft analysis of the significance of the Northern Securities prosecution and the coal strike in *The Age of Reform*, New York, 1955, 232–236.

27. George E. Mowry, *Theodore Roosevelt and the Progressive Movement*, New York, 1960, 22.

28. Quoted in John M. Blum, *The Progressive Presidents*, New York, 1980, 41. See also Blum, *The Republican Roosevelt*, 73–105.

29. Quoted in Mowry, *The Era of Theodore Roosevelt and the Birth of Modern America, 1900–1912*, New York, 1962, 211.

30. Morris, *Roosevelt*, 717.

31. Roosevelt's view of power and his own sense of self and office is best caught in Blum, *The Republican Roosevelt*, 106–124, and Blum, *The Progressive Presidents*, 30–60.

32. *New York Times*, November 9, 1904.

CHAPTER 2

1. Henry F. Pringle, *The Life and Times of William Howard Taft*, vol. 1, New York, 1939, 57.

2. Ibid., I, 96.

3. James T. Patterson, *Mr. Republican*, Boston, 1972, 3–16.

4. Pringle, *Taft*, vol. 1, 138.

5. Ibid., 143.

6. 29 C.C.A. 167.

7. 29 C.C.A. at 170–171.

8. 175 U.S. 211.

9. Pringle, *Taft*, vol. 1, 235–236.

10. Theodore Roosevelt, "Governor William H. Taft," *Outlook*, September 21, 1901, 166.

11. Roosevelt to Taft, November 26, 1902, *TRL*, vol. 3, 382.

12. Pringle, *Taft*, vol. 1, 261.

13. Roosevelt to Taft, March 15, 1906, *TRL*, vol. 5, 184.

14. Philip C. Jessup, *Elihu Root*, vol. 1, New York, 1938, 428.

15. Pringle, *Taft*, vol. 1, 350–351.

16. Ibid., 354.

17. Ibid., 356.

18. Ibid., 365–366.

19. Ibid., 378.

20. Archie Butt to Mrs. F. B. (Clara) Butt, March 11, 16, 1909, in Archie Butt, *Taft and Roosevelt: The Intimate Letters of Archie Butt*, vol. 1, Garden City, N.Y., 1930, 9, 14.

21. Pringle, *Taft*, vol. 1, 378.

22. Taft to William Allen White, March 22, 1909, quoted in Donald F. Anderson, *William Howard Taft: A Conservative's Conception of the Presidency*, Ithaca, N.Y., 1973, 159.

23. Roosevelt to Taft, November 10, 1908, *TRL*, vol. 6, 1341.

24. Taft to Roosevelt, March 21, 1909, *WHT/LC*.

25. George E. Mowry, *The Era of Theodore Roosevelt and the Birth of Modern America, 1900–1912*, New York, 1962, 266.

26. William Allen White, *The Autobiography of William Allen White*, New York, 1946, 445.

27. Pringle, *Taft*, vol. 1, 454.

28. Mowry, *The Era of Theodore Roosevelt*, 254.

29. Anderson, *Taft*, 289–306. Taft outlined his views in Taft, *Our Chief Magistrate and His Powers*, New York, 1916. Roosevelt's more rambunctious view appears in his *Autobiography*, *TRW*, vol. 22, 404–405.

30. Martin F. Sklar, *The Corporate Reconstruction of American Capitalism, 1890–1916*, Cambridge, Mass., 1988, 364–367.

31. See "President on Tour" and "Trust Law Uncertainty," *Independent*, October 5, 1911, 721–722, 776–777.

32. Roosevelt to Cecil Arthur Spring Rice, August 22, 1911, *TRL*, vol. 7, 333–334.

CHAPTER 3

1. John Milton Cooper, Jr., *The Warrior and the Priest*, Cambridge, Mass., 1983, 69.

2. Theodore Roosevelt to Henry Cabot Lodge, April 11, 1911, *TRL*, vol. 7, 73, 74.

3. Theodore Roosevelt, "The New Nationalism," August 31, 1910, *TRW*, vol. 19, 10–30.

4. William Manners, *TR and Will*, New York, 1969, is the standard account of "A Friendship That Split the Republican Party."

5. *New York Times*, June 8, 1911.

6. "A Washington Journalist," "Men We Are Watching," *Independent*, April 13, 1911, 778–779; Norman M. Wilensky, *Conservatism in the Progressive Era*, Gainesville, Fla., 1965, 12–31.

7. Robert M. La Follette, *La Follette's Autobiography*, Madison, 1913, 338.

8. "Republican 'Progressives,' " *Independent*, February 2, 1911, 2. A contemporary view of proposed reforms appears in James W. Garner, "Progressive Republicanism: The New Democracy," ibid., March 23, 1911, 605–608.

9. La Follette, *La Follette's Autobiography*, 515–516.

10. "The Conference of Progressive Republicans," *Outlook*, October 28, 1911, 439.

11. Theodore Roosevelt to Theodore Roosevelt, Jr., September 22, 1911, *TRL*, vol. 7, 345.

12. Quoted in Kenneth W. Heckler, *Insurgency*, New York, 1940, 23.

13. Elting E. Morison, *Turmoil and Tradition*, Boston, 1960, 178–190, has an astute analysis of Roosevelt's moment of decision.

14. George E. Mowry, *Theodore Roosevelt and the Progressive Movement*, New York, 1960, 188.

15. Theodore Roosevelt to Hiram Johnson, October 27, 1911, *TRL*, vol. 7, 420–422.

16. Theodore Roosevelt to James R. Garfield, December 1, 1911, *TRL*, vol. 7, 445–446.

17. Theodore Roosevelt to Henry Cabot Lodge, December 13, 1911, *TRL*, vol. 7, 457.

18. Theodore Roosevelt to Henry Cabot Lodge, December 23, 1911, *TRL*, vol. 7, 465.

19. Theodore Roosevelt to Benjamin Ide Wheeler, December 21, 1911, *TRL*, vol. 7, 462.

20. Theodore Roosevelt to Joseph Bucklin Bishop, November 21, 1910, and December 13, 1911, quoted in Bishop, *Theodore Roosevelt and His Time*, vol. 2, New York, 1920, 308, 312.

21. Roosevelt to Wheeler, December 21, 1911, *TRL*, vol. 7, 462–463.

22. Morison, *Turmoil and Tradition*, 182.

23. Theodore Roosevelt to Frank A. Munsey, January 16, 1912, *TRL*, vol. 7, 484.

24. Elihu Root to Theodore Roosevelt, February 12, 1912, quoted in Philip E. Jessup, *Elihu Root*, vol. 2, New York, 1938, 173–176.

25. Theodore Roosevelt to Chase S. Osborn, January 18, 1912, *TRL*, vol. 7, 485.

26. Seven governors (an eighth endorsed the appeal) to Roosevelt, February 10, 1912, quoted in *TRL*, vol. 7, 511. The maneuvers surrounding the governors' appeal gets good coverage in Robert M. Warner, "Chase S. Osborn and the Presidential Campaign of 1912," *Mississippi Valley Historical Review*, June 1959, 26–32.

27. Owen Wister, who was at the dinner, gave a poignant account of the incident in "Roosevelt and the 1912 Disaster," *Harper's Magazine*, May 1930, 669–670.

28. Robert S. Maxwell, *La Follette and the Rise of the Progressives in Wisconsin*, New York, 1973, 183.

29. *New York Times*, February 6, 1912.

30. Ibid., February 24, 1912.

31. Ibid., February 22, 1912.

32. Ibid.

33. Roosevelt to the Republican governors, February 24, 1912, *TRL*, vol. 7, 511.

34. Amos Pinchot to Louis D. Brandeis, February 9, 1912, quoted in Pinchot, *History of the Progressive Party, 1912–1916*, New York, 1958, 138.

35. *New York Times*, February 18, 1912.

36. *Independent*, March 21, 1912, 600–603; March 28, 1912, 653–655; April 25, 1912, 877.

37. *New York Times*, March 17, 1912.

38. Ibid., March 21, 1912.

39. Ibid., March 27, 1912.

40. Ibid., April 9, 1912.

41. Ibid., April 7, 1912.

42. Ibid., April 29, 1910.

43. Ibid., April 7, 1912.

44. Ibid., April 10, 1912.

45. Ibid.

46. Ibid., April 15, 1912.

47. Ibid., April 16, 1912.

48. Ibid., April 26, 1912.

49. Ibid., May 5, 1912.

50. Henry F. Pringle, *The Life and Times of William Howard Taft*, vol. 2, New York, 1939, 779, 781.

51. *New York Times*, April 30, 1912.

52. Taft to Horace D. Taft, May 12, 1912, quoted in Pringle, *Taft*, vol. 2, 784.

53. *New York Times*, May 14, 1912.

54. Ibid., May 23, 1912.

55. Ibid.

56. Quoted in "National Politics," *Independent*, May 30, 1912, 1137.

57. *New York Times*, May 29, 30, 1912.

58. Quoted in Robert P. Dunbar, "Teddy Challenges the President," *Harvard Magazine*, March-April 1980, 32.

59. Theodore Roosevelt, "A Naked Issue of Right and Wrong," *Outlook*, June 15, 1912, 330.

60. The Washington *Times*, a Munsey newspaper, described the process candidly, June 9, 1912, quoted in Victor Rosewater, *Backstage in 1912*, Philadelphia, 1932, 64–65.

61. Jessup, *Elihu Root*, vol. 2, 189.

62. Nicholas Murray Butler, *Across the Busy Years*, vol. 2, New York, 1932, 244.

63. Roosevelt, "The Case against the Reactionaries," July 17, 1912, *TRW*, vol. 19, 285, 293, 317.

64. Charles Moreau Harger, "The Two National Conventions: I. The Republicans at Chicago," *Independent*, July 4, 1912, 9.

65. Maxwell, *La Follette and the Rise of the Progressives in Wisconsin*, 187–188.

66. Richard W. Leopold, *Elihu Root and the Conservative Tradition*, Boston, 1954, 86–87.

67. *New York Times*, June 19, 1912. The formal report on the convention, which conceals as much as it reveals, is the *Official Report of the Proceedings of the Fifteenth Republican National Convention*, New York, 1912.

68. Jessup, *Elihu Root*, vol. 2, 198.

69. Ibid., 202.

70. William Howard Taft to Fred W. Carpenter, June 27, 1912, *WHT/LC*.

71. *New York Times*, June 21, 1912; Claude G. Bowers, *Beveridge and the Progressive Era*, Cambridge, 1932, 419–420.

72. Jessup, *Elihu Root*, vol. 2, 185.

73. The platform is reprinted in Arthur M. Schlesinger, Jr., *A History of American Presidential Elections, 1789–1968*, vol. 3, New York, 1971, 2178–2185.

CHAPTER 4

1. *New York Times*, April 21, 1912.

2. Henry Wilkinson Bragdon, *Woodrow Wilson: The Academic Years*, Cambridge, Mass., 1967, 99.

3. Arthur S. Link, *Wilson: The Road to the White House*, Princeton, 1947, 11.

4. Woodrow Wilson, *Congressional Government*, Boston, 1887, 56.

5. Link, *Wilson*, 19.

6. Wilson to Moses Tyler Pyne, December 25, 1909, *WWP*, vol. 19, 630.

7. George Harvey's role is fully chronicled in William Inglis, "Helping to Make a President," *Collier's Weekly*, October 7, 14, 21, 1916.

8. Woodrow Wilson, "Credo," August 6, 1907, *WWP*, vol. 17, 335–338.

9. Quoted in Link, *Wilson*, 116.

10. Woodrow Wilson, *Constitutional Government in the United States*, New York, 1908, 64, 65–66.

11. Ibid., 70, 73.

12. "Looking Ahead," *Harper's Weekly*, May 15, 1909, 4.

13. Quoted in Link, *Wilson*, 142.

14. John Maynard Harlan to Woodrow Wilson, June 11, 1910, *WWP*, vol. 20, 519.

15. Woodrow Wilson to John Maynard Harlan, June 23, 1910, *WWP*, vol. 20, 540.

16. Newark *Evening News*, July 15, 1910, *WWP*, vol. 20, 550.

17. James Kerney, *The Political Education of Woodrow Wilson*, New York, 1926, 36–37, 49–51.

18. Quoted in Link, *Wilson*, 159.

19. Woodrow Wilson to Edgar Williamson, August 23, 1910, *WWP*, vol. 21, 59–60.

20. Link, *Wilson*, 168.

21. Trenton *True American*, September 16, 17, 1910, *WWP*, vol. 21, 91–94, 119.

22. John M. Blum, *Joe Tumulty and the Wilson Era*, Boston, 1951, 22; Joseph P. Tumulty, *Woodrow Wilson as I Knew Him*, Garden City, N.Y., 1921, 21–22.

23. Link, *Wilson*, 179.

24. George L. Record to Woodrow Wilson, October 17, 1910, *WWP*, vol. 21, 338–347.

25. Woodrow Wilson to George L. Record, October 24, 1910, *WWP*, vol. 21, 408, 411.

26. Link, *Wilson*, 195.

27. Woodrow Wilson, "A Statement on the Senatorship," December 8, 1910, *WWP*, vol. 22, 153.

28. "Governors and Governors," *Independent*, January 19, 1910, 165.

29. Ransom E. Noble, Jr., *New Jersey Progressivism before Wilson*, Princeton, 1946.

30. Woodrow Wilson, "A Statement on the Work of the New Jersey Legislative Session of 1911," April 22, 1911, *WWP*, vol. 22, 579.

31. Woodrow Wilson to Mary Allen Hulbert Peck, April 23, 1911, *WWP*, vol. 22, 581–582.

CHAPTER 5

1. Robert W. Cherny, *A Righteous Cause*, New York, 1945, 273.

2. Woodrow Wilson, "A Political Address in Indianapolis," April 13, 1911, *WWP*, vol. 22, 568, 563–564.

3. Woodrow Wilson to Mary Allen Hulbert Peck, April 23, 1911, *WWP*, vol. 22, 519.

4. Burton J. Hendrick, *The Life and Letters of Walter Hines Page*, vol. 1, Garden City, N.Y., 1922–1925, 106–107.

5. Wilson to Mrs. Peck, April 2, 1911, *WWP*, vol. 22, 533.

6. Denver *Rocky Mountain News*, May 9, 1911, *WWP*, vol. 23, 25.

7. Kansas City *Star*, May 5, 1911, *WWP*, vol. 23, 4–5.

8. Quoted in *WWP*, vol. 23, 32.

9. San Francisco *Chronicle*, May 16, 1911, *WWP*, vol. 23, 54.

10. Woodrow Wilson, "Press Release," June 15, 1911, *WWP*, vol. 23, 157–158.

11. *New York World*, July 31, 1911, *WWP*, vol. 23, 243.

12. William Jennings Bryan to Woodrow Wilson, January 5, 1911, *WWP*, vol. 22, 307.

13. Woodrow Wilson, "An After-Dinner Political Address in Burlington," New Jersey, April 5, 1911, *WWP*, vol. 22, 536.

14. Lewis L. Gould, *Progressives and Prohibitionists*, Austin, Texas, 1973, 58–84.

15. New York *World*, December 24, 1911, *WWP*, vol. 23, 610–611.

16. New York *World*, December 24, 1911, and *New York Times*, December 24, 1911, *WWP*, vol. 23, 607–629.

17. Edward M. House to William Jennings Bryan, November 25, 1911, in Charles Seymour, ed., *The Intimate Papers of Colonel House*, vol. 1, Boston, 1926, 49–50 (hereafter, *House Papers*).

18. Edward M. House to William Jennings Bryan, December 6, 1911, ibid., vol. 1, 50–51.

19. Edward M. House to William F. McCombs, February 10, 1912, ibid., vol. 1, 56.

20. House's efforts for Wilson are chronicled in Alexander L. George and Juliette L. George, *Woodrow Wilson and Colonel House*, New York, 1956, 88–112.

21. Woodrow Wilson to Mrs. Peck, April 9, 1911, *WWP*, vol. 22, 545.

22. Woodrow Wilson to Marion J. Verdery, April 12, 1911, *WWP*, vol. 22, 553.

23. Arthur S. Link, "The Underwood Presidential Movement of 1912," *Mississippi Valley Historical Review*, May 1945, 230–245. See also, "A Washington Journalist," "Men We Are Watching: Oscar W. Underwood, M.C.," *Independent*, January 18, 1912, 144–145.

24. John Temple Graves, "Democratic Presidential Possibilities: Speaker Champ Clark," *Independent*, November 2, 1911, 959–963; Champ Clark, "The Duty of the Democrats," ibid., January 25, 1912, 177–179; John E. Lathrop, "The Views of Champ Clark," *Outlook*, May 11, 1912, 65–73.

25. 61st Congress, third session, U.S. House of Representatives, *Congressional Record*, 2520 (February 14, 1911).

26. James Bryce, *United States Annual Report*, 1912, quoted in *WWP*, vol. 24, 508.

27. Woodrow Wilson to Mrs. Peck, March 5, 1911, *WWP*, vol. 22, 479. The *Nation* showed similar skepticism in an editorial, "Champ Clark as Chantecler," June 22, 1911, 618; later, so did the *Independent*: "One of the Democratic Candidates," June 13, 1912, 1336–1337.

28. *New York Times*, April 7, 1912.

29. Arthur S. Link, *Wilson: The Road to the White House*, Princeton, 1947, 382; Frank Parker Stockbridge, "How Woodrow Wilson Won His Nomination," *Current History*, July 1924, 570.

30. Alfred Henry Louis, "The Real Woodrow Wilson," *Heart's Magazine*, May 1912, 2265–2274.

31. Woodrow Wilson to Adrian H. Joline, April 29, 1907, *WWP*, vol. 17, 10.

32. Woodrow Wilson, "An Address in Washington," January 8, 1912, *WWP*, vol. 14, 10.

33. Link, *Wilson*, 356.

34. Cherny, *A Righteous Cause*, 124.

35. Woodrow Wilson to Mrs. Peck, January 14, 1912, *WWP*, vol. 24, 43.

36. Woodrow Wilson to Mrs. Peck, January 31, 1912, *WWP*, vol. 24, 99.

37. Des Moines *Register and Leader*, March 2, 1912, *WWP*, vol. 24, 221.

38. Woodrow Wilson, "An Address in Richmond," February 1, 1912, *WWP*, vol. 24, 108.

39. Woodrow Wilson to John W. Wescott, February 18, 1912, *WWP*, vol. 24, 179.

40. Kansas City *Star*, February 22, 1912, *WWP*, vol. 24, 187.

41. Woodrow Wilson, "An Address in Topeka," February 23, 1912, *WWP*, vol. 24, 189.

42. Des Moines *Register and Leader*, March 2, 1912, *WWP*, vol. 24, 221.

43. Woodrow Wilson to Harper and Brothers, March 4, 1912, *WWP*, vol. 24, 223.

44. C. Vann Woodward, *Tom Watson: Agrarian Rebel*, New York, 1938, 426–427, 430.

45. William Jennings Bryan to Woodrow Wilson, April 1, 1912, *WWP*, vol. 24, 273.

46. 62d Congress, third session, U.S. Senate, Subcommittee of the Committee on Privileges and Elections, *Campaign Contributions*, vol. 2, Washington, D.C., 1913, 912.

47. Edward M. House to Woodrow Wilson, March 6, 1912, *House Papers*, vol. 1, 58.

48. William G. McAdoo to Woodrow Wilson, March 8, 1912, *WWP*, vol. 24, 237.

49. Woodrow Wilson to George Foster Peabody, March 26, 1912, *WWP*, vol. 24, 265.

50. Chicago *Daily Tribune*, April 7, 1912, *WWP*, vol. 24, 299.

51. *New York Times*, April 10, 1912.

52. Woodrow Wilson to George Foster Peabody, May 15, 1912, *WWP*, vol. 24, 401. The pessimism in May is aptly caught in Ray Stannard Baker, *Woodrow Wilson: Life and Letters*, vol. 3, New York, 1931, 309–321.

53. *New York Times*, May 30, 1912.

54. Woodrow Wilson to Edith Giddings Reid, May 26, 1912, *WWP*, vol. 24, 446.

55. *New York World*, May 30, 1912, quoted in Link, *Wilson*, 429.

56. Frank I. Cobb to Woodrow Wilson, June 6, 1912, *WWP*, vol. 24, 463.

CHAPTER 6

1. Arthur S. Link, "The Underwood Presidential Movement of 1912," *Journal of Southern History*, May 1945, 242–243.

2. On Murphy, see Nancy Joan Weiss, *Charles Francis Murphy, 1858–1924*, North-hampton, Mass., 1968; Alfred Connable and Edward Silberfarb, *Tigers of Tammany*, New York, 1967, 231–268; and J. Joseph Huthmacher, "Charles Evans Hughes and Charles Francis Murphy: The Metamorphosis of Progressivism," *New York History*, January 1965, 25–40.

3. *New York Times*, June 24, 1912.

4. Dewey W. Grantham, *Southern Progressivism: The Reconciliation of Progress and Tradition*, Knoxville, Ten., 1983.

5. Quoted in William G. McAdoo, *Crowded Years*, Boston, 1931, 143.

6. T. W. Gregory to Edward M. House, July 9, 1912, in Link, ed., "A Letter from One of Wilson's Managers," *American Historical Review*, July 1945, 771.

7. *New York World*, June 22, 1912.

8. Woodrow Wilson to John Haslup Adams, June 21, 1912, *WWP*, vol. 24, 491.

9. Wilson to Bryan, June 22, 1912, and Bryan to Wilson, June 21, 1912, *WWP*, vol. 24, 493, 492.

10. Woodrow Wilson to Mary Allen Hulbert Peck, June 9, 1912, *WWP*, vol. 24, 466.

11. The *Official Report of the Proceedings of the Democratic National Convention*, Chicago, 1912, also conceals as much as it reveals.

12. William F. McCombs attached special significance to the victory, see McCombs, *Making Woodrow Wilson President*, New York, 1921, 128–130.

13. Ellen Maury Slayden, *Washington Wife*, New York, 1963, 179.

14. *New York Times*, June 28, 1912. Charles W. Bryan, "The Morgan-Ryan-Belmont Resolution," ibid., March 6, 1921, explains the Bryans's attempts to enlist other progressives.

15. *New York Times*, June 29, 1912.

16. Ibid.

17. Virgil V. McNitt, ed., *A Tale of Two Conventions*, New York, 1974, 48.

18. Link, *Wilson: The Road to the White House*, Princeton, 1947, 451.

19. McAdoo, *Crowded Years*, 155.

20. Ibid., 153–154.

21. *New York Times*, June 29, 1912.

22. William J. Stone to Wilson, June 29, 1912, *WWP*, vol. 24, 507.

23. New York *World*, June 30, 1912, *WWP*, vol. 24, 510.

24. Wilson to Bryan, June 29, 1912, *WWP*, vol. 24, 508.

25. *New York Times*, June 30, 1912.

26. Richard Washburn Child, "Mr. Bryan Says, 'Boo!,'" *Collier's Weekly*, July 13, 1912, quoted in Paxton Hibben, *The Peerless Leader*, New York, 1929, 315.

27. Connable and Silberfarb, *Tigers of Tammany*, 238.

28. Alfred Lief, *Democracy's Norris*, New York, 1939, 135.

29. *New York Times*, June 30, 1912.

30. Ibid.

31. Link, *Wilson*, 457.

32. *New York Times*, July 1, 1912.

33. Charles H. Gratsy to Woodrow Wilson, July 1, 1912, *WWP*, vol. 24, 519.

34. Baltimore *Evening Sun*, July 1, 1912.

35. New York *World*, July 1, 1912.

36. Ibid., quoted in *WWP*, vol. 24, 513.

37. Ibid.

38. Charles W. Gratsy to Woodrow Wilson, July 1, 1912, *WWP*, vol. 24, 520.

39. Francis G. Newlands to Wilson, July 1, 1912, *WWP*, vol. 24, 521.

40. 62d Congress, third session, U.S. Senate, Subcommittee of the Committee on Privileges and Elections, *Campaign Contributions*, vol. 2, Washington, D.C., 1913, 918–925.

41. *New York Times*, July 2, 1912.

42. Link, ed., "A Letter from One of Wilson's Managers," 770.

43. *New York Times*, July 2, 1912.

44. Ibid.

45. Link, ed., "A Letter from One of Wilson's Managers," 769.

46. Maurice F. Lyons, *William F. McCombs, The President Maker*, Cincinnati, 1922, 102.

47. *New York Times*, July 3, 1912.

CHAPTER 7

1. Chase S. Osborn to Theodore Roosevelt, June 24, 1912, quoted in Robert M. Warner, "Chase S. Osborn and the Presidential Campaign of 1912," *Mississippi Valley Historical Review*, June 1959, 34.

2. Chase S. Osborn statement, July 3, 1912, quoted in ibid., 39.

3. *New York Times*, July 3, 1912.

4. Theodore Roosevelt to Chase S. Osborn, June 28, 1912, *TRL*, vol. 7, 566–567.

5. Ibid., 566.

6. Theodore Roosevelt to Chase S. Osborn, July 5, 1912, *TRL*, vol. 7, 569–570.

7. Theodore Roosevelt to Madison Clinton Peters, July 9, 1912, *TRL*, vol. 7, 574.

8. Roosevelt to Osborn, July 5, 1912, *TRL*, vol. 7, 569.

9. Quoted in Sylvia Jukes Morris, *Edith Kermit Roosevelt*, New York, 1980, 381. See also Henry L. Stoddard, *As I Knew Them*, New York, 1927, 307.

10. Theodore Roosevelt to Horace Plunkett, August 3, 1912, *TRL*, vol. 7, 593.

11. Theodore Roosevelt to Edwin A. Van Valkenburg, July 16, 1912, *TRL*, vol. 7, 577.

12. Theodore Roosevelt to William A. Prendergast, June 25, 1912, *TRL*, vol. 7, 563.

13. Quoted in George E. Mowry, *Theodore Roosevelt and the Progressive Movement*, New York, 1960, 257.

14. John Allen Gable, *The Bull Moose Years*, Port Washington, N.Y., 1978, 19–57.

15. *New York Times*, July 8, 1912.

16. *La Follette's Magazine*, June 29, July 20, July 27, 1912, cited in Robert S. Maxwell, *La Follette and the Rise of the Progressives in Wisconsin*, New York, 1973, 189–190.

17. Roosevelt to Julian La Rose Harris, August 1, 1912, *TRL*, vol. 7, 584–590.

18. *New York Times*, August 5, 1912.

19. Ibid., August 6, 1912.

20. Ibid.

21. Ibid., August 8, 1912.

22. Claude G. Bowers, *Beveridge and the Progressive Era*, Cambridge, Mass., 1932, 426–430.

23. *New York Times*, August 7, 1912.

24. Theodore Roosevelt, "A Confession of Faith," August 6, 1912, *TRW*, vol. 19, 358–411.

25. New York *Sun*, August 7, 1912.

26. Theodore Roosevelt to Arthur Hamilton Lee, August 14, 1912, *TRL*, vol. 7, 597.

27. Mowry, *Theodore Roosevelt and the Progressive Movement*, 271–272.

28. George E. Mowry, "Election of 1912," in Arthur M. Schlesinger, Jr., ed., *History of American Presidential Elections, 1789–1968*, vol. 3, New York, 1971, 2152. John A. Garraty describes the incident at the convention in *Right-Hand Man*, New York, 1960, 268–270. See also, Gable, *The Bull Moose Years*, 100–103.

29. *New York Times*, August 7, 1912.

CHAPTER 8

1. H. Wayne Morgan, *Eugene V. Debs*, Westport, Ct., 1962, 121.

2. Anon., *Debs: His Life, Writings and Speeches*, Girard, Kan., 1908, 41.

3. Quoted in Ray Ginger, *The Bending Cross*, New Brunswick, N.J., 1949, 84.

4. Four inmates to Eugene V. Debs, November 22, 1895, in *Debs: His Life, Writings and Speeches*, 66.

5. New York *Socialist*, June 20, 1908, quoted in ibid., 67.

6. Quoted in Ginger, *The Bending Cross*, 190.

7. Quoted in Nick Salvatore, *Eugene V. Debs: Citizen and Socialist*, Urbana, Ill., 1982, 161–162 (hereafter, Salvatore, *Debs*).

8. Morris Hillquit, *Loose Leaves from a Busy Life*, New York, 1971, 53–54.

9. Quoted in Salvatore, *Debs*, 229–230.

10. Daniel Bell, "The Background and Development of Marxian Socialism in the United States," in Donald Drew Egbert and Stow Persons, eds., *Socialism and American Life*, vol. 1, Princeton, 1952, 278.

11. Quoted in Ronald Radosh, ed., *Debs*, Englewood Cliffs, N.J., 1971, 115.

12. Quoted in Salvatore, *Debs*, 206.

13. Eugene V. Debs, "Arouse, Ye Slaves!", *Appeal to Reason*, March 10, 1906, in Arthur M. Schlesinger, Jr., *Writings and Speeches of Eugene V. Debs*, New York, 1948, 256–258.

14. Quoted in Ginger, *The Bending Cross*, 251.

15. Ibid., 252.

16. Ibid.

17. David Karsner, *Debs*, New York, 1919, 186.

18. Quoted in Ginger, *The Bending Cross*, 291.

19. Eugene V. Debs, "Working Class Politics," *International Socialist Review*, November 1910, quoted in Jean Y. Tussey, ed., *Eugene V. Debs Speaks*, New York, 1970, 173–176.

20. Eugene V. Debs, "Danger Ahead," *International Socialist Review*, January 1911, in ibid., 177–182.

21. Eugene V. Debs, "Sound Socialist Tactics," *International Socialist Review*, February 1912, in ibid., 189–199.

22. "The National Socialist Convention of 1912," *International Socialist Review*, June 1912, 808.

23. Ibid., 822.

24. Ibid., 823.

25. John Spargo, ed., *Fifth National Convention of the Socialist Party*, 1912, 122.

26. "The National Socialist Convention of 1912," 825.

27. Spargo, *Fifth Convention*, 133.

28. Ibid., 130.

29. Ibid., 134–135.

30. Arthur M. Schlesinger, Jr., ed., *History of American Presidential Elections, 1798–1968*, vol. 3, New York, 1971, 2198–2203.

31. Editorial, "The Compromises of the Socialist Convention," *Independent*, May 30, 1912, 1182.

CHAPTER 9

1. *New York Times*, July 14, 1912.

2. Champ Clark, *My Quarter Century of American Politics*, vol. 2, New York, 1920, 424–425, 442.

3. Arthur S. Link, *Wilson: The Road to the White House*, Princeton, 1947, 485–486.

4. Michael E. McGerr, *The Decline of Popular Politics: The American North, 1865–1928*, New York, 1986, 69–106.

5. Woodrow Wilson, "A Speech Accepting the Democratic Nomination," August 7, 1912, *WWP*, vol. 25, 3–18.

6. The party used this passage as a frontespiece for *The Democratic Text-Book, 1912*, New York, 1912.

7. *New York Times*, August 8, 1912.

8. Ibid., August 29, 1912.

9. Quoted in Melvin I. Urofsky, *Louis D. Brandeis and the Progressive Tradition*, Boston, 1981, 71.

10. *New York Times*, September 3, 1912.

11. Woodrow Wilson to Louis Wiley, September 5, 1912, and Wiley to Wilson, September 6, 1912, *WWP*, vol. 25, 107, 114.

12. *New York Times*, August 30, 1912.

13. Ibid.

14. Ibid.

15. Woodrow Wilson to Mary Allen Hulbert, September 1, 1912, *WWP*, vol. 25, 77.

16. Wilson, "Labor Day Address in Buffalo," September 2, 1912, *WWP*, vol. 25, 77.

17. Wilson, "An Evening Address in Buffalo," September 2, 1912, *WWP*, vol. 25, 83, 87, 82.

18. *New York Times*, September 10, 1912.

19. William G. McAdoo to Wilson, September 5, 1912, *WWP*, vol. 25, 111.

20. *New York Times*, September 3, 1912.

21. Woodrow Wilson, "An Address at a Workingmen's Dinner in New York," September 4, 1912, *WWP*, vol. 25, 100, 101.

22. Woodrow Wilson, "An Address to the New York Press Club," September 9, 1912, *WWP*, vol. 25, 121, 123–124.

23. *New York Times*, September 10, 1912.

24. Woodrow Wilson, "Statement to the Democrats of New Jersey," September 8, 1912, *WWP*, vol. 25, 116–118.

25. *New York Times*, September 13, 1912.

26. Woodrow Wilson, "A Talk to the New York State Leaders in Syracuse," September 12, 1912, *WWP*, vol. 25, 144.

27. *New York Times*, September 13, 1912.

28. Ibid., September 14, 1912.

29. Ibid., September 16, 1912.

30. Ibid., September 17, 1912.

31. Ibid.

32. Ibid.

33. Ibid., September 20, 1912.

34. Woodrow Wilson, "A Campaign Address in Columbus," September 20, 1912, *WWP*, vol. 25, 209, 206–207.

35. Woodrow Wilson, "A Campaign Address in Sioux City, Iowa," September 17, 1912, *WWP*, vol. 25, 152.

36. Woodrow Wilson, "An Afternoon Address at the Parade Grounds in Minneapolis," September 18, 1912, *WWP*, vol. 25, 179.

37. Wilson, "A Campaign Address in Sioux City, Iowa," September 17, 1912, *WWP*, vol. 25, 150–151.

38. *New York Times*, September 19, 1912.

39. Wilson, "An Afternoon Address at the Parade Grounds in Minneapolis," September 18, 1912, *WWP*, vol. 25, 181.

40. Wilson, "A Campaign Address in Columbus," September 20, 1912, *WWP*, vol. 25, 208–209.

41. *New York Times*, September 21, 1912.

42. Ibid.

43. Ibid.

44. Ibid.; Woodrow Wilson, "A Speech in Hoboken, New Jersey," September 21, 1912, *WWP*, vol. 25, 219–220.

45. *New York Times*, September 24, 1912.

46. Ibid., September 25, 1912.

47. Ibid.

48. Edward M. House, "Diary," September 25, 1912, in Charles Seymour, ed., *The Intimate Papers of Colonel House*, vol. 1, New York, 1926, 74.

49. Quoted in Urofsky, *Louis D. Brandeis and the Progressive Tradition*, 71.

50. Woodrow Wilson, "An Address in New Haven," September 25, 1912, *WWP*, vol. 25, 250–251.

51. Woodrow Wilson to Louis D. Brandeis, September 27, 1912, *WWP*, vol. 25, 272.

52. Woodrow Wilson to Louis D. Brandeis, October 4, 1912, *WWP*, vol. 25, 339.

53. Philippa Strum, *Louis D. Brandeis*, Cambridge, Mass., 1984, 199, 201–202.

54. Woodrow Wilson, "A Campaign Speech on New Issues in Hartford," September 25, 1912, *WWP*, vol. 25, 245.

55. *New York Times*, September 27, 1912.

56. Wilson, "An Address in New Haven", September 25, 1912, *WWP*, vol. 25, 248.

57. Ibid., 247.

58. Ibid., 248.

59. Woodrow Wilson to Mrs. Hulbert, September 29, 1912, *WWP*, vol. 25, 285.

60. Woodrow Wilson, "A Statement on the New York Democratic Situation," September 29, 1912, *WWP*, vol. 25, 284.

61. Woodrow Wilson to William Sulzer, October 3, 1912, *WWP*, vol. 25, 329.

62. Charles Willis Thompson to Mrs. Thompson, October 6, 1912, quoted in *WWP*, vol. 25, 361.

63. *New York Times*, October 3, 1912; Frank Freidel, *Franklin D. Roosevelt: The Apprenticeship*, Boston, 1952, 145.

CHAPTER 10

1. Theodore Roosevelt to Arthur Hamilton Lee, August 14, 1912, *TRL*, vol. 7, 596.

2. Alfred D. Chandler, Jr., "The Origins of Progressive Leadership," *TRL*, vol. 8, 1462–1465.

3. Roosevelt to Lee, August 14, 1912, *TRL*, vol. 7, 598.

4. *New York Times*, September 14, 1912.

5. Roosevelt to Lee, August 14, 1912, *TRL*, vol. 7, 598.

6. *New York Times*, September 21, 1912.

7. Ibid., September 18, 1912.

8. Ibid., September 11, 1912.

9. Ibid., September 6, 1912.

10. Ibid., September 7, 1912.

11. Ibid., September 8, 1912.

12. Ibid., September 21, 1912.

13. Ibid., September 17, 1912.

14. Ibid., September 23, 1912.

15. Owen Wister, "Roosevelt and the 1912 Disaster," *Harper's*, May 1930, 663.

16. *New York Times*, September 28, 1912.

17. Quoted in ibid., September 30, 1912.

18. Ibid., September 20, 1912.

19. Oscar King Davis, *Released for Publication*, Boston, 1925, 355–358.

20. Woodrow Wilson, "Address to the New York Press Club," September 9, 1912, *WWP*, vol. 25, 124.

21. Theodore Roosevelt, "Limitation of Governmental Power," *TRW*, vol. 19, 419–429.

22. *New York Times*, September 24, 1912.

23. Ibid., September 14, 1912.

24. Ibid.

25. Roosevelt to Lee, August 14, 1912, *TRL*, vol. 7, 598.

26. *New York Times*, September 22, 1912.

27. Ibid., September 11, 1912.

28. Ibid., September 3, 1912.

29. Ibid., September 5, 1912.

30. Ibid., September 18, 1912.

31. Ibid., September 20, 1912.

32. Theodore Roosevelt, "The Minimum Wage," *TRW*, vol. 19, 431.

33. *New York Times*, September 18, 1912.

34. Roosevelt, "The Minimum Wage," *TRW*, vol. 19, 430.

35. *New York Times*, September 3, 1912.

36. Ibid., September 5, 1912.

37. Ibid., September 8, 1912.

38. Ibid., September 18, 1912.

39. Ibid., September 17, 1912.

CHAPTER 11

1. William Howard Taft to Fred W. Carpenter, June 27, 1912, *WHT/LC*.

2. William Howard Taft to Mrs. Taft, July 14, 1912, *WHT/LC*.

3. William Howard Taft to J. D. Long, July 5, 1912, quoted in Henry F. Pringle, *The Life and Times of William Howard Taft*, vol. 2, New York, 1939, 816.

4. William Howard Taft to Mabel Boardman, August 9, 1912, quoted in Pringle, *Taft*, vol. 2, 816.

5. William Howard Taft to Mrs. Taft, August 9, 1912, *WHT/LC*.

6. William Howard Taft to Mrs. Taft, August 26, 1912, *WHT/LC*.

7. William Howard Taft to Mrs. Taft, July 16, 1912, *WHT/LC*.

8. William Howard Taft to Delia Torrey, August 1, 1912, quoted in Pringle *Taft*, vol. 2, 823.

9. *New York Times*, August 2, 1912.

10. Ibid.

11. Ibid., August 29, 1912.

12. Ibid., October 2, 1912.

13. Ibid., September 11, 1912.

14. Michael E. McGerr, *The Decline of Popular Politics: The American North, 1865–1928*, New York, 1986, 161–162.

15. *New York Times*, September 6, 1912.

16. Ibid., September 7, 1912.

17. Ibid., September 25, 1912.

18. Ibid.

19. Ibid., September 29, 1912.

20. Ibid., October 1, 1912.

CHAPTER 12

1. Eugene V. Debs, untitled box, *International Socialist Review*, August 1912, 128.

2. Eugene V. Debs to J. Mahlon Barnes, July 2, 1912, EVDF.

3. Ray Ginger, *The Bending Cross*, New Brunswick, N.J., 1949, 311.

4. "Minutes of the National Campaign Committee," June 15, 17, July 7, 1912, *Socialist Party Monthly Bulletin*, July, August 1912.

5. *National Ripsaw*, June 17, 1912.

6. Ibid.

7. Ibid., July 10, 1912.

8. Ibid., July 22, 1912.

9. Eugene V. Debs to the editor of the *New York Times*, August 10, 1912, *New York Times*, August 14, 1912.

10. Quoted in *National Ripsaw*, August 14, 1912.

11. 62nd Congress, second session, U.S. House of Representatives, *Congressional Record*, 9241–9248 (July 18, 1912).

12. Eugene V. Debs, "Debs' Speech of Acceptance," *International Socialist Review*, October 1912, 304–307.

13. Quoted in "Lincoln Steffens Learns about Debs and Socialism," Ronald Radosh, ed., *Debs*, Englewood Cliffs, N.J., 1971, 117.

14. *Socialist Party Handbook*, 1912, passim. See also, Algernon Lee, "The Successful Methods of Socialism," *Independent*, March 9, 1911, 515–518.

15. Elizabeth Gurley Flynn, "Eugene V. Debs," in Radosh, ed., *Debs*, 98–99.

16. Haywood Broun, "The Miracle of Debs," ibid., 141.

17. *National Ripsaw*, September 21, 1912.

18. Terre Haute *Star*, September 17, 1912.

19. *New York Times*, September 3, 1912.

20. Woodrow Wilson, "An Evening Address in Buffalo," September 2, 1912, *WWP*, vol. 25, 82.

21. Los Angeles *Citizen*, September 6, 1912.

22. New York *World*, September 30, 1912.

23. *New York Times*, September 30, 1912.

CHAPTER 13

1. Theodore Roosevelt to Arthur Hamilton Lee, August 14, 1912, *TRL*, vol. 7, 598.

2. *New York Times*, October 5, 1912.

3. Roosevelt to Moses Edwin Clapp, August 28, 1912, *TRL*, vol. 7, 623.

4. Paterson, New Jersey, *Morning Call*, October 8, 1912.

5. *New York Times*, October 8, 1912.

6. Ibid., October 5, 1912.

7. Ibid., October 8, 1912.

8. Ibid.

9. Ibid., October 9, 1912.

10. Ibid., October 11, 1912.

11. Ibid., October 8, 1912.

12. Ibid., October 9, 1912.

13. Woodrow Wilson, "A Campaign Address in Indianapolis Proclaiming the New Freedom," October 3, 1912, *WWP*, vol. 25, 321–329; John Wells Davidson, ed., *A Crossroads of Freedom*, New Haven, Ct., 1956, 10.

14. *New York Times*, October 6, 1912.

15. Ibid., October 12, 1912. The original form of the judgement came from Senator Jonathan P. Dolliver of Iowa: Taft was "a large amiable island surrounded entirely by persons who knew exactly what they wanted." Elting E. Morison, *Turmoil and Tradition*, Boston, 1960, 179.

16. *New York Times*, October 7, 1912.

17. Ibid., October 12, 1912.

18. Woodrow Wilson, "A Campaign Address in Detroit," September 19, 1912, *WWP*, vol. 25, 192–193.

19. *New York Times*, October 9, 1912.

20. Woodrow Wilson, "An Address in New Haven," September 25, 1912, *WWP*, vol. 25, 251. John Milton Cooper, Jr., has a balanced discussion of "The New Nationalism versus the New Freedom" in *The Warrior and the Priest*, Cambridge, Mass., 1983, 206–221. How Wilson and Roosevelt narrowed the gap between them is apparent in William Henry Harbaugh, *Power and Responsibility*, New York, 1961, 446–448.

21. Woodrow Wilson, "Baccalaureate Address," June 13, 1909, *WWP*, vol. 9, 245.

22. *New York Times*, October 10, 1912.

23. Ibid., October 11, 1912.

24. "Mr. Taft on the Issues," *Harper's Weekly*, October 26, 1912, 9.

25. *New York Times*, October 12, 1912.

26. Ibid., October 15, 16, 1912; Oscar King Davis, *Released for Publication*, Boston, 1925, 376.

27. Davis, *Released for Publication*, 378.

28. Theodore Roosevelt, "The Leader and the Cause," *TRW*, vol. 19, 441–452.

29. *New York Times*, October 16, 1912.

30. New York *World*, October 22, 1912.

31. *New York Times*, October 16, 1912.

32. Quoted in Sylvia Jukes Morris, *Edith Kermit Roosevelt*, New York, 1980, 388.

33. *New York Times*, October 16, 1912.

34. New York *Call*, October 16, 1912, quoted in ibid.

35. "Diary of Edward M. House," October 18, 1912, in Charles Seymour, ed., *The Intimate Papers of Colonel House*, vol. 1, Boston, 1926, 78 (hereafter, *House Papers*).

36. *New York Times*, October 16, 1912.

37. Theodore Roosevelt, "The Fight Goes On," *TRW*, vol. 19, 454–455.

38. *New York Times*, October 17, 1912.

39. *Harper's Weekly*, November 2, 1912, 6.

40. *New York Times*, October 17, 1912.

41. Edward M. House to Bill McDonald, October 15, 1912, quoted in *House Papers*, vol. 1, 79.

42. Woodrow Wilson, "A Speech in Dover, Delaware," October 17, 1912, *WWP*, vol. 25, 424–425.

43. *New York Times*, October 18, 1912.

44. Woodrow Wilson, "A Campaign Address in Wilmington, Delaware," October 17, 1912, *WWP*, vol. 25, 428.

45. Ibid., 426.

46. Woodrow Wilson, "A Campaign Address in Burlington, New Jersey," October 30, 1912, *WWP*, vol. 25, 490.

47. Woodrow Wilson, "A Campaign Address in Montclair, New Jersey," October 29, 1912, *WWP*, vol. 25, 470–471.

48. B. M. Anderson, Jr., to Woodrow Wilson, October 15, 1912, *WWP*, vol. 25, 420.

49. *New York Times*, October 22, 1912.

50. Woodrow Wilson, "A Campaign Address in Brooklyn, New York," October 19, 1912, *WWP*, vol. 25, 438.

51. Woodrow Wilson, "A Campaign Address in New York," October 19, 1912, *WWP*, vol. 25, 441.

52. Woodrow Wilson to Alexander Walters, October 21, 1912, *WWP*, vol. 25, 449.

53. *New York Times*, October 22, 1912.

54. "Diary of Colonel House," October 20, November 2, 1912, quoted in *WWP*, vol. 25, 448, 507.

55. *New York Times*, October 21, 1912.

56. "Mr. Taft on the Issues," *Harper's Weekly*, October 26, 1912, 9–10.

57. *New York Times*, October 29, 1912.

58. Theodore Roosevelt, "The Purpose of the Progressive Party," *TRW*, vol. 19, 456–463.

59. *New York Times*, November 1, 1912.

60. Woodrow Wilson, "A Campaign Address in New York City," October 31, 1912, *WWP*, vol. 25, 493–501.

61. "Vagueness and reiteration, symbolism and incantation, I take to be the chief secrets of Mr. Wilson's verbal power." William Bayard Hale, *The Story of a Style*, New York, 1920, 247.

62. *New York Times*, November 3, 1912.

63. *National Ripsaw*, October 29, 1912.

64. Ibid., October 30, 1912.

65. Newark *Evening News*, November 4, 1912, quoted in *WWP*, vol. 25, 510.

66. Ray Stannard Baker, *Woodrow Wilson: Life and Letters*, vol. 3, Garden City, N.Y., 1931, 408–409.

67. Woodrow Wilson, "Remarks to Princeton Students and Neighbors," November 5, 1912, *WWP*, vol. 25, 520–521.

CHAPTER 14

1. Some implications of these figures are explored as "the era of electoral demobilization" in Paul Kleppner, *Who Voted? The Dynamics of Electoral Turnout, 1870–1980*, New York, 1982, 55–82.

2. Elihu Root to Theodore Roosevelt, February 12, 1912, quoted in Philip C. Jessup, *Elihu Root*, vol. 2, New York, 1938, 175.

3. Theodore Roosevelt to Elihu Root, February 14, 1912, *TRL*, vol. 7, 504.

4. Quoted in George E. Mowry, *Theodore Roosevelt and the Progressive Movement*, New York, 1960, 255.

CHAPTER 15

1. Woodrow Wilson, "Planks for a Democratic Platform," June 16, 1912, *WWP*, vol. 24, 479.

2. Arthur S. Link, *Woodrow Wilson and the Progressive Era, 1910–1917*, New York, 1954, 72–76.

3. 247 U.S. 251; 259 U.S. 20.

4. Link, *Woodrow Wilson*, 227.

5. Quoted in Richard Lowitt, *George W. Norris: The Persistence of a Progressive, 1913–1933*, Urbana, Ill., 1971, 282.

6. See, for example, Norman Thomas, "Our Welfare State and Our Political Parties," *Commentary*, April 1954, 351, 342.

7. Charles R. Morris, *A Time of Passion*, New York, 1984, 139–143.

8. David Vogel, "The 'New' Social Regulation in Historical and Comparative Perspective," in Thomas K. McCraw, ed., *Regulation in Perspective*, Cambridge, Mass., 1981, 155–185.

9. Randall Rothenberg, *The Neo-Liberals*, New York, 1984, 239–247.

Bibliographic Essay

To catch the sustained drama of the campaign for the presidency in 1912, no single source rivals the intimacy of contemporary newspapers and periodicals, especially the *New York Times*, then, as now, the preeminent newspaper of record. In addition, and especially for the Democrats, the *New York World* and the *Baltimore Sun* are excellent. Among periodicals, *Harper's Weekly* and the *Independent* made politics a central theme.

For depth beyond day-to-day coverage, the record is now quite full. For Woodrow Wilson, Arthur S. Link, ed., *The Papers of Woodrow Wilson*, 58 vol., Princeton, 1966–1988, especially volumes 19–25, are a mammoth source, one of the great editorial undertakings of this era. The record on Theodore Roosevelt is less full, but Elting E. Morison et al., eds., *The Letters of Theodore Roosevelt*, 8 vol. Cambridge, Mass., 1951–1954, is also superbly crafted; it may be supplemented by *The Works of Theodore Roosevelt*, 24 vol., New York, 1923–1926. William Howard Taft's papers have not been similarly arrayed. The extensive quotations in Henry F. Pringle, *The Life and Times of William Howard Taft*, 2 vol., New York, 1939, may be supplemented by the William Howard Taft Papers in the Library of Congress (also available on microfilm at other libraries). For Eugene V. Debs, small snatches of correspondence have survived at the Eugene V. Debs Foundation, Terre Haute, Indiana. Several collections of his writings and speeches are available, including Arthur M. Schlesinger, Jr., ed., *Writings and Speeches of Eugene V. Debs*, New York, 1948; anon., *Debs: His Life, Writings and Speeches*, Westport, Conn., 1962; Ronald Radosh, ed., *Debs*, Englewood Cliffs, N.J., 1971. The Debs Foundation also has extensive scrapbooks of newspaper clippings.

Biographies of each candidate use and go beyond the primary record. Arthur S. Link's *Wilson: The Road to the White House*, Princeton, 1947, draws on Link's mastery of the Wilson papers, substantially replacing the older Ray Stannard Baker, *Woodrow Wilson: Life and Letters*, 8 vol., New York, 1927–1929. Henry Wilkinson Bragdon, *Woodrow Wilson: The Academic Years*, Cambridge, Mass., 1967, focuses on Wilson's prepolitical years. John M. Mulder, *Woodrow Wilson: The Years of Preparation*, Princeton, 1978, draws on thirty years of scholarship since Link; it is especially useful in putting Wilson's religious views in perspective. John Milton Cooper, Jr., *The Warrior and the Priest*, Cambridge, Mass., 1983, uses a striking metaphor (with which I disagree) to differentiate Wilson from Roosevelt. Edwin Weinstein, *Woodrow Wilson: A Medical and Psychological Biography*, Princeton, 1981, a controversial book, raises issues that I gloss over in my own work.

For Roosevelt, Edmund Morris, *The Rise of Theodore Roosevelt*, New York, 1979, replaces all previous accounts for the prepresidential years. Henry F. Pringle, *Theodore Roosevelt: A Biography*, carries the story further, but not reliably. George E. Mowry, *Theodore Roosevelt and the Progressive Movement*, New York, 1960, does much to fill the gap, especially if supplemented by the shrewd analysis in John Morton Blum, *The Republican Roosevelt*, Cambridge, Mass., 1967, and *The Progressive Presidents*, New York, 1980, 30–60. Cooper, *The Warrior and the Priest*, is as useful for Roosevelt as it is for Wilson.

For Taft, the pickings are thinner. In addition to the Pringle biography noted above, Donald F. Anderson, *William Howard Taft: A Conservative's Conception of the Presidency*, Ithaca, N.Y., 1973, and Paolo E. Coletta, *The Presidency of William Howard Taft*, Lawrence, Kansas, 1973, have thoughtful comments. Archie Butt, *Taft and Roosevelt: The Intimate Letters of Archie Butt*, Garden City, N.Y., 1973, catches both presidents in formal and informal moments. William Manners, *TR and Will*, New York, 1969, records the deterioration of the Taft-Roosevelt friendship.

Nick Salvatore, *Eugene V. Debs: Citizen and Socialist*, Urbana, Ill., is wonderful both in its range and in its empathy. The much older and briefer volume, Ray Ginger, *The Bending Cross*, New Brunswick, N.J., 1949, still stands up well.

For the period as a whole, two classic volumes carry their years admirably: George E. Mowry, *The Era of Theodore Roosevelt and the Birth of Modern America, 1900–1912*, New York, 1962, and Arthur S. Link, *Woodrow Wilson and the Progressive Era, 1910–1917*, New York, 1954. In addition, Arthur M. Schlesinger, Jr., *History of American Presidential Elections, 1789–1968*, 4 vol., New York, 1971, is an admirable compendium, particularly for the texts of the parties' platforms, and even more particularly, for this book, for George E. Mowry's excellent essay on the election of 1912.

On the larger topic of progressivism, everyone will now have to contend with the new boy on the block, Martin J. Sklar, *The Corporate Reconstruction of American Capitalism, 1890–1916*, Cambridge, Mass., 1988, a comprehensive analysis of the forces that struggled for primacy in 1912. Though better on Roosevelt than on Wilson, Sklar has reset the terms for the discussion of progressivism. Nonetheless, older books and articles still deserve attention: Richard Hofstadter, *The Age of Reform*, New York, 1955; Samuel P. Hays, *The Response to Industrialism, 1885–1914*, Chicago, 1957; J. Joseph Huthmacher, "Urban Liberalism and the Age of Reform," *Mississippi Valley Historical Review*, March 1958, 664–685; Gabriel Kolko, *The Triumph of Conservatism*, Chicago, 1967; Grant McConnell, *Private Power and American Democracy*, New York, 1967; Robert H. Wiebe, *The Search for Order, 1877–1920*, New York, 1967; John D. Buenker, *Urban Liberalism and Progressive Reform*, New York, 1973; Alfred D. Chandler, Jr., *The Visible Hand*, Cambridge, Mass., 1977; Thomas K. McCraw, ed., *Regulation in Perspective*, Cambridge, 1981.

Index

About the Author

FRANCIS L. BRODERICK is Commonwealth Professor Emeritus at the University of Massachusetts at Boston. He is the author of several books, most recently *Reconstruction and the American Negro* and *Black Protest Thought in the Twentieth Century*.